MW00561194
intangible

the story behind Virginia's
bigger-than-basketball program

articulated by:

Ritchie McKay
Barry Parkhill
Jason Williford
Jontel Evans
Ronnie Wideman
Will Sherrill
Joe Harris
Thomas Rogers
Akil Mitchell
Johnny Carpenter
Grant Kersey
Will Gent
Rob Vozenilek
Angus Mitchell
Evan Nolte
Mike Curtis
London Perrantes
Kevin Oberlies
Ben Buell
Devon Hall
T.J. Grams
Isaiah Wilkins
Jack Salt
Marial Shayok
Alex Peavey
Ty Jerome

with Robert Friddell

MOUNTAIN ARBOR
PRESS
Alpharetta, GA

ISBN: 978-1-6653-0288-3 - Paperback
eISBN: 978-1-6653-0289-0 - eBook

Printed in the United States of America 082721

♾This paper meets the requirements of ANSI/NISO Z39.48-1992 (Permanence of Paper)

Cover Art by Mollie and Evan Burch

for Laura, Coach (our pup), Dad, friends, family,
and friends who become family

"Yet it is not our part to master all the tides of the world,
but to do what is in us for the succour of those years
wherein we are set,
uprooting the evil in the fields that we know,
so that those who live after may have clean earth to till.
What weather they shall have is not ours to rule."

- *Tolkien*

contents table

intro

March 2009

articulated by:
Ronnie Wideman

"Are you sittin' down?"

I'm like, "Oh, funny you say that – I'm actually sitting in the lobby of a bank. Yeah, I'm sittin' down."

He's like, "Pack your bags; we're goin' to Virginia."

I said, "What?! What do you mean? Last night, you told me you weren't! Now, what happened?!"

He said, "I slept on it, prayed about it. I just woke up this morning and felt as though I should go."

The night before, he had called me and said, "Hey, look..."

Obviously, I knew what was going on. He'd come out here to Charlottesville and visited. He called me the night before it was announced, and he said, "You know, I just don't feel like the time is right."

So, I go into the bank the next day because I was going to buy a new car. I'm like, *Alright, cool. We're going to be here [in Washington] for a little bit.*

I'll never forget the day that Tony told me that he was going to come out to Virginia.

So, you know, here we are.

letter

Between Tony Bennett's "Are you sittin' down?" in March 2009 and Ronnie Wideman's, "So, you know, here we are," in May 2020, things happened, a thing got built, and things and thing remain underway.

In April 2019, I set out to learn what made the thing tick. What were the pivot points, why the pivots, what stayed the same, and what still sticks with those involved along the way?

Originally, I planned on writing supplemental paragraphs and pages, but as the twenty-six interviews progressed through July 2020, what these guys said started to sound like a story in its own right. So, apart from this letter and [bracketed] words throughout the chapters, I didn't write or say a word of what follows; instead, the people who lived the story get to tell it.

Structurally, it wound up like a written documentary or a paper play, but to me, it's like reading the blues: some of it aches, some of it soars, and all of it's real. It's worth a listen.

To those who took the time to talk with me: thanks a lot for your earnest thoughts, have fun, I loved this, and I hope you enjoy reading your story.

cast

Ritchie McKay
Associate Head Coach
2009-2015

Barry Parkhill
Associate Athletic Director
1998-Present

Jason Williford
Assistant Coach
2009-2018
Associate Head Coach
2018-Present

Ronnie Wideman
Assistant Director of Men's
Basketball Operations
Associate Athletic Director
2009-Present

Mike Curtis
Strength and Conditioning
Coach, 2009-Present

T.J. Grams
Assistant Director of
Academic Affairs
Director of Academics
2010-Present

Alex Peavey
Mindfulness Coach, VCU
2017-Present

Johnny Carpenter
Basketball Technology
Assistant, 2015-2018
Director of Player Personnel
2018-Present

Jontel Evans
#1, 2009-2013

Will Sherrill
#22, 2007-2011

Joe Harris
#12, 2010-2014

Thomas Rogers
#30, 2010-2014

Akil Mitchell
#25, 2010-2014

Grant Kersey
#1, Manager,
2016-2020

Will Gent
Manager,
2014-2018

Rob Vozenilek
#23, 2011-2015

Angus Mitchell
#21, 2011-2012

Evan Nolte
#11, 2012-2016

London Perrantes
#32, 2013-2017

Kevin Oberlies
Manager,
2014-2016

Ben Buell
Manager,
2015-2019

Devon Hall
#0, 2013-2018

Isaiah Wilkins
#21, 2014-2018

Jack Salt
#33, 2014-2019

Marial Shayok
#4, 2014-2017

Ty Jerome
#11, 2016-2019

One

articulated by:
Ritchie McKay

Ritchie McKay: We experienced the doubt, and the frustration, and the possibility that we weren't going to be a National Champion because the agenda was never being a National Champion – the agenda was the process of becoming. There's where I think the story lies.

I think it's a noble story that he won't talk about. Not many of us who are [coaching] descendants, if you will, of Tony will talk about it because of the propensity that it would seem like it lacked humility. We're just an offshoot of the tone that he set from Day One, hence why most are very guarded about talking about it or taking credit for it.

Most people will have a barometer of success that's based on a scoreboard [and] not based on the heart of man, or the character of an individual, or the preparedness that I think that our program is. The way we operate isn't usually the plodded.

Look, I'm older than Tony Bennett, but I learned a great deal from him. His sense of integrity is fabulous. I take pride in knowing that I'm a part of their family tree. I don't want to insert myself and call me a family member – that's not what I mean by that – I mean that family has impacted my life, and I think Ron Sanchez would say the same.

I was [the head coach] at Liberty [in 2008-2009]. I loved my experience at Liberty. I wasn't looking to move. I've always had a penchant for the right fit. Because I moved so many times, I had good relationships with Athletic Directors that had hired me, and I kind of knew the process. Post-basketball coaching, I think I'll be involved in a search firm one way or another or in some advisory role for coaches because it's my heart to try and connect people.

So, Tony and I got on the phone, and in all the years that we had known each other, he had never really talked about leaving a job or getting a job – other than going with his dad to Washington State as an assistant, which I had no voice in.

Although I did talk to Jim Sterk, the AD [Athletic Director] at Washington State. I mentioned to him and Anne McCoy, "The way to get Dick Bennett might be to offer his son a coach-in-waiting role." And I don't know if there was a better fit for Washington State than Dick Bennett.

Anyway, Tony calls me, and we talk, and he said, "Hey, what do you know about Virginia?" He was rumored at a bunch of different places. Virginia wasn't one of them. And he said, "Do they care about basketball? Is it a Stanford of the east?"

So, I could tell in his probing he had a little bit of interest. And I asked him about another job or two that I'd heard about, and he said, "Nah." And if you know Tone, he's not looking for advancement. He's looking for fit.

So, I reached out to an Assistant AD [at Virginia] that I knew, and I said I had a name for him, and I asked him about that name, and he said, "I'll call you back. I'll call you back in twenty-four hours."

Early the next morning: "What do we got to do?"

I shared some of that with Tone, and Tone went through the process, and I didn't know if he was going to take it. We had talked very briefly about, "Would you consider joining me?"

And I said, "Tone, that's not why I'm doing this. I really like it where I am. I like being a head coach."

But I always felt this appreciation for what his dad had done for me from a distance and how inviting his dad had been to help me. And I was a nobody to him – like a *nobody*. But he opened his door, and I just had a sense of gratitude and appreciation for that. It instantly connected me with the Bennett family.

Tone and I had become friends. I'd offered him a job at Colorado State after his playing career. So, I think we trusted one another.

So, Tone takes the job, and I tell him, "I'm just not ready. I'll pray about it." When I said, "I'll pray about it," it meant, *How do I tell him no?*

He said, "Well, could you and Julie just come to the hotel and talk to us?" He was in Virginia at the time. This is either the day before or the day after the press conference – I can't remember. We went to the hotel, we talked, and my daughter came with us. She was looking after Anna, his daughter.

When I left there, Julie and I kind of thought, "Mm, yeah, man – he's a pretty good salesman. I love his vision. But I've only been here [at Liberty] two years."

So, then when we got up in the morning – and I couldn't sleep – both of us kind of heard a verse, and I'll summarize it for you: that Christ came to this earth to serve, not to be served. And it was in that place – or that space – that I called him and said, "Man, I'm coming."

I didn't expect the effect it would have on our campus in Lynchburg – it was tough. Telling players, telling my AD... man, it was tough! Seth Curry had just decided to transfer. That probably led into my decision a tiny bit, but I was still ready to keep trying to build our program.

I get [to Charlottesville], and it's just [Tony] and I, and he's talking about staff hires. We have a brief meeting with the team, and I'm like, *Woah. This is not ready-made.* No indictment to the previous staff; no shaming the guys that we inherited – there was just not a connection.

I thought to myself, *I don't know if I made the right decision,* but I kept hearing what Tone said about building a program: "Get guys you can lose with first. Let's be about the process of building something special." And to him, special meant: whole person special, men of character, being able to get guys that would sacrifice maybe what they dreamed about for what we dreamed about. And staying in that lane was the origin of what he accomplished.

The greatest role that I think I played for him was just having an older coach that believed in him [and] that could help avert wrong exits. If you're driving down the freeway, and it says, "Get off on Exit 47 to go to this game," and you miss Exit 47, and you see that next sign, "12 miles to the next exit," you've got a choice to make: *Do I make an illegal U-turn, or do I go, frustrated, doing the right thing, turning back around, and taking the consequence behind being late?* And I think that's what he had an incredible ability to do: to stay doing the right thing.

The Pillars [Humility, Passion, Unity, Servanthood, and Thankfulness] mean something to the Bennett family. They are not words on a piece of paper [or] signage on a wall. He wants to live them out. And every man has conflict in his life – both external and internal. Tony's not exempt from that.

But when we lead our lives based on our convictions, our convictions influence our circumstances. When we lead our lives based on our circumstances, they influence our convictions. And Tony had the emotional maturity to stay true to his convictions (not perfectly).

I just remember those Pillars meant something to me, too, because I was a descendant of his dad. His dad was one of the reasons why I enjoyed coaching. I had great mentors.

[For] the first six years, we had the same staff. It was me, Jason [Williford], Ron [Sanchez], Ronnie, and Brad Soucie, who's been a longtime assistant of mine [and] who helped a ton in shaping the culture from a really invisible standpoint. He's gifted like that. Johnny Carpenter came from a manager to a support role.

There was a learning curve for us as assistants. Although I knew Tony relationally, I had never worked for him. I was part of the interview process with every candidate, and there were many who were interested. Jason Williford stood out. His passion for UVA [and] the pride that he had in the basketball program – it was infectious. Jay Willy, he's a special dude.

[Tony] was deciding on what role Coach Sanchez would have and what role Ronnie would have. He decided on those fairly soon. I remember talking to a bunch of people at the beginning, but it was spinning so fast for him. I think Jay really just emerged as the right fit for us. But he hired relatively quickly – I don't think Jay Willy waited long.

Those Pillars are how he hires. He wants men that have humility, who can be a part of something bigger than themselves, who will unite not divide, who are over themselves, if you will, and who are passionate. He wants to hire, he wants to recruit, [and] he wants to live the Pillars.

That first staff was really connected. We had our disagreements, but we knew who Tone wasn't as much as we knew who he was. Our desire as an assistant coaching staff was to allow him to focus on the things that he was great at, so he wouldn't have to focus on things that would distract him from being great. I think we served in a capacity that allowed him to be who he was.

Jay Willy and I may disagree or have a different view, but I can tell you I love and respect him a ton! So, even if I thought [a player] should play more [and] he thought he shouldn't, we didn't skip a beat. And that was honestly the [crux] of building community: that our staff was connected. There was no disrespect from those relationships that could be viewed by the ones we were shepherding or stewarding, and I think that laid a little bit of the foundation.

The learning curve in the recruiting process was who Tony could coach. I tell our staff [at Liberty] that all the time: "There are certain guys that I don't do well coaching," and I learned that at New Mexico. So, I think we missed on a few guys, but the guys that stayed, Joe Harris and Akil Mitchell, those guys cut nets. And not to say the other guys couldn't have done it either, but they were fully invested, and great teammates, and wanted to be a part of something bigger than themselves.

Joe Harris was the player catalyst for Virginia's National Championship. You talk to Justin Anderson, Malcolm Brogdon, [and] London Perrantes, [Joe] would be intentional about, "Let's do stuff together." And this is a kid from *Chelan,* [Washington]. There's not a lot of brothers in Chelan. But he didn't care about any of that. He cared about, "Man, these guys are my brothers."

In seeing how those initial years were shaped, learning who Tony could coach, staff connection, Joe Harris and his intentionality to unite the brethren, all that started to swirl into a little bit of a dust storm – and it eventually became a tornado ten years later.

Two

articulated by:
Barry Parkhill

Barry Parkhill: I never met Tony before he came here. In a former life, I coached. I think I met his dad at a clinic but didn't really know his dad either.

When he, Laurel, and the kids moved here, we were neighbors. We lived on the same street – he was a couple of doors up. So, I got to know the family. We are still colleagues, but I got to know him as a friend early on.

About five years into their move here, they moved in town, so I don't see them nearly as much, but we talk occasionally. I've gotten to know Tony better than other family members, but I've spent a lot of time with his dad and gotten to know his mom.

It's just been an incredible journey that he's put our basketball program on, and as I've said, he's the best coach on the planet, but he's a better person. He amazes me all the time. It's not just coaching and what he's built – which is extraordinary – but how he handles everything: how he handles adversity [and] how he handles success.

As he preaches, he's very humble. He's very competitive. You don't have the success that Tony has without being competitive. When you're competitive, if you keep score, you play to win. Sometimes, once that's in your blood, it never leaves.

But he's just got a way in practice, in dealing with coaching, [and in] whatever he's working on. I've seen a lot of coaches perform and a lot of great coaches. They're all different. But just the way he handles things is... he's one of a kind, really is.

Obviously, I'm invested in a lot of different ways in our basketball program. Everybody knows about his defensive philosophy – which is phenomenal – but it goes way beyond that. He's very consistent in the kind of kids he recruits.

I was on a Zoom call last night with a bunch of Virginia folks – probably seven hundred people on it. I was a moderator, and Carla Williams, Tiki Barber, and Joe Harris were on the call. Carla's my boss, and Tiki's a great friend, but my wife and I have gotten very close to Joe.

I think if you look at a pyramid of the success [of the program] – if you look at it that way – Joe's at the bottom of the pyramid. He and Akil Mitchell came in with [Tony's initial recruiting] class of [seven] kids. Joe's just an amazing human being – let alone a great player.

He's a Tony Bennett kid, but all his kids are great kids – everything about them. They just happened to be really good basketball players.

And I got to say, he's got a great staff. I mean, I've known all those guys. He's got a phenomenal staff. And those guys, I think maybe they're underrated. I don't know if that's the right word or not, but he's got great people around him, and that makes a huge difference.

What he does with his team, those things are amazing – just with the team. The things he does after a practice or before the [National] Championship Game in Minneapolis. The guy's got something that nobody else has. It's really hard to describe, and he's as down to earth as anybody you'd ever want to be around – that's what makes it really, really cool.

As someone who works in athletics and works with basketball and all the other sports, having played here, and knowing just about every former basketball player, and the pride that's out there with the success, and the way it's done, and the kids we have, I can't tell you how many people I've talked to over the years who are fans of other schools in the ACC, but when we're not playing their school, they're fans of Virginia because of Tony Bennett and the kind of players that we have that he's coaching. You can't help but love the guy.

Listen, everybody loves a winner, but it's also the way it's done with the kind of kids we have. It's just such a joy to be involved and to watch. And again, success certainly helps, but he never ceases to amaze me.

How many head coaches of any sport – let alone CEOs of

companies – would turn down a major salary increase and then turn around with his wife and make a half-million-dollar commitment to what we're working on with the Master Plan?

Probably one.

It was part of the Master Plan, but the Center for Leadership and Sports Ethics. It's an overwhelming project, but one that we're into. If you break it down for basketball only, he's made our job [in Development] a heck of a lot easier. Tony doesn't ask for a whole lot, but we've renovated the locker room in the John Paul Jones Arena, we are in the process of expanding the weight room, and we've also had some success in endowing the head coaching position, which provides long-term support for our basketball program.

Listen, I'm not uncomfortable saying we are an elite men's basketball program, but it takes a lot to get there, and it takes a lot to stay there, and that's what we want to do. We want to keep Tony happy with what he's got to work with.

And you know what? It's hard for people to say no when we're asking them to help Coach Bennett and the basketball program. Success is something that people enjoy being a part of.

It always starts at the top, and we've got the best on the planet at the top. So, the whole thing's amazing. Good things happen to good people.

He's just a regular guy that happens to be the best basketball coach in the world and a great human being. I think people see someone like him who's had that incredible success, you sort of envision a certain personality.

But if you continually watch him – even if you're not a Virginia fan and you live in Timbuktu – you watch his press conferences, you watch the way he handles himself on the bench, you gotta say, "That's a pretty good guy." But knowing him, he's a regular guy! He's just great at what he does.

He's just a very level-headed guy who kind of keeps everything on an even keel, which I think is really good. He doesn't get real, real high or get too low (you know, George Welsh was like that quite a bit: just keep focused and keep moving forward).

You go back to his mom and dad: I've spent more time with his dad than his mom, but she's a sweetheart; his dad: very successful coach, really good guy. I'm sure he was – my guess would be – pretty intense on the sideline. But Tony's got all the great qualities of both his mom and dad, and Laurel's as down to earth as Tony is.

It's just a great storybook – certainly a feel-good story, for sure.

Three

articulated by:
Jason Williford

Jason Williford: I interviewed with Coach [Dave] Leitao prior to Tony being the head coach on two different occasions – didn't get the job. The first time was my doing, the second time, he chose someone else. I kept thinking, *I'll never get back home. I'll never get back to UVA. It's not going to happen.* Because ultimately, this is where I wanted to be after stints at Boston University and American.

I was kicking myself that the first time I didn't take it: *God, I should have taken it. What was I thinking?* I wanted to be back in the ACC, and part of it is wanting to coach at the highest level. As you get into this profession, you want to be at the highest level, and there's nothing higher than the ACC when it comes to basketball.

So, Tony gets the job. And it's funny because there were all kinds of rumors that Tubby Smith was going to be the guy. I knew some folks that knew Tubby, and I was trying to get to Tubby, and out of the blue, Tony Bennett is the candidate. He is the guy that they pegged to be the next [head] coach. And I'm like, "Who the heck is Tony Bennett?" I had no clue.

I remember watching Tony play when he was in Charlotte [in the NBA with the Hornets]. I didn't watch him play in college, but I knew who he was – you know, the little point guard backing up Muggsy Bogues. I had not watched a whole lot of Washington State prior, but I knew Ron Sanchez.

Ron and I stayed in touch over the years when I was at American. We'd met each other on the road recruiting, and just by happenstance, we're talking, and we exchanged numbers, and he would often call me about guys in the DMV, that D.C., Maryland, Virginia area that's a hotbed for basketball. He'd be like, "Hey, you know this kid? How good is he?"

And I'd be like, "That kid is not your level. I'm recruiting that kid at American." So, I think he respected my eye [for] people that I knew in that area.

And when Tony was the guy, I called Ron, and I said, "Ron, I'd love to have a chance to come back to my alma mater. Tell me what I need to do. Can you help me out?"

Well, Ron had no idea that I played at Virginia. And he was like, "I had no idea. Hold tight. I'll get back to you."

Maybe two days pass, and he texts me back. At this point, Tony's going [to Charlottesville] for the [introductory] press conference. And everything in me is like, *Get to Charlottesville. Drive down. Be at the press conference. As soon as Tony's done with the press conference, make sure he knows who I am and introduce myself.*

And Ron sends me a text: "Tony knows who you are. We've done some homework. He's interested, but don't come to Charlottesville."

I'm like, "Don't come?!" *What is he talking about?*

He said, "Tony's overwhelmed. He's got a lot of guys that are doing exactly what you want to do. Don't come. We'll be in touch."

And so, I end up watching the interview on my computer at American. Jeff Jones, who was the [head] coach [at American] and my former coach at UVA, said, "Why aren't you in Charlottesville?"

I said to him, "Because they told me, 'Don't come.'"

He said, "Then you do what they tell you."

And my wife is telling me to go, everybody is telling me to go, and I don't go.

Long story short, I finally get an interview, and I come down, and Tony says, "The fact that you didn't come and you listened meant a lot to me."

And Tony is different. He walks to his own beat, and he doesn't always do things traditionally. And that was one of them. And I guess the fact that I was a good listener and obviously, my ties had a lot to do with me being able to come back.

In a nutshell, that's the story of how I got here. Tony had no idea who I was; I had no idea who he was. It was all Ron Sanchez. I'm so thankful for that opportunity.

I think it's been a good choice (laughs). I've been able to be with [Tony] now going on twelve seasons. It's been fun to be back, and this is where I wanted to be.

Playing here, doing my four years here, growing as a man, met my wife here – it was home. A lot of good friendships – a lot of the same folks that were working in the Athletic Department and on Grounds are still some of the same people that are here today.

The culture that Jeff [Jones] established when I was a player was a family atmosphere, and I wanted to bring that back. I wanted all former players to feel like they could come back.

I always looked at the Duke's, the [North] Carolina's, the Kentucky's, the Kansas's of the world – those "Blue Bloods." I wanted to help Virginia establish themselves as a Blue Blood. We had some really good years when I played, Ralph [Sampson] had some really good years, but there wasn't consistency.

I wanted to help bring consistency to the program and build a program that could compete with those big boys night in and night out and win National Championships. I told Tony, "I'm going to be with you until we win one."

My goal was to do that but also have the basketball alumni feel like they could always be a part and come around. Naturally, having someone that played [at UVA] on the staff helps bridge that gap. Even if I didn't play with those guys in those different eras, I think I can relate to their experience. You know all of the names, even if you don't know them. You've seen all the names, you know their records, you know everything that they've accomplished, and you've watched some old film.

I told Tony, "I'd love to make sure we got alumni back," and those guys felt like they were part of this.

You want those guys to pass on to the young guys what it was like and that there's something bigger than themselves. You're doing this because somebody else laid that foundation. You guys are laying a foundation for guys behind you. And I think that's what builds a program. That's what builds sustainable success.

You see it with some of those other programs. I don't want to give them too much credit, but some of those other programs have been able to do it. I think that's how you do it: you take pride in being a part of something bigger than yourself, and you take pride in being part of that Wahoo Family, that basketball family.

There were some good players in the program [when we got here]. There have been great players throughout the history of the program. Again, the sustainability and the consistency are what I wanted to see. Teams were good, then we'd drop off a few years, and we'd have a good team. Virginia always attracted good basketball players, and there were good players in the program.

Part of what we had to do: Tony had to lay the foundation of how he wanted to play, and the kids that bought in to that were a good fit for the University as a whole, outside of basketball. And Tony wasn't going to put up with a whole lot of nonsense as far as character. There were some guys that chose to leave when we got here, and some guys that obviously chose to stay, and they helped start laying that foundation of this version of Virginia Basketball.

It was hard work, but it was guys giving of themselves to be a part of something bigger. And those Five Pillars that we have, the principles of our program, it started with that. Knowing who you are, the humility piece, and being in service – they had to serve each other.

From there, we just kept building and getting our guys bought in – guys that all wanted to ultimately win and win at a high level. But I think Tony's vision, and his master plan of the Virginia Pillars, and building a program based on those Pillars is what was the foundation, and that was the start.

We made mistakes in recruiting early, and we had some turnover, but ultimately, we had the right guys who all bought in to be a part and have gotten us to where we are. And we don't do it without that first crew of Mike Scott, and Jontel Evans, and Mustapha [Farrakhan], and Sammy Zeglinski and Jerome Meyinsse, and Will Sherrill, and Assane Sene. Those guys helped lay that foundation. Those are some of the guys that trusted us and believed in us.

They could have easily have gone, but they stayed, and they bought in, and then we reaped the benefits of Ty Jerome, Kyle Guy, and De'Andre Hunter because of all of those guys and alllll of those dudes in between that were part of this.

Four

articulated by:
Jontel Evans

Jontel Evans: When he got the job, everybody [said], "You know who Tony Bennett is?"

I'm like, "I can't say that I do," and I know for *damn* sure he didn't know who I was.

We were coming into it together, not knowing one another, but I heard through the grapevine: "Oh, he's really a defensive guy." And that's what stood out to me. I was like, *Okay, that can work.*

When Coach Bennett first got there, a lot of the players that were on the team just weren't really buying in to his philosophy, his system, [and] what he was trying to bring to the table, and Coach Bennett is not that type of guy or coach that's going to get rowdy and all in your face.

I just remember some people just pushing him, tryin' him, and then one day, he just stopped practice, and he was like, "You know what? I'm in it for the long haul. I'm here for a while. And if you guys don't want to be part of that, then there's the door," and we just continued to practice.

Right there at that moment, I'm like, *Alright, this guy is the real deal.* Even though it was subtle, it said a lot. And then as the season went on – when he suspended pretty much the best player in the conference at that time – it was just like, *Okay, this guy is serious. His bite is way bigger than his bark.* And that's the type of guy I want to play for because he doesn't play favorites, and he's fair, and he wants to build a program.

It's just one of the many stories that really stood out to me from when I was like, *I'm locked in; I'm ready. What can I bring to the table to help this team and help this program?* And it ended up being a miraculous ride.

I think what gets me is: I remember where it was ten years ago because I was part of that. We didn't have social media digging us up; we didn't have all these accolades. We had a whole bunch of L's and hope – that's it. We had a new coach. We had a new system. That's all we had: hope, hope in our coach, our leader.

One thing that Coach Bennett always told us: "Keep knocking. Keep knocking." And that's what we did the first two years: we just kept knocking. [My] third year, we kicked down the door. And that's what they've been continuing to do year-after-year-after-year.

UVA basketball means a lot to me. I get really excited talking about UVA because when I was at school and like two years after I graduated, I never really understood or accepted the fact when people were like, "Thank you. You set the foundation."

I'm like, *I don't really care about that... I wish I could be part of this right now, like ACC Champions* – that's what I'm thinking in my head, which was very selfish.

But then, as I got older, I started to realize that being the foundation… I'm like, *Dude, you were the start of this. This is the reason why it's like this now,* and it just makes me appreciate my time and everything I went through at UVA so much more.

A lot of people say, "Oh, UVA basketball is boring. They don't run up and down."

When did winning become boring? I don't care what type of talent Coach Bennett has; it's the system that he has implemented in this program that will always give his team a chance.

We could be playing against the [Los Angeles] Lakers right now with the team we have, and if we're down 4 points, [or] if it's a two-possession game with 3-4 minutes left, my money is on the Cavaliers because our system is going to work. We're going to make you play 30 seconds of defense, and we're going to make you play 30 seconds of offense. That's our system; that's our way: we're going to slow it down.

A lot of teams nowadays, they like to get out of transition. We're stopping you from getting in transition. We're stopping you from getting easy buckets [and] stopping you from getting in the paint. We're making you play defense. The system works. And a lot of people say, "Oh, it's boring, it's boring" – it's boring until you have to practice it.

Coming out of high school, I was bigger, stronger, quicker, faster, and more athletic than a lot of those guys. But then, when I got to UVA, my first summer here, I'm guarding Sammy Zeglinski, and I'm like, *Man, I can own him* (in my head!), but he was so much more experienced than me at the college level.

It was like, *Damn, dude. This guy is really, really good.* Like [he's] running off screens, I'm running into screens, and my conditioning wasn't the best, and I was just like, *Man, I have a loooong way to go.*

I wasn't disciplined. I always relied on my athleticism. But once I settled down and used the Pack Line principles to my advantage with the talent that I already had, man, you're looking at a lights-out defensive player.

So, it took a while because I was still caught in that high school phase of, *Alright, you can be dominant because of your talent and your athleticism.* But at the next level, everybody has the same talent and athleticism or maybe even more, so then it becomes a from-the-neck-up type of game, which I truly had to sit and learn from my teammates, my coaches, just being around the game of basketball, and watching everything.

Five

articulated by:
Ronnie Wideman

Ronnie Wideman: My role here, really, is to serve. I've been with Tony for... gosh, we'll be going on eighteen years this season. So, I've seen a lot. I've been able to go through the hills and the valleys with him. It's definitely been a journey.

One of the Pillars is Servanthood, and I really just try to embody that. I enjoy being a part of something bigger than myself. My fulfillment comes from serving others and seeing these young men reach their full potential, whether it be the NBA, or the business world, or pursuing an MBA, or whatever it is, real estate, all those types of things that these guys have aspirations to do – that's the joy in it for me. Of course, winning is great, and it makes it enjoyable, but for us, it's bigger than basketball. It's bigger than wins and losses.

So many people have played an important role in it: Ritchie, his perspective as a former head coach [and] coming out of that role as an assistant coach and serving Tony, and then, obviously, Coach Sanchez.

It's in line with what Tony said in his [introductory] press conference [in 2009] about finding players he could lose with first before you can win. I think he did a great job in building his staff the same way.

He had to find individuals that he knew because he knew, *This is going to get hard. And there is going to be a temptation to do things differently, but I need to know I can trust these men to do what is holistically in line with what our program is about.*

So, it's identifying the right type of people to be on your staff that you can trust, and the reason being is simple: again, it was to build a program, not a team. And Tony doesn't bring us in every year, "We're going to follow the rules." You know that expectation because of how Tony carries himself and lives his life.

I was twenty-four/twenty-five [years-old] at the time [in 2009]. [I] packed three bags, jumped on a plane, and came out here [to Virginia]. I'll never forget: when you get into a program, you don't know anybody's name. I'm like, *How am I gonna learn all these players' names?*

There are fifteen-to-sixteen guys on the roster, and I don't even know their names – I'm stressed about *that*. I'm like, *I got this undertaking! How am I going to know all these names?*

Coach Sanchez, and myself, and Coach Bennett, the three of us stayed in a one-bedroom apartment for probably – I don't want to exaggerate – probably two weeks when we first got here. So, Sanchez and I slept on the floor in the living room area, and Tony, of course, had the room.

You can imagine there's three guys crashing in a one-bedroom apartment. We've got different recruiting ideas; we're trying to recruit – so much is thrown at you at such a fast pace. So, it was drinking from a firehose at the beginning.

I kid you not, every day something came up: a kid transferring or a commitment that didn't want to come. You had to re-recruit Jontel Evans and Tristan Spurlock. Every day there was something. It was like, *Good-gosh, what are we doing here?*

I say that with all due respect to the young men that were in the program and the staff before. It was a whirlwind at the beginning – still is to this day. As you have more success, there's more demand [and] more responsibility in my role.

No joke, a week in, Coach Sanchez's car got broken into. Someone stole his GPS and some other stuff. It was like, *Wait a second, what is happening?* We were scratching our heads, *Alright, these are signs that maybe it wasn't the right time.*

There was a lot going on. And I'll never forget looking at the players. [The] first day I walked in the gym, we had our first workout, and you could just see the type of athlete and player that was already in the program. And again, that's a credit to Dave Leitao and the previous staff.

[The] only thing I had to compare it to was what we had at Washington State. And again, that's not a disrespect to Washington State. I mean, we had guys like Klay Thompson. We had some good players at Washington State, but it was just a different type of player: physicality, length, athleticism. I'll never forget seeing Jerome Meyinsse in a workout. I'm like, "Gah-lee! Who's this guy?!"

And I don't know who I was talking to, maybe one of the former Academic Coordinators. He was like, "Oh, that's Jerome. But he never plays."

I'm like, "Dang, if that guy's not playing, we're going to be really good," because I remember seeing him in a workout and thinking, *That guy's a monster.* He was a great person. Jerome was all about the student-athlete.

And the experienced guys like Will Sherrill, I'll never forget him – he was a walk-on, but just what he did for our program – [and] Sammy Zeglinski, I can go down the list. But there were really good players and good young men in the program at the time.

The beginning was such a whirlwind. And it's still... sometimes you have to stop and think back to where it was. One thing I want to do is: I really want to be careful and intentional in not disrespecting the previous staff, Dave Leitao, and even those before him, like Pete Gillen. I don't want to disrespect them at all because there were some good things in the program. I don't want to say that we had to completely revamp everything.

Of course, Tony brought a philosophy more so around the Pillars that we had to try to get our guys to believe in. Mike Scott was a little bit resistant to it at the beginning: *Can I trust these guys? What is this they're saying? This is a little bit foreign to me.* And I just want to be respectful and appreciative of what those guys did – Coach Leitao and his staff – in laying some foundational pieces that we came in and built on. So, I want to make sure I give them their credit where it's due.

It wasn't about completely changing them as people or recruiting different types of players; it was more just getting them to buy in to A) the Pillars and the way that Coach Bennett wanted to build this program, but then, B) the system. And that takes time.

There are no shortcuts for that. I mean, you've heard it a hundred times: you've got to find guys you can lose with first before you can win. And those guys did – to their credit. Was it easy? No.

Mike Scott bucked the system. I remember I'm up in the office administering study hall for him and [another player] as the other guys are downstairs practicing.

Again, that was just trying to get them to buy in, and we had different expectations: you gotta get to class, you gotta be on time, you gotta be prepared in the same way that you wouldn't be late to practice or you wouldn't come without your court shoes or your jersey to practice. We had the same expectation for class and your studies, and that was important. It was just the message that we were trying to send: the academics [piece] is just as important as the basketball piece, and you're not going to get one without the other.

Again, I don't know if Coach Leitao did or didn't. I'm not trying to judge one way or the other. Those are things that we were trying to improve as quickly as possible, but not rushing it. You can be quick, but you don't want to hurry or be rushed in a way that you cut corners or make mistakes.

Tony had a plan, and he was going to stick to it. He wasn't going to deviate from what he believed in, regardless of what people said. Everything from whether it's his system, like, "Oh, your system will never win in that league," to the types of guys that he's recruiting.

And that's one word that I always like to use about Coach Bennett: consistency. He's always consistent, and that's one of his greatest strengths. He came here with a plan, and he was going to stay true to that plan and be consistent from Day One, and just steady, steady, steady.

The same message, the Pillars – we talk about those every day. It's a consistent message that the players start to understand:

Okay, this isn't just lip service. This is how this coach is living his life. This means a lot to him. It's important to him. That's one reason why I think there has been so much success: that level of consistency.

[The Pillars] are important because they apply to life. They're not just sports, they're not just about basketball, they're applicable to life, and they have stood the test of time. They're Biblical principles, and that's not a secret – Coach shares that. His father came up with them forty years ago.

And it's a cool story: he and his staff, I think they're at a Denny's (of all places), and – on a napkin – he was writing down things that he had been reading in Scripture. And he just said that he wants to have constancy in his program – again, coming back to consistency – "What can I continue to share with my guys?" And he wrote these down at a Denny's on a napkin: [Humility, Passion, Unity, Servanthood, and Thankfulness].

And here they are, forty years later, on walls everywhere. Other programs are using them. They're transforming lives, is the hope and the desire. But they're important because they've stood the test of time, they're Biblical, and they apply to life across the board – bigger than athletics. They're applicable to anybody's life.

And I mentioned the academic and the athletic side of things – I don't think you can have one without the other. They're not mutually exclusive. And it shows a level of responsibility and respect: respect for your professors, your teachers, your classmates, respect for even the principle of being a student-athlete.

But academics is going to be important. And that's the type of student-athlete that Tony wanted to recruit. That's why it's such a good marriage: because of who Tony wants to coach and the type of young man that the University of Virginia attracts. The two go well together – hand-in-hand. So, that's why I feel like that was so important to set the tone and the expectation early on: to [make sure] that the young men understood that this was bigger than basketball.

And it may be like, "Well, yeah… it's just going to class," but going to class, being on time, being prepared, being respectful, those are signs of maturation, responsibility, and development as a young man, and they require time management skills. Holistic development is the biggest takeaway from what we're trying to do. And yeah, of course you're trying to develop these young men to become the best basketball players they can be, but we're also holistically trying to develop them to become great husbands, fathers, [and] friends down the road.

And I think it requires some young men to be pushed out of their comfort zone. You've got to be pushed outside of your comfort zone to improve, and academically, Virginia does that. For the general student population, I believe UVA requires their students to be pushed out of their comfort zone to learn and grow in the four-to-five years that they're there.

When you have a vested interest in something, you have those types of transformational experiences. When you have a relationship with a professor or you've invested time in a coach/player relationship, if you trust and believe in somebody, that's the only way you can become transformational. It's hard to overcome some hurdles, or barriers, or guardrails that you put up without a level of trust and commitment.

And those are some of the hurdles that we had to overcome when we first got here: *Can I trust these men? Do they believe in me?* And that's just part of it. We didn't recruit them.

Recruiting, that's when you kind of build that trust, but we didn't. [The players] inherited us just as much as we inherited them, whether they wanted to or not – that was the reality. Winning games, of course, is the fruit of the labor, but just simply trying to reach your full potential, complying with expectations, and those types of things were things that you could see gradually taking shape [and] taking hold. Again, not easy, but you could see it over time.

I think it was a bit complicated because nobody knew who Tony Bennett was. So, not only did he have to earn the trust, but he had to earn some credibility. I could be wrong, but I don't know if there was a player in that locker room that knew who Tony Bennett was.

I think he's thirty-seven at the time, thirty-eight, maybe? So, you have a relatively young head coach from out west who nobody knows – very little credibility and street cred as you walk into a locker room. You're not – one of the names that was rumored for the job was Tubby Smith – you're not Tubby Smith. You're not walking into a locker room with "National Title" behind your name, and a ton of experience, and street credibility – just credibility in general – name recognition, that type of thing. So, not only did you know these guys inherited him and we inherited them, no one knew of him!

Again, I want to be careful because I don't want to say a breath of fresh air in a disrespectful tone. I think there was a bit of fresh air in the way that Tony handled the transition. Tony is one of the most competitive guys you'll ever meet, period. However, the way he handles adversity, success, or setbacks is different. He has some peace about him. He has a different demeanor – much calmer demeanor – than even his father. Again, I'm not a hundred percent sure, but I think it's different than what they saw with Coach Leitao. And again, I don't want that to come across as disrespectful, but I think it was a bit of fresh air for them – the way Tony handled adversity.

And expectations, when they weren't met, his disciplinary actions were more grace and forgiveness rather than berating them, and dog-cussing them, and that sort of thing. That, along with the consistency, were the two biggest things: his demeanor and approach, and being consistent through the highs and through the lows.

Summer 2009

articulated by:
Will Sherrill

Will Sherrill: If I had to say one characteristic that Tony had and his staff had from Day One for their first two years, which were my last two years, was that, yes, they have the Five Pillars, and that's all gotten a ton of press, and rightfully so, because those are really important. That's what the program is built on.

But almost immediately, there was a sense that players trusted every single day they knew who was walking through that door as a coach and as his coaching staff, and they knew exactly where the coaching staff was at. We knew exactly what to expect every single day, and that was from, "Hey, this is how we're going to approach things tactically, strategically on the basketball floor, playing defense, rebounding, sharing the ball, offensive strategy, et cetera," to, "This is how you're going to carry yourself off the floor, going to class."

The summer before Tony's first year, so after they'd been there for a spring, guys were going into the dining hall the back way [and] sneaking a free meal here and there. Very little thing – wasn't an issue at all. But they said, "Hey, you got to do every single thing by the book," because everything reflects on the program.

And that consistency was applied to everyone. There was no star treatment; there was no favoritism. And basically, the coaching staff's and Tony's viewpoint was, "This is how I'm going to do it, and if you don't get on board with that, then you can go. But this is the only way I know how to do it, and this is how I'm going to do it. And I'm not kind of changing or bending my objectives or my principles because this guy is a great player or x, y, z."

The first year, it was tough. We had come from an environment where everyone was kind of out for themselves. I'm sure that's not dissimilar from other programs where the coaching staff gets fired. We had two pretty bad [seasons].

We were like second-to-last in the ACC my freshman year; we were last the next year. That's probably pretty similar with other teams that are in last place in their conference: people are probably out for themselves, it's a bad culture, and players are certainly a part of that.

So, a lot of Tony's first year was about instilling, "This is how we're going to do things," over-and-over-and-over-and-over-and-over – and making no exceptions.

One of the best players on the team heading into the year was kicked off the team before we even played a game because he wasn't going to class [and] was kind of acting out. We had guys who were highly touted [as] either players or recruits who were not getting playing time because they were not doing what was asked of them.

I mean, I started getting playing time. I was not individually as talented as some other guys that I was playing ahead of, [but] I was executing the plan that Tony wanted from a coaching standpoint. Two games before the end of the season, we had our best player – who had won ACC Rookie of the Year the year before – get kicked off the team because he's not going to class.

Every single day you knew that trust was built and that players walked into the gym and said, "This is the program that we're a part of, and we can either get on board or not." In my view, that's really the only way to build a program from the ground up. And you have to do that in the face of some serious losses.

Every single day, there's just consistency. Every single day, you practice the same. You know what you're going to get every day. And that feeling of trust between the coach and the players – that's table stakes for being able to build any sort of program.

It's that consistency: I trusted the person coming in that day. I knew what they were about. I knew exactly what they deemed to be important. You know, I had a great relationship and have a great relationship with Ron Sanchez – same with Ronnie. You have good relationships with the other coaches.

And I have a good relationship with Tony [but] didn't have a great personal relationship with Tony. Probably now, with the players while they're in school, he will probably talk to them more [and] text them more. I think in two years, I went into Tony's office one time.

But that's kind of okay because I knew when I was going to practice what I needed to do, I knew the things that I was going to be evaluated on, I knew the things that would determine whether or not I go on the floor, and that stuff never changed and never changed for anybody.

So, you were able to go out, and perform, and play cohesively as a team because you knew exactly what you were expected to be doing on a daily basis. Then it becomes, "Okay, are you able to recruit good players? Are you able to develop good players? Are your strategies successful? Are your tactics successful?" And obviously, the answer has been yes.

I knew when I graduated, *It's just a matter of time,* because Tony is an unbelievable person – all his coaches are great people. If I was their teammate in college, we'd all be boys. Those are the types of teammates you would love to have. You can have fun shootin' the shit.

They were good at developing talent. I mean, Mike Curtis is a genius. And I worked a good amount on my own to get better, but Mike Curtis, what he does with the players – he's a genius. And it was only a matter of time, in my view, that the program would be where it's at today. People ask me, "Is it surprising to see what's happened?"

I'm like, "No, actually, not at all."

I thought in 2016 they were going to win the National Championship. I thought in 2014 they were going to win the National Championship. But, you know, the ball bounces as it does.

A lot has been made about coming back from UMBC to winning the Championship last year. It's kind of the same thing:

the approach, it doesn't change. That's what he believed he had to do to be successful in terms of an approach and having the willpower and the determination to maintain that approach and not massively reexamine the program after a loss like that or after a number of earlier-than-maybe-should-have-been NCAA Tournament exits – and I say, "should have been," in terms of being a #1 seed and not yet making it to the Final Four.

But it wasn't surprising for me to see the team come back last year and have a tremendous year. Obviously, I was never expecting a National Championship, but I mean, they had the horses, and they have the coaching staff.

I think the thing has always been, "Do they have enough playmakers to win?" That just comes down to getting good players. But you know that the team is going to be a real beast to knock out because everyone knows what they're supposed to be doing. And that was evident from Day One.

Year 1

(2009-2010)

articulated by:
Ronnie Wideman
Will Sherrill
Ritchie McKay

Ronnie Wideman: In '09, we went to a tournament. St. Thomas, maybe?

Will Sherrill: Oh man. Yeah, we were down in Cancun [for] Thanksgiving.

Ronnie: We were going to go do something fun. We're going to jet ski. We're at a tournament, [so] we're going to an island and going to hang out on the beach or something.

So, we go to practice, and we had a fight during practice, and it's like, "What are we doing?" Again, looking at each other like, *What have we got ourselves into?*

Will: Somebody was fouling or hacking somebody, and two guys just squared up, and it was a legit fistfight – you know, punches thrown. I don't think anything connected, but a legit fistfight. And we'd been planning to practice in the morning and then go jet skiing as a team. So, that got totally scrapped.

Ronnie: We just had a team meeting and had really one of the most powerful and transformational team meetings where guys just let out what they thought, like, "What do you think about us as a staff? Do you trust us? What do you think about each other? Your teammates? You got to love each other. We're in this together."

That was the first time you [could] see some vulnerability. That was November. We got the job in April, so it took [seven] months.

Will: But we had had fights all the time, [previously]. We had a drill called "One-on-One Box" that basically was one person is on defense, and they've got to get three rebounds in a row, and they're going one-on-one against a person. Guards would go against bigs. Anyone could go against anyone.

You've got to get three [rebounds] in a row, and if you can't get three in a row, you go back to zero. But also, in order to end the rep, you had to get the ball. So, if a guy scored, he could get the ball and then keep scoring – that devolved into fistfights all the time.

Sean Singletary, one time, was getting put in the blender, and he squared up Mamadi Diane and clocked him right in the jaw. He got kicked out of practice, but we just kept practicing. Mo didn't fall down. Mo's pretty tough. I wouldn't mess with Mo.

That's just one example, but that happened a bunch – kind of normal. But that was the environment, though, coming in, where it was very much just chaos.

Will: I think Coach McKay called the meeting. At that time, you have to remember, Tony was only forty-years-old. He had been a head coach for three years at Washington State.

So, he's a relatively new head coach, and he had Coach McKay, who had been a head coach for a long time. We had a lot of meetings early on – especially that first year – with Coach McKay, where it was basically – and Coach McKay doesn't curse – "What are you guys doing? What's wrong with you guys?"

Ronnie would have been there, too. Tony wasn't in that meeting.

Ritchie McKay: I was surprised that a teammate would punch another teammate and felt like it had to be addressed. My role for Coach Bennett was not in my X's and O's prowess, or offensive strategy, or philosophy. It wasn't in my ability to recruit. I did those things because that's what you do when you're trying to build a program.

When I was passionate about something, he let me talk, and I was passionate about unity. A house divided cannot stand, and who punches their brother?

I had two brothers, and I got in fights with them, but my brother Darryl could knock me out. He'd never hit me in the face. He might wrestle me to the ground. I would do the same to my younger brother, but punching a brother in the face? That ain't right.

So, I remember that being said in the meeting: "The buy in to the Pillars and the buy in to who we are as a family is what will be the next step in our journey."

Brad Stevens said, "You're either a great teammate and fully invested, or you're not." Those dudes that were not fully invested or not great teammates, they wanted to leave.

Ronnie: But that was the first time our guys could be vulnerable with each other. And I thought it was so important with setting the tone with what was to come. Of course, you don't want a fight in practice between student-athletes to be the trigger for something like that, but it's what it was.

And what came of it was so powerful because it did allow these young men to be vulnerable with us and for us to be vulnerable with them and just tell them, "Hey, look, guys, we're not perfect. We got a lot of things we're trying to figure out, too. But we're in this together. We're a family." So, there was a lot that came from that.

Again, that was our first year in November. So, you're in the first four weeks of your season, and that lent itself to really changing the way those current players saw us as a coaching staff, and quite frankly, how we saw those young men – realizing, *These guys have true feelings, and there are things that they're going through, but we're going to get through this together.*

And quite frankly, we wouldn't have had that conversation any other way. Things would have kind of gotten brushed under the rug, and we'd have kept going. But no, "We're not going to go jet skiing. We're going to come into a meeting space, and we're going to talk [and] figure this out together."

I was disappointed – I gotta be honest with you. I wanted to go jet skiing.

Will: Then we played Stanford the next day [in Cancun], and then Cleveland State. And actually, that was kind of my coming out party with 20 points against Cleveland State. I made like 7 threes in the second half, and that was the first time I'd ever really played. So, I have very fond memories of that trip (laughs).

Will: There was another meeting early on. The summer before their first year, people were skipping class or something like that. And we had a meeting, and Coach McKay said, "Who thinks they're going to go to the NBA?"

I think I was the only one that didn't raise my hand (laughs). I mean, we'd been last place in the ACC the previous year. I think the coaches were like, *Jeez. What's going on here?*

But we had been in an environment previously where it was very antagonistic. Everything was antagonistic, and it was motivation by saying, "You can't do this." So, the question, "Who thinks they're going to go to the NBA?" – that was like a gauntlet came down [or] a challenge.

If you didn't raise your hand, you don't think you can go to the NBA, [and] that's like, "You don't have any confidence," and, "Why do you even belong on this team?"

So, it wasn't even that, inherently, people who raised their hands really thought, *If I had to put a million dollars on it, I'm going to the NBA.* It was just the environment that we'd been in, where everything was antagonistic, everything was in conflict, and there wasn't cohesion. It was, "You suck. Prove me wrong."

And after a while, it was chaos. Everyone was just kind of looking out for themselves. So, Tony and his staff had to break that mindset and instill in us that we were all in this thing together.

Ritchie: Did we start the ACC like 3-0, or 4-1, or something like that?

Will: We started the ACC season 3-0, and then 5-2 in conference play. We were in first place, and we beat North Carolina at North Carolina for the first time in a bunch of years. We beat Georgia Tech, who was highly ranked – they had Derrick Favors and Iman Shumpert on their team. We beat... maybe it was Miami? I mean, we had some good wins.

Ritchie: I remember being in the locker room where a lot of meetings took place. That's when Tone would kind of pour out his emotions. And I came in that locker room, and there was somebody from Sports Illustrated – maybe it was John Feinstein – and he was talking to Tony about, "How'd you build it so quick?"

And I remember sitting there thinking, *Yeah! Yeah, Tone! This is good for recruiting! Tell him we've arrived, and you better recognize!*

He was like, "No. We don't need it. It's too much too soon for us."

And I was thinking, *What? You're missing an opportunity here, dude! This is how you grow!*

He said, "It's too much too soon."

Sure enough, I think we lost [nine] in a row after that. So, it was my realization that, *Wow, there's still a lot of work to do.*

Will: We just got hot, and those teams ended up not being as good as previously thought, then we started a [nine-game] losing streak [in conference play to end the regular season]. A weaker coaching staff would have started trying to change things and started trying to fill here and there or compromising: "Hey, maybe we need to adjust to this player as this player is really talented, but we'll give him a pass for not wanting to play defense." There were no excuses made [and] no changes made.

Every day was constant: "This is what we're going to do as a program." And so, everyone on the team, slowly but surely, had to jell as a unit. The one takeaway coming out of that first year was that everyone knew exactly what Tony and his coaches were about.

So, at the end of that first year, guys had a choice, and a lot of guys transferred, [and] we had a few graduates. But you have basically six or seven guys who, over the course of the year, either were kicked off the team, left midseason, or transferred. And so [from] the outside perspective, people were like, "What's going on? It's a dumpster fire."

But on the inside, I'm sure it was exactly what Tony wanted: he wanted people who wanted to be there because it was very clear what type of program he was building. That was kind of the first step to changing the culture.

And it wasn't about Humility. It wasn't about Servanthood. It wasn't about Passion. It wasn't about Unity. It wasn't about Thankfulness. It was about being consistent every single day in: "This is what you're going to do. You're going to play defense. You're going to move the ball. You're going to go to class. You're going to not get in trouble. You're going to do these things. And there are no exceptions." So, the people that stayed, either they had no better options, or they really bought in to it and wanted to stay.

At the end of the year, we played probably our best four games of the season. We lost to Maryland, who won the ACC that year – Greivis [Vasquez], Jordan Williams, and a bunch of good players. We lost to them by [6] on our home floor – played a really tight game.

We go to the ACC Tournament, [and] we win our first game against Boston College. And then we played Duke, and played Duke really tight, and lose to Duke by [11]. Duke ends up winning the National Championship that year. And so, at the end of that, there is a real excitement: "This group of guys that we have now, it's exciting. We're excited for the next year."

Summer 2010

articulated by:
Will Sherrill
Joe Harris
Thomas Rogers
Akil Mitchell
Ronnie Wideman

Will Sherrill: Coming back, we only had six guys. And coming in, I think there were six-to-seven freshmen. So, to a certain extent, that was almost a whole new first year for the program. There had been a little bit of weeding out of people who didn't fit with the culture in the program, but then, in Tony's second year, you basically have a brand-new program.

No one coming back had really done anything in their career. Mike, that [first] year, had been in and out of the starting lineup. I was a walk-on, and I ended up playing a lot, but I averaged 20 minutes a game [and] 4 points a game. Sammy Zeglinski and Mustapha [Farrakhan] had been kind of marginal players.

I mean, we finished last in the ACC two years in a row, and our best individual player had left, and Jerome [Meyinsse] was the second-best player that year. He graduated – would have been great to have him another year.

So, you had six guys on the team who hadn't done anything in their careers up to that point, you've got a relatively new coaching staff, and then you've got seven freshmen coming in who are the first recruiting class in Coach Bennett's era. And they're coming in with their own kind of confidence and maybe cockiness in some scenarios as well.

Joe Harris: I was in Coach Bennett's first recruiting class to Virginia. The Six Shooters! The six of us, it was is K.T. Harrell,

James Johnson, Akil [Mitchell], Will Regan, Billy Baron, and myself.

Thomas Rogers: I came in with the class, "The Six Shooters," or whatever they called it, and I was number seven, so I was always a little offended by that... I'm just kidding.

Joe: And T-Rog! It should've been seven! We all came in a huge recruiting class because Coach Bennett had taken over the program. A lot of the guys that were in the program prior to him didn't necessarily abide by a lot of the rules that he instilled.

So, he was a pretty strict disciplinarian in terms of guys not being late, guys going to class, [and] guys not really having any sort of issues off of the court. And then anything that happened internally or on the court, obviously, those are big things for him as well.

So, we got there, and there was a weird dynamic between us and the former players. It took them a little while to warm up to us because it's always different when you come in, and you know that the guys that are coming in are all the guys that Coach Bennett recruited, and they're all his guys, you know? Not that there was any sort of animosity, they just had us doing stuff a lot of times separate from the guys that were previously there. And it took a little bit of time to jell together.

Will: Also, this was not a recruiting class of Kyle [Guy], Ty [Jerome], and De'Andre Hunter. I mean, obviously, there are some great players in that class: Joe, mainly, and Akil Mitchell.

Our first open gym playing pickup with Joe, I was like, "This dude is a pro." You could see he was athletic, he was bouncy, [and] he could really shoot it, but everyone else in the class was a ways away.

Akil was super raw, and K.T. Harrell was pretty skilled, but no one else in the class was a guy that you're like, *This is great*. So, we had to then find leadership, and we had to come together as a group and build on the principles that we, as returners, had begun to become ingrained in.

Akil Mitchell: I might just ramble a little bit. The first couple of days on Grounds, I still remember having no clue what I was getting myself into – like at all. Not being ready for college – I was seventeen when I got there, so I turned eighteen that summer. So, [for] the first month of workouts and class, I was still a seventeen-year-old.

At that point, Tom [Thomas Rogers] might have been twenty-one. If he wasn't twenty-one, he was about to turn twenty-one, but he was the only guy that I really hung out with. I remember he had an old Cash Money Records album that he had in his car. And every morning – he was the only person that had a car – he would drive all six of us in his little Honda Accord to workouts.

Somehow, all of us would pile into his car. Billy's sitting in my lap, Tom's driving with knees in his seat, and it's like five o'clock in the morning going to our first few workouts. And I just remember being exhausted for the first month.

Like I said, it's like five o'clock in the morning. James is still half-asleep. Billy's either complaining or, who knows, talking to himself. Joe never really talked. At that point, I'm probably still asleep. So, our first three or four weeks, it was just like that.

That's all we did: we would wake up early, go work out, [and] go to class. 5:00 a.m. is with Coach [Mike] Curtis – strength and conditioning stuff. At that time, that was the most important thing for all of us. I was a seventeen-year-old kid against Mike Scott – no chance.

My first class was a weather class or something like that. We were really just there hoopin', man. It was a great time.

Thomas: Summer school was four weeks of class from 9:00 a.m. to 4:00 p.m. every day. So, my first class was one of those – like, jeez.

That summer, you could do two hours a week of on-court with

the coaches. At first, we would do an hour a week of full-team drills and practice, and an hour a week of four-man groups with one of the assistant coaches or Tony, where we're doing two-on-two stuff [or] one-on-one, which is... crazy. The five-on-five stuff looks easy compared to trying to guard Joe Harris one-on-one in the half-court: he's got the entire court and unlimited dribbles – he doesn't need them, but, yeah.

Coach Bennett's dad, Dick, is incredibly important to him, but he was also incredibly important to us. Halfway through that summer, Dick came in.

For like two-to-three weeks, he would take us for an hour a night, and we wouldn't do any basketball. We'd just be on the court, and he'd just talk to us about the Pack Line. It was like a class. It was a Pack Line class.

So, he would walk us through things, even stuff like getting through screens, or the angles your body needs to be at to prevent guys from going baseline, or a post trap, which is obviously pivotal, but I thought that was a lot of information.

Akil: We were going through boot camp. We had Dick Bennett's Boot Camp. Man, talk about the mental strength that it took to get through that one.

It was an hour, but there [are] no basketballs. It's literally every minute detail about where we needed to be on the court.

We were drilling every day for two weeks straight – however much time we were allowed on the court. It was little stuff: James just couldn't figure out how to hedge a ball screen, Joe just couldn't close out right. And you could see it, like, "Wrong. Do it again. Wrong. Do it again. Do it again. Do it again. Do it again." You can see guys either start to figure it out or really kind of go inside of themselves and struggle with it.

I definitely struggled, but we grew together, man. I remember those first couple of months, the seven of us – if you include Tom – we did everything together: ate lunch together, we would come back [to the gym] at night to get shots and stuff, and then walk back to the dorms, or again, all of us would pile into the car, or order Domino's – honestly, some great times.

Thomas: And it's funny because after that, it never happened again. After those two weeks, we never did a class like that with Dick, but he did that – and Tony did that – so that we could teach the next... it just got easier.

You didn't have to break it down like that. That was ground zero. That was blank slate; blank canvas – over half the team doesn't know what they're doing on the court.

Ronnie Wideman: I actually forgot that summer we did that. It was so important because that was our first recruiting class. For Tony, that shows how much respect he has for his dad and what he thinks of him. And they talk all the time – X's and O's.

I don't want to say no one else can emulate it, but it's one of the reasons why not many other teams are as successful running the Pack Line defense. You can watch a video about the Pack Line, but there [are] things you just can't figure out from watching a video.

Tony recognizing the importance of that was a display of humility, obviously, the trust he had in his dad, and the importance of building a solid foundation – that was so important with that young group of guys. And again, just a tip of the hat credit to Tony for his big picture thinking in that moment.

That investment in 2010 was an investment he was making for... the first eight years had to happen before the last two. And that had a huge part in it, I believe. So, I'm glad Thomas brought that up.

Really, it just takes that much time. Time lends itself to the fruit in trying to build a program. It takes time. It's just the way that Tony builds his programs, and that's just the way that his philosophy takes shape.

There are different ways to do it – some that are much more time-friendly – but Tony was trying to build a program, not necessarily a team. Building a team is more of a short-term thing.

Tony was committed to building a program, which is a long-term investment and takes time.

And that commitment in 2010 – that summer when he brought his dad in to teach the foundational pillars of the Pack Line that are so important – that was a commitment to the process, falling in love with the process, knowing that there were going to be some hard times, and there were going to be opportunities to take shortcuts, but we couldn't fall victim to that. We had to stay the course.

Thomas: [Here's] one story that puts into perspective what the athlete experience [is like] and how much you sacrifice from being a normal student – not in a bad way, it just is what it is. I spent two years at a military boarding school. I was so excited to get to college. I lived in SAE [fraternity] that summer before – I lived in the Launchpad. So, I lived there for a month, and I lived in Dinsmore [Row] in July.

So, that summer was fun, but then regular school is about to start, and I'm like, *Oh, this is gonna be awesome.* They have the First-Year Orientation in JPJ [John Paul Jones Arena], and they had B.o.B come play, and then Block Party was after that.

A day before, I was pumped. None of the other six freshmen went out at that time. Joe and Billy were in serious relationships, K.T. and James didn't like to do that stuff, Akil was like sixteen-years-old and afraid of girls at that point, and Will Regan didn't dabble either. But I was excited. I was a little older (I was twenty), so I was like, *Let's go.*

So, the day before, Ronnie was like, "I need five guys to come in and work out with a recruit tomorrow night."

I was like, *Are you serious?*

And it was maybe me, Joe, Billy, K.T., Akil, and Will. We go in, and play three-on-three with this recruit, and meet his family and everything in JPJ.

While the concert is going on, we're on the practice court behind it, so I'm just like listening to the concert. I'm not a big B.o.B fan or anything, but it was like, *That'd be fun.*

The recruit was Malcolm [Brogdon]. So, it was worth the investment. We played with Malcolm, he was obviously good, big, and I went to the B.o.B concert, and he wanted to go back to his hotel [and] didn't want to go out (of course), but my first Friday night of college was ruined by Malcolm.

I guess it was worth it.

Year 2

(2010-2011)

articulated by:
Joe Harris
Akil Mitchell
Thomas Rogers
Will Sherrill
Ronnie Wideman
Johnny Carpenter
Jason Williford

Joe Harris: That first year that I was there, we were one game below .500. We had a mixed sort of season. ACC was pretty tough – like it normally is. We were competitive, we were in a lot of games, and we just didn't have anything to get us over the top. We didn't necessarily have that belief in ourselves as players yet. And everybody – even the coaches – was trying to find their footing with everything that was going on.

Akil Mitchell: We were all going a little crazy. In summer school, you're kind of there by yourself. There's not a lot of girls. There's really nobody to talk to outside of the team. That's really all we were thinking about: *Man, I can't wait for the girls to get here. Classes are going to start, but whatever, once we start playing, everybody is going to recognize us, and life's going to be great.*

Did not go that way. At all.

I remember my first semester, I had Calc 2 for God knows what reason. I was in a Comm School [McIntire School of Commerce] class. It kicked my ass, man. The first couple of weeks were horrible, just *terrible*.

I wanted to do the Comm School. I didn't realize at the time how difficult the Comm School would be on top of basketball. It was an animal. And then on top of it, like I said, we were chillin' in the summer.

So, I go into the fall thinking, *This'll be a breeze.* It was not at all. But again, I was doing it with guys that I really enjoyed being around and really trusted.

We were in Kellogg [dorm] our first year, and all of us were in the dorms together. There's just nothing better than dorm life.

I was with Will Regan [in] the same room on the third floor, and Tom was on the other side. Across from him, Joe Harris and Billy Baron had a room together, and at the time, both had girlfriends who had moved in and were living with them for a part of the semester – four people in a dorm room at one point. And then K.T. and James Johnson were in the same room. And those two fools, they would be up until like four o'clock every night playing video games – just ridiculous.

But once the games started rolling around, I honestly don't remember much of that first year. I remember sitting on the bench a lot. I remember a lot of practice. But honestly, I don't remember a whole lot from that semester just because I was trying to get adjusted. I remember calling home, like, every day trying to figure it out.

My parents were like, "You know, it's just an adjustment. It's a period of adjustment. Kinda got to go through it."

School is not easy. There were a few times where – like I said, Tom was twenty-one at this point – I remember Tom going to buy beers. I didn't drink at that point. I don't think any of us did. James didn't; K.T. didn't. None of the guys went out except Thomas. I liked to go meet people at least. But the rest of the guys would just stay in their rooms.

So, it was just me and Tom. We forged this friendship, and it worked because he was cool with anything, and I was cool with anything. Some Wednesday nights, we'd go hit Boylan [Heights], and sneak in, and go to Dance Night, and just hang out, [and] blow off my math homework for whatever reason. Tom ended up being my go-to guy – and still is.

Thomas Rogers: That first year was pretty rough. We went to Maui, and in the first game out in Maui, we just got absolutely destroyed by Washington. I think they were [17-26] from three. They had Isaiah Thomas, Terrance Ross, Justin Holliday – they had four-to-five guys that were in the NBA – and that was the best team we'd played at that point and by far the best team I'd seen in my life up to that point – or played against at least.

Will Sherrill: They had studs. We got beat by [43 points]. We got absolutely annihilated, and we went into the hotel meeting room afterwards. Also, we were the last game of the day, so like a 7:30 p.m. game, and we played Oklahoma the next day at noon.

Tony rarely screams, and even his first year, [he] never really screamed. He lit into people in that meeting because of playing selfishly [and] not adhering to everything that we'd been working on for the last year and a half.

Thomas: Tony was very, very upset (laughs). I have not seen him yell like that. He's got a vein in the middle of his forehead that comes out. I've never watched that game film, but I imagine we quit to lose by that much.

We also weren't as good that year. [Tony] took that year as, "The freshmen are what's important here," like developing Joe, and K.T., and Akil. Not all his investments paid out, but Joe and Akil did in a big way.

It wasn't a conscious decision, but I think a lot of people, especially the scholarship freshmen guys – and now, looking back at it, definitely – if they're not playing as much as they want to, they're like, *What's the point of this? My buddy's at School X, and playing a lot of minutes, and doing well. If we're going to lose by 50 to Washington, why am I even here?*

Will: But then, we've got a game in like fifteen hours, and the next morning, [we] wake up, [and] it's the same Tony that next day, saying, "Okay, we've got a game to play. These are the things that we've got to do. This is how we got to play. We got to play the Pack. We got to move the ball. We got to do a lot of things."

It's the same thing regardless of the fact that we just got annihilated the night before, where – and I can only speak from personal experience of my first two years – that would [normally] require deep, deep soul searching, and re-examination of everything we've been doing as a team, and new strategies, and a new starting lineup, and drastic changes, and going person-by-person and saying, "This is why you're fucking up."

And that wasn't it at all. It was, "Okay, let's go." You call out bad play, selfish play, whatever, but the next morning, it's like, "Alright, let's get to work, and let's play."

We started the same five guys the next morning, and we end up coming back and beating Oklahoma by [18] points. Now, Oklahoma wasn't great that year, but it was still like, "Hey, we're right there."

Thomas: And then [in] the last game of the tournament, we were playing Wichita State, and we started the game up like 22-0 or something like that, and we lost. So, as awesome as Maui is, that was rough.

But then the next week, we went to Minnesota, and we beat like the [#15] Minnesota on the road, and Mike Scott was just unreal. Joe and Mustapha had like 25 each or something [24 and 23, respectively]. That was the first time when we were like, *Oh, maybe he knows what he's talking about. Maybe this could work.*

Will: I end up breaking my leg against Minnesota, which for me personally, it's still something I think about. I had come in as a recruited walk-on, but freshman year [2007-2008], I'm the last guy on the bench to get into the game in garbage time. There was one other walk-on on the team. My goal for the end of freshman year was to be the second-to-last guy to get in the game off the bench – so just leapfrog over that other guy – and I did that.

My goal for sophomore year is to get in the game in the first half of the game because that means I'm kind of in the rotation – I'm not just getting garbage time. I did – I got into the game in the first half in one game, but I still got it.

[In] my junior year, I got into the rotation, and I was getting minutes, but I was a hustle guy. And then, my senior year, I was finally an actual player versus just the hustle guy and had double-digit scoring in a few games: Oklahoma and Wichita State. And then, against Minnesota, I broke my leg.

I sat out for only about two weeks, and I came back and played basically the whole season with a fiberglass shell around my leg and the bone still broken. We didn't have any guys because Mike then got hurt [two games after Minnesota and] was out for the season.

Thomas: So, we go from being: we thought we were bad, to, we thought we were good, to, we *know* we're bad. Because Mike was – and still is – unreal. He would wear Ray-Bans in Boylan. He's one of my favorite people – hilarious.

Will: We had one freshman redshirting, then we had all these other freshmen. It was kind of an all-hands-on-deck situation. I ended up playing seventy-five percent the whole year. I always think about: if Mike and I hadn't gotten hurt, I think we would have gone to the [NCAA] Tournament that year, which would've been a great experience.

And I end up breaking my leg again against Miami in February – just broke the [same] bone in a different place – and then actually played that entire game – didn't come out of the game.

Ronnie Wideman: In the ACC Tournament, we played Miami, and we were up 10 (or whatever it was) with like 50 seconds left and ended up losing the game – one of the worst fails in the last seconds of the game.

Johnny Carpenter: I feel like Mustapha or Sammy, one of them stole the ball from the other one, and the ball went rolling out of bounds – just what-the-heck stuff.

Ronnie: I'll never forget Tony bringing us up to the hotel room after that – this is in Greensboro – and he said, "This is going to make us better."

I mean, this is the head coach. He's got to be just angry and upset because that was the end of our season. We had no postseason. For him in that moment to bring us up to his room after one of the most embarrassing losses and say, "This is going to make us better"? I mean, what a perspective!

Those are the life lessons that, as a twenty-seven-year-old at the time, I'm like, *Dang, okay. I didn't think that was coming*. It's so good for our staff to hear those words from your leader.

But even more so, it's great for him to share that with the players at a later date: "Hey, yeah, that happened. We're going to be better because of it." And we wouldn't be where we were in Year 9 and 10 without those experiences because they make us as a staff better, too.

Tony is a much better coach now than he was eight years ago and a much better coach now than he was last year. He just continues to get better. He's so driven to be the best he can be, and that's the attention to detail and iron sharpening iron – just finding ways to find even one percent to get better.

Will: We ended up having an okay season. We were like 17-15 or something like that. The first two years, things did not go as planned. And certainly, that second year, things did not go as planned.

We were finally playing well. We beat Minnesota, who I think was ranked [#15] at the time. We go into their place and beat them in the ACC/Big Ten Challenge. Mike was really playing well, and he had really come into his own as a stud.

He and I actually played pretty well [together] because I just stood at the three-point line and waited for him to get double-teamed. I didn't have to do anything. He was a great passer, and Joe was a good player, and Sam and Mustapha Farrakhan were coming into their own as good players, but injuries took a toll.

Honestly, my senior year, we didn't have a great leadership structure in place. I'll just speak for myself: I tried to be a leader. I am fairly vocal, so I tried to be a leader, but I got hurt pretty early in the season. It's hard to be a leader when you're hurt. It's hard to be a leader when you're back on the floor but you're kind of limping around [as] a marginal player.

When that six or seven [returning players] came back [for Year 2], it wasn't like after one year we were all like, "Oh, totally all in. Servanthood, Togetherness, Thankfulness..." The second year, on an individual level, each player was figuring themselves out as well.

Mike was becoming the leader at that time, and he had really improved as a player. It always helps to have the best or one of the best players be the leader. He was really coming into his own, but Mike got hurt eight games into the season. And prior to that – you think about that summer and into that fall – Mike was figuring out how to be a leader because he had never been in that situation before.

I was a senior, I was an upperclassman, but I had not been in a situation where I merited being a leader. So, I was trying to figure that out. Mustapha Farrakhan was the other senior. His career up until then had been up-and-down, and he hadn't been in that leadership position before. So, no one coming back had really been a leader. We were still adjusting to a new coaching staff and a new culture.

And in my view, frankly, the freshmen that came in, they had a bit of a cockiness, like, *I could be coming in and playing 20-30 minutes a game. I'm coming into a last place team. They got six guys coming back.* And with few exceptions, none of them were that good. And for the exceptions, you can look at who stayed [Joe, Akil, and Thomas]. But that created dynamics internally where you had people still having individual agendas that needed to get worked out. And you see, in that first freshman class, only [three] guys lasted.

We almost went through the same thing in Tony's second year as we did in his first year, except we had a bit more consistency from that returning group [and] a little bit more cohesion. We were starting to jell together, and we had a-little-bit-better players. Joe was better – especially in that system – than players that we had had previously. Mustapha was a year older, a year better; Sam [Zeglinski], the same thing. We finished middle of the pack. It wasn't like we were great. But in my view, that really set up that next year.

You had Mike coming back, and that's when that real leadership torch started getting passed. It was Mike, to Joe, to Malcolm, to London [Perrantes], to Ty and Kyle. And obviously, Anthony Gill, and Akil, and other guys were tremendous.

Our senior year, Mike had started to really come into his own and be a fucking beast, but also, from a leadership standpoint, he had really bought in, and that continued.

Jason Williford: Obviously, we didn't recruit Mike, so there was just a difference in philosophy in how we went about doing things and what he was accustomed to. He just had to trust a little bit, and we had to trust him. And there was some middle ground. It's a partnership. Mike rebelled a little bit, but it wasn't too bad, and ultimately, he bought in.

He had bigger goals for himself. He wanted to play at the next level, and he wanted to make sure we knew that's what he wanted to do, and how could we help him get there?

That was our job, but also it was our job to build a team. It wasn't just about getting you to the next level, but if you buy in and you do these things, you'll get to the next level because we'll win, and winning is ultimately what gets you there. I think it took him some time – not a whole lot of time – to adjust, but he became our go-to guy his last year.

And then I think guys watched [Mike's] progression and his

work ethic. Going into his fifth year, Mike really worked on his game. He spent a lot of time in the gym. Obviously, his shooting improved – he was able to make shots from all over the floor. And I think guys just saw his work ethic, and they followed that.

Then we had young guys by the names of Joe Harris and Akil Mitchell that joined the program when Mike was here. Those guys just kind of followed that work ethic, and they got better.

I don't like to toot our own horn too much, but I think we do a good job with developing guys. I think the track record speaks for itself. If you're here for a few years, you definitely develop, and you get better. I think that's so much of our success.

Summer 2011

Part One: Transfers

articulated by:
Joe Harris
Akil Mitchell
Ritchie McKay

Joe Harris: [From] the recruiting class that had come in, Billy [Baron] left my first year. He left literally halfway through the first year, and guys just slowly started trickling out after that.

Akil Mitchell: That was tough. That was really tough because for a year and a half – I mean, everybody kind of left at different periods – those were my best friends. I was with them twenty hours a day. Billy was sitting in my lap every morning. We were thick as thieves.

And I felt it, too. We were all struggling to figure it out.

I remember catching a bus after a morning workout, and [Billy] was catching the same bus, and he was like, "Hey, man, I'm out of here."

I was like, "What are you talking about?"

He was like, "I called my dad. I'm transferring. I'm going to Rhode Island. I'm out of here."

It didn't really sink in until we got to practice, and his name was off of the locker.

You could see it really hurt Coach Bennett, too, because he had plans for what we were going to be for the program's future, and he was really excited about all of us. We were his guys. You know, Jontel and those guys really fit in, but we were kind of the guys that he wanted to build the program around. So, to see Billy go really hurt him.

Joe: Will Regan was next: he transferred.

Akil: I saw Will go. We were roommates, so I saw him struggle every day. He had some other issues and wanted to be closer to home. For me, it was kind of a mindset switch: *Alright, I gotta step up my game, or I'm going to get left behind.* So, I really focused in, locked in that summer, [and] added some weight.

Joe: And then James [Johnson] and K.T. [Harrell] transferred halfway through our second year.

Akil: I [was] K.T.'s and James's roommate [in my second year]. It was me, K.T., James, and Tom all in the same building.

I can't remember what game it was, but K.T. didn't play well. Malcolm ended up playing really well that game, though, and it was kind of a shift. Everybody's looking at Malcolm like, *Okay, Malcolm's here to stay. He can play.*

I think maybe a day or two later, K.T. announced he was transferring. Maybe a week later, James was out of there – they kind of did it together.

Again, that one hurt, too, because we'd had so many great memories [and] so many great times together. But at the same time, I understood. It was just kind of the way it went. And guys wanted to see themselves in a different role and play a different way.

I'd lie if I said I didn't think about it. I definitely thought about it, but I was happy with the progress I was making. I was happy sticking through it. And I had no clue where I was going to go. So, I was like, *I'll stay. We'll tough it out. We'll figure it out. But I'm not running from it.*

I'm proud of it. I'm proud of the fact that Joe, Tom, and I got to stay and see the fruits of it all.

Ritchie McKay: In my six years [at UVA], Tony never ran anyone off – in spite of maybe an inclination from other coaches on the staff, yours included, that said, "He ain't one of us." [Tony's] too compassionate.

I don't remember him ever telling a guy, "This isn't the place for you."

So, I think all of the transfers were [of] their own volition, and no negativity was cast on them from any of the coaches in a public setting. Were there private conversations about, "Yeah, that's probably best for him"? Absolutely.

But I can tell you the integrity in which those transfers were cared for was right. And we never rooted against them. As a matter of fact, a few of those transfers I've stayed in contact with. And they knew we rooted for them.

Joe: It was interesting, though, because in that second year, we could feel that we had gotten a lot better. We had been improving a lot. We had taken significant strides.

We had brought in Malcolm. We brought in Paul Jesperson. We had Mike Scott back playing because he had been hurt [my] first year. We knew we were going to have a chance to be pretty good.

All these guys decided to leave for various reasons. Some of them didn't think that it was the best style of play to get them to the NBA – I remember K.T. saying that, specifically. He was probably the most talented guy that left.

It's crazy [when] I look back on it: K.T. left and went to Auburn, [and] Billy left and went to [University of Rhode Island] – both of them were First Team All-Conference players. Billy almost led the nation in scoring. K.T. led the SEC in scoring. So, they could have made it work had they stayed in Virginia.

It was more of a difference in terms of philosophy, I guess, and just the whole mental approach. Because it was tough for us. You go in, [and] everybody's in this foreign situation – even for the coaches and stuff, too. And aside from all the basketball stuff, it was difficult from an academic and lifestyle perspective as well.

We were getting up really early every day. We would go to class, and Coach Bennett didn't have a lot of bullshit with any of the classes that we were taking. He was checking and making sure everybody was going. He wanted to know what our grades were – making sure that we were actually putting in significant work on that end.

I don't want to speak ill on any other programs, but a lot of guys that I'm with in the NBA now, they talk about their college experience, and the academics are not even mentioned. So, our experience with Coach Bennett was a little bit different in the priority that he put on that sort of stuff, along with being demanding on the court and conditioning.

I think it's important to him because [of] the way that Coach Bennett views his program. Obviously, he wants guys to have success playing basketball, but for him – and he would mention it all the time – the bigger picture is, "What are you going to be doing ten years from now when you're not able to be playing basketball? I hope every single one of you guys comes in here, is able to play, [and] have long careers, but I want you to have sustained success afterwards. I want you guys to find something that you're interested in or enjoy, study it, and make sure that not everything is totally dependent on what you do on the floor."

He wanted guys to add other forms of value to their lives. He's also straightforward with that when you come into the program, too. I mean, he's not sitting here like some college coaches and telling them, "Y'all, you don't have to worry about class. We're going to make sure the curriculum is easy enough for you."

That's just not his approach. He wants guys to come in and prioritize [education] first and foremost. And I think that was instilled in him by his dad. His dad would come back all the time my freshman and sophomore year, and that was the message that he was always reiterating to us.

Pillars

Humility Passion Unity Servanthood Thankfulness

articulated by:
Johnny Carpenter
Thomas Rogers
Grant Kersey
Joe Harris
Will Gent
Rob Vozenilek

Johnny Carpenter: Coming in as a manager was unique because what you find out over time is that it's very special to be a manager at Virginia. Managers are not treated well at most schools. So, when you start talking about your experience as a manager at Virginia, and you start talking about, "Yeah, the coaches know me by name," and, "Yeah, if the players were to ever talk poorly or treat a manager disrespectfully, coaches will ream him," every other manager is like, "What? Wait – the coaches know your name?"

It starts with Coach Bennett, and he'll defer to the Pillars. Even culturally, he recruits kids to the Pillars. We look for kids that are humble, and that's a hard trait to find. Coach Bennett describes humility as, "Knowing who you are," like, straightforward, but what does that mean?

The way he breaks it down is, "Know your strengths, but also know your weaknesses." Know what you need to work on, know you might not be the best in anything [and] that someone else can do something better than you – and that's okay. It still gives you room to improve. It means not thinking so little of yourself – definitely not too highly of yourself, but also not too low of yourself – thinking of yourself less, and having a healthy perspective of yourself.

Thomas Rogers: Humility is an easy one. I think every young athlete needs to understand humility because it is more than just [being] a passive guy – you can be confident and be humble. What is it, Sun Tzu, "Know yourself"?

Humility is – I don't want to pick on Akil – but it's like Akil not shooting 4 threes a game, something like that: "Akil, you're quicker and more athletic than everyone that's ever guarded you. Stop shooting jump shots." And that's just a general example, but same with Justin [Anderson]: Justin's the best athlete I've ever seen in person, and early in his career, before his jump shot had really developed, he would take some questionable shots, and his percentages showed it. He's a better shooter than he showed.

So, yeah, it was like, know yourself in a lot of different ways because people misuse and misdefine humility so much. When Coach Bennett is preaching humility to them, some guys take that as a confidence hit, but the best version of yourself is great, but the version of yourself that you *think* is the best is *not* great.

Ty's strength is: he knows himself so well, and he's so confident to the point where people sometimes are like, "Ty's playing hero ball again. He's walking the clock down to 5 seconds and then double-crossover, thirty-footer." It's great that he has that confidence, and that's how he made all the shots he made because he's got so much swag, but let's reel it in a little bit.

Kyle, too. Dude, Kyle would drive me crazy early in his career, but Tony wants to empower these guys to be confident and take shots they can make because Kyle can get *so* hot. If Kyle is hot, we're gonna win the game. So, it's all about balance with Tony: finding the balance between high and low, and hot and cold, and aggressive and patient.

Johnny: [Coach Bennett] looks for passion. Passion means to him, "Do not be lukewarm." In whatever you do, do not be lukewarm – like intrinsically-motivated self-starters on and off the court, people who love to play, the fiery, the competitive.

I think one of the first ultra-competitive guys we got under Coach Bennett was Joe Harris. I mean that dude's competitiveness – not just effort. Competitiveness is that aggressive desire to win.

And then the Malcolm Brogdon's, Ty Jerome's – he's Tom Brady. Ty Brady is one of the nicknames I call him because of that will to win, the passion, the fire. And it's not just rah-rah. They just love the game, they love to win, and they love to compete more than anything else.

Unity: the quote Coach Bennett always throws around is, "If you want to go fast, go alone; if you want to go far, go together." I've never seen a guy more level-headed. Highs, he can get excited, but he also doesn't get too high. Lows, he doesn't get like, *Woe is me. The world is falling over.* How does a human being go from losing to a #16 seed [for the] first-ever time [in 2018] to be able to go and say, "Credit to UMBC – they kicked our butts. This is what happens in the arena. Hats off to them – don't want to take away from Devon [Hall] and Isaiah [Wilkins]"? It was unbelievable.

Even Syracuse [in the 2015 Elite Eight], you're knocking on the door. You blow a 14-point lead with 8 minutes to go, and Coach Bennett says, "There will be pain in the night; joy comes in the morning." Like, who says that? Every other coach I see is crying on TV or, "I love the kids!" And Coach Bennett loves the kids and cares about the kids, it's just been unbelievable to see those Pillars of guys who want to go the distance: they're not too high, they're not too low, [and] they have a quiet confidence, a hunger, a humility.

Servanthood: it's crazy to think that a manager can go from being a manager for a team to being a groomsman in one of the players' weddings – that kind of stuff happens. It's such a unique atmosphere where former players and managers stay in contact with each other. It's unbelievable. It's a true family in the sense of the managers will go a hundred-ten percent for the players in whatever they do. Whatever the players need, the managers will take care of it.

Grant Kersey: Especially for me being a manager, Servanthood really speaks to me because that's what managers do. We're there to serve. We're there to serve whoever: the players, the coaches, the trainers. I mean, anyone in the program, whoever needs anything, our commitment is to serve them and make their lives easier.

When you take on the role of being a manager, you accept that some of the work isn't going to be glamorous. Not many want to wipe up sweat from the court or clean out water bottles. It's all part of the program that leads to success. We like to stay under the radar most of the time. We try to be proactive and take great pride in what we accomplish.

That's why some of it speaks to me, but the other thing is Thankfulness and the way that the program – Coach Bennett, and his staff, [and] the players – they all really respect the managers.

We're part of the family like everybody else – nobody is greater than the other. That's super cool for the managers to see the way they approach Thankfulness, and they make us, the managers, know how thankful they are for us – all the guys.

Johnny: Thankfulness [is] being thankful through the great times and the hard times. We've had our fair share of heartbreaking losses over ten years, like [the] ACC Tournament against Miami [in 2011] – we blew that lead. Obviously, you think of UMBC [in 2018]. Shoot, there was when we lost to Florida State on a last-second shot in Charlottesville, and that probably kept us out of the [NCAA] Tournament in the 2012-2013 season. Just so many hard losses.

And we've also had so many good wins, but being able to handle it and be truly thankful for it – anybody can say they can learn from something, but to actually learn from it, and to be put back in not a similar spot but the *exact same spot*, #1 vs. #16 [against Gardner-Webb in 2019]: you're down by a lot, do you do what you did the first time and give in, helter-skelter, or do you keep fighting no matter what?

Eventually, we broke through. And once our guys broke through, I think we all kind of knew something just changed – the weight was lifted.

Joe Harris: Coach Bennett would talk about all five of them all the time, and you try to conduct yourself in a way where you're abiding by them when you played, but then also off of the court. The managers certainly were the Pillar of Servanthood.

I mean, they never got any credit for anything they did, but they put in more work than we ever did. They sacrificed for us all the time without ever getting any credit, and that was continually instilled in us. We genuinely had such an appreciation and respect for all of those guys because of everything they put in.

As players, it's probably going to be different depending on which players you talk to, but I'd say when I was there, Thankfulness is one of them. I remember Akil and I, [and] Thomas, we were all just real appreciative to see what was going on [and] to see the transition that had been made to trust in Coach Bennett and the process.

Obviously, we knew that we had played a big part of it, but at the end of the day, it was the managers, it was the coaches, it was all the people that came in, it was the people that were there before, and there was just a level of gratitude and genuine thankfulness to be a part of that program and to see it get to where it did.

Will Gent: I ought to ask Coach one day how he did it, how he got us all to – maybe he had to ask his dad – how he got us to buy in to these Pillars. As a coach, I'd be concerned about a level of cheesiness, but they just resonated with me.

Rob Vozenilek: There was certainly a stress on those things throughout the whole year. They're in the locker room above all of our lockers. I think they're in the film room, too. So, whether it was in a film session or one of Coach Bennett's pregame talks, there was always some sort of reference to it.

All of them have some direct kind of source from the Bible. It was always some passage where his dad pulled these things from. There was always some sort of reading, whether it was from a book, from the Bible, or something that would correlate to those

Five Pillars. They were everywhere. They're all over the locker room, they're on shirts that we had, [and] they're certainly everything that is promoted about the program.

I wouldn't say they're cliché. It's not like he's always trying to be like, "Come on! Thankfulness!" But he'll recognize the Green Team [practice squad] as kind of that Servanthood Pillar. It's usually [in] postgame comments where he's always being thankful for what happened and then also for film: to learn from the loss [and] being thankful for having the ability to learn from our mistakes. Humility was the thing that was always stressed in relation to the Green Team, in terms of us knowing exactly what our roles were. There were a lot of things that would be talked about off the court. It was stuff that Coach Bennett tries to live by. I think everyone can carry them throughout the rest of their life.

The one thing I always try to tell about Coach Bennett is: he's exactly who he is. Off the court, on the court, whatever you see or hear about him, that's who he is. There's no fluff to him. He's not out there preaching about these Five Pillars just so people hear it and think about it. It's how he lives his life. It's how he runs our program. It is exactly one equals one. Everyone believes it, everyone understands it, but it's certainly not like "the code," and it's not a bunch of bullshit either.

We don't talk about it a ton. From a player-to-player standpoint, we're not always referencing them directly. There are certainly references to it, like Humility – understanding what your role is – but it was so much more about how you approached the game and how you carried yourself off the court, in the locker room, and how you treated other people.

When you think about Servanthood and Thankfulness, those immediately applied off the court. The Passion, the Unity, [and] the Humility, those you can look at as tangible things on the court. It wasn't like we were always thinking about these things in the back of our minds – they weren't omnipresent. They weren't things that we lived and died by, but everyone understood that they were kind of bigger than basketball as well.

I think I saw it with some football recruit that committed the other day or something, but he was just referencing how you know, when you go to Virginia, it's more than football, or it's more than basketball. Guys are understanding that they're about life and not just basketball.

I mean, gosh, I've used those [Pillars] in every job interview since I graduated. There's no reason not to. They really are applicable to everything in life moving forward.

Grant: When I think back on the UMBC loss, the overwhelming feeling of defeat and despair, and how Coach Bennett immediately focused on lifting us and supporting us by using The Pillars as our guide, he turned one of the most devastating losses into a life-changing moment for many of us. That was a big moment for me, thinking about the Five Pillars and how impactful they are in all aspects of life – that is a lesson that will stay with me forever.

The Pillars are the building blocks for the whole program. On and off the court, they help guide us so much. I know personally over my four years, these lessons have made me a better man, just seeing how they incorporate day in and day out, on and off the court, with everything.

Summer 2011

Part Two: Walk-ons

articulated by:
Angus Mitchell
Rob Vozenilek

Angus Mitchell: Out of high school, I had zero intention of trying to walk on. I'd been recruited by some [Division]-III schools, but I didn't want to go to a small, random school. Kenyon was recruiting me, but I didn't want to go to Kenyon. So, I had zero intention of playing. And then it was two years in, and ZY [fraternity] had just gotten kicked off, and I was kind of like, *Alright, what are you doing?*

At that point, my body felt a lot better because I felt really worn out in high school. My knees always hurt; my back always hurt. I felt better, somehow, after two years of college.

[Will] Sherrill used to hang out with some of the ZY guys. They would play [basketball] with us occasionally. He told me as he was graduating that year, "Look, next year, there's only going to be ten scholarship guys. They're definitely going to take walk-ons. So, if you want to try out, at least you'll know that they will be taking somebody – there will be a chance."

So, he put me in touch with Ronnie, and then I talked to Ronnie in Spring of 2011, [the] second half of [my] sophomore year. I met with him, and he was like, "Yeah, we're gonna have tryouts in the fall. If you want to try out, I would recommend getting in really good shape."

That summer, the first half of the summer, I did study abroad in Valencia – very good for conditioning (laughs). I did work out a lot there because you have a ton of time. So, I was just running and doing a lot of push-ups, but still not in good shape. I was maybe staying afloat.

I got back to Houston and had like a month and a half at that point, and I didn't have a job lined up. I told my parents, "Look, I want to try to walk on. I want to take this time to train."

They were like, "Okay, that's fine."

There's a guy I played with in high school who walked on at Arizona State. He was a really good AAU basketball player. I got in touch with him, and he put me in touch with a skills development coach. So, then I started working out with that guy every day.

He used to coach at U of H, and at [Texas] A&M, and a couple other places, so he had this collection of guys who would still come back to him in the summer. It was me and these four other dudes who played in Europe at a very high level. In the morning, I would go run with them and go run sprints in the park in Houston in like a 105-degree heat, then we would go do these workouts in an un-air-conditioned gym – so fucking miserable.

I had already made this plan and told people about it, so then I was like, *Ah, fuck. I kind of have to go through with this.*

And it was also alarming how out of shape I was and how badly these other dudes were kicking my ass. It was very bad.

For the first two weeks, the coach was like, "You should not be doing this. I'd recommend against this."

So, that was a good motivator because I was like, *This is going to be really fucking embarrassing if I can't do this or if I go into the tryout and can only run up and down the court three times.*

I was grinding pretty hard for six-to-eight weeks – basically doing nothing but working out and sleeping.

Then I actually tweaked my back when I got to Charlottesville, and there's no way I would have been able to try out. Randomly, tryouts got pushed back like three weeks, and then I got better and tried out. It was an open tryout with ten-to-twelve people, and me, Rob Vozenilek, and Ryan Wright got picked. They invited us back for practice, and it kind of went from there.

Rob Vozenilek: I had spoken to Coach Williford, being a Richmond guy, before I went to school, but there were obviously no assurances for me that I was going to make the team [as a walk-on]. So, all that really did was give me a part in the tryout, which is an open tryout, but it's not publicized.

You have to go through some NCAA and medical testing beforehand in order to make sure you're cleared to participate, and I was fortunate enough to be on the team that first year. The tryout is like forty-five minutes to an hour long after a practice, and [you] basically go one-on-one, two-on-two, three-on-three, four-on-four, and five-on-five.

Pretty quickly, they can narrow it down to: "These are the three guys that get it. These guys know how to play, they can run an offense, [and] they can just roll the ball out and have a feel for the game." I mean, they're certainly looking for people with skill and people that will work hard, but they need people that can be taught, and can pick up an offense every single week, and change into a new one two days later.

That first year, me, Angus, and Ryan Wright were on the team, and that was a weird year. It was the first year we made the [NCAA] Tournament, and we had a ton of guys transfer.

We were initially just suiting up for home games, and then, when K.T. and James left, Paul [Jesperson] burned his [red]shirt, so he was off the Scout Team, then I joined the Scout Team, and I actually traveled the rest of that whole year.

We played that [Tournament] game in Omaha against Florida with like seven scholarship players. Doug Browman was ready to go, [and] I was ready to go as a third point guard. I was a freshman walk-on who barely played the whole year.

I fortunately did not play, so I never played in a loss in my whole career. I was at the table ready to check in with Tom and Doug, and then something happened, and we got pulled back because they were dribbling out the clock. So, dodged a bullet there.

Year 3

(2011-2012)

articulated by:
Jontel Evans
Joe Harris
Thomas Rogers
Jason Williford
Akil Mitchell
Will Sherrill
Johnny Carpenter
Angus Mitchell

Jontel Evans: The first two years, I remember [Coach Bennett] always stressed to us: "Before we can win with each other, we have to lose."

Those first two years, they were rough. First year, we went 15-16. We were trying to settle into his philosophy [and] his system. Year 2, [we] kind of had the same record, but flip-flopped: the first year, we went 15-16; [the] second year, we went 16-15.

[In] the third year, we were like, *Alright, we got some players. We have Mike Scott coming back. This is our third year in the system. We understand it. The guys that are coming in should know what we're about [and] what Coach Bennett wants, and it's on us to help them get used to the system that he's trying to teach.*

Joe Harris: [My] second year, we obviously got a lot better. We had better players, though. Malcolm came in. Mike Scott was finally playing for us.

We just had a really well-rounded team. Sammy Zeglinski, who had tons of experience and had been playing for a long time, was really good for us – [and] Assane Sene. We had finally meshed the former regime with the new one.

Basically, everybody that was there at this point was bought in. We were all on the same page with Coach Bennett and the rest of the staff in terms of how he wanted us to play, how he wanted us to conduct ourselves outside of the court, and everything started jelling together.

Jontel: That year was a turnaround year. We actually got that on shirts towards the end of the year, but that was perfect because that's what it was. It was a turnaround year, and it was a turnaround for the program, the city, the whole school, actually.

Thomas Rogers: It started my second year. Either at the start of the season or at the end of the season, [Coach Bennett will] have this one little saying or acronym that we'll use as a bonding thing. So, my second year was TAY.

We had a shirt that said, "TAY," which was Turnaround Year, and that was a thing: *It's on us. This is the year we turn the program around. This is the year we get back to the Tournament for the first time since 2007*. And we did.

Jason Williford: It gives it focus, and [it's] one of the things that I think Tony is really good at and we've done over the years. Yes, it's ultimately big picture, but you want to make it so that there's something that you're constantly focusing on.

Those themes that he gives them, regardless of what happens in a game, or in a practice, or let's say you have a bad stretch for a couple games, you can always go back to "Turnaround Year," and *What's our focus?* So, we may have one or two bad games, but this is the ultimate focus. It puts your attention there.

We like to say, "Improve daily, and don't worry about the end result. The end result will take care of itself, and we'll be fine. We'll bounce back. Win or lose, we'll be fine. But just play the game, and respect the game, and do it in the right way, and the results will follow. But never disrespect the game."

"It's in the dirt," we like to call it. It's the daily grind of practice and practicing the right way. And if you practice hard and your practice habits are the right way, games are easy. Enjoy the game because you put in the work, and in the process of preparing to compete and play the right way, you'll be able to play with anybody.

Tony is: what you see is what you get. He's as cool and calm and collected as anyone, but when you don't play the right way, if you don't prepare the right way, if you don't practice [the right way], that's when he loses it.

I think the guys understand it's bigger than whatever opponent we're playing – it's the game. Play the game; don't disrespect the game.

When you do that, I think you'll have more success than you will failures. That's what all those acronyms that we use at the beginning of the year do.

It's funny. I can't remember all of them. [Tony] gives us one every year.

Akil Mitchell: I was confident going into that second year. I had gotten more minutes [in my first year] than I expected to. Coming out of high school, I was seventeen. I was scrawny – athletic, but raw, just super raw. So, everybody thought I would redshirt, but I guess I picked up some things quicker than everybody expected, and defensively, I could do some stuff that we really needed. So, I knew going into my second year I was going to play. I just didn't expect to play as much as I did.

That would have been the year that Mike was going crazy. That was Mike Scott's fifth year. I remember every day, Coach Curtis, Coach McKay, [and] Coach Sanchez, their goal was to get me to push against Mike. So, whatever I could do to get under Mike's skin or to make him a better player, that was my job at that point.

I feel like that's when I really noticed, *Okay, I could be a really good defender.* Trying to guard him, and his fadeaways, and his post moves every day… like I said, at that point, he was twenty-one. He was an adult. He's strong, smart, and a really good shooter. So, I learned a whole lot playing against him every day.

If you don't [get the pressure and timing right], he's going to score on you every time. He will embarrass you.

In that program, you can't take a step back; you've got to get stops. So, I really dove in my second year. I was starting to get comfortable.

Throughout the year, I played here and there, but I don't think I started until Assane Sene got hurt going into ACC games, kind of late in the ACC schedule. I got a few starts, and then that was it. I was playing every night after that.

I remember watching [Mike] work. I remember watching him coming off the injury – even *with* the injury – doing all of his rehab stuff, and us having conversations like, "Yeah, this is my last go. I'm going to make a push for this now."

He completely changed – everything about himself: his demeanor [and] the way he approached the guys on the team. You can tell all he wanted to do was win. And there's nothing better than an older guy who kind of approaches you like that. It's cool to watch. It was really cool to see.

I learned a lot from him. But all the guys: Assane Sene was a great leader, Mustapha Farrakhan – still guys that I talk to – Sammy Zeglinski, all these guys. And when we catch up, we catch up about all the stories but also talk about how important Mike's fifth year was for all of us. So, I'll give him a lot of credit.

[Jontel is] one of my favorite teammates ever. He's got your back in anything. I love that kid – definitely one of the best defenders in the Tony Bennett era, too. Don't dribble around him; just get rid of it.

Will Sherrill: I was still really close to the program because I was so close with Mike and also Sam, who had a fifth year and who I lived with for four years. [Mike] really started taking that mantle of, *This is my program, and that's how we're going to do things.* It had started my senior year, but it kind of got put on hold while he was hurt.

And that's when you start bringing in the Five Pillars because the coaches can talk about the Five Pillars, but you need a couple of those standard-bearers, as the best players on the team, to embody those. And then the rest of the guys will follow, and new guys coming into the program will follow them. But that first step was the guys who were there and the freshmen coming in figuring out that trust and that consistency that we've got in the coaching staff.

Jontel: Mike Scott was our leader. That was our go-to guy. I remember like it was yesterday, we're at warm-ups, and he was just like, "You mf'ers are tryin' to be cool in warm-up lines," and everybody just looked at him like, *Alright, let's get it together. Our leader said we're tryin' to be too cool. Let's get it together.*

When we had open gyms in the practice facility, and guys were being lukewarm, we could count on Mike to start trash talking, get everybody involved, and get the competitive nature going. That's what type of year it was: everything was clicking. I'm getting goosebumps thinking about it because it was a great time to just be a part of something that was bigger than ourselves.

[Mike] didn't always have it, but when he came back for that fifth year, he knew what was at stake for not just our program but for himself. So, he knew he had to grow into a leadership role and lead us on and off the court.

He did an astounding job doing that because he raised the level of play of all of us in practice, games, everything. We see this guy going; we want to help him out. In practice, we see him getting after us; we want to get after him as well. It was just making each other better. And I feel like during his fifth year, that's when he really stepped into that leadership role and led us the whole season.

Joe: Mike even mentions it, too. I don't know if he's ever said it in the press, but Mike mentions Coach Bennett is pretty much the main reason why he was able to make it into the NBA and have such a long career because of the habits that [Coach] instilled in him while he was at UVA that last year. He was a talented player, [but] he was just a little bit of a shithead leading up to that last season until Coach Bennett had gotten there.

Jontel: That year right there was amazing. We had just won big against Winthrop at home before we went to the Thanksgiving tournament in the Virgin Islands, and everybody was on a high horse like, *Yeah, you know, we're pretty good. We're gettin' it down pat.*

We go in, and we lose to TCU in the first game of the tournament: 47-45. Everybody plays terrible, and I'm like, *Dang.* Everybody was looking around like, *Are we gonna have a repeat of the years before?*

But then we just all came together as players. I don't even think the coaches know this, but we came together, and we looked at the schedule, and we were like, "If we're going to turn this thing around, we cannot lose another game until we get to conference play." And it was against Duke and stuff.

Next thing you know, we're just racking off W's, and we're getting closer with each other on and off the court. A lot of people don't know that year, we were close on the court, but we did a lot of things outside of basketball like movies, bowling, hanging out at Chipotle, a lot of things.

One of the things that I thought was very important and imperative to our team's success was the player meetings with our team chaplain, George Morris. I feel like those meetings that we had on the road before games allowed us to get closer together and feel comfortable with each other on and off the court. And I think that's what really brought us success, on top of what Coach Bennett was doing with his system and how he was implementing it through us.

It was team building. I remember vividly: there was one [meeting] where we all had these cards, and you had to pick a card that had a name of one of the players, and you had to say something very positive about that player. Hearing a teammate think that about you, it automatically raised your confidence: *Dang, he thinks I'm this good. I want to be even better – not just for myself but for him and this team.*

The morale was just right there that year – you could feel it. You could feel it when we went out to The Corner or when we went to parties and stuff. It was like, "Ayyy basketball team! Let's take pictures!" We kind of felt like rock stars.

It was like, *Dang, nine months ago, it wasn't like this.* And we had just suffered that loss to Miami in the ACC Tournament [the year before]: we were up 10 with like 50 seconds left. And it was just how that changed in a short period of time. Things were clicking for us. It was awesome. Everything was clicking after that TCU loss.

It was a lot of blood, sweat, and tears, man. I remember vividly: guys were really pushing each other in practice, and outside of practice, we wanted to be our best versions on and off the court. But in those practices, we were battling each other. It was so competitive, but it was great competition for us.

Everybody was pulling for one another. It didn't matter in practice who had a great practice [or] who had a bad practice. If somebody had a bad practice, it was like, "Alright, I'll get you next time," or if somebody had a great practice, it was like, "Keep working. Keep working."

It was just that type of moral togetherness. It was truly special. And now, every time I think about it, it gets better and better as I explain it because that was the turnaround point for where it is right now.

It took me a while to learn [the defense], but once I got it, it was just like, *Alright.* The defense is there to help people that aren't as quick with their feet. If you can guard a guy for two-to-three dribbles, you will thrive in that defense. You just have to give effort – that's it. You can't coach effort. If you give effort, you're good in the Pack Line, and if you know the principles, you're good. That's all you need: effort and to get the principles down pat, then you'll be good. And once everybody starts buying in to it: woooo, lights out. There's no stoppin' us – one 24-second violation after another.

That's one of the greatest feelings of all time. When you sit down in a stance, and you stop a team from [even] getting a shot off, when you hear that 24-second shot clock go off, it's a rush.

It's like, "AHHH! I want another one." It's like a drug. It's like I'm a fiend: "I want another one. Let's get another one." It just revs us up. I know JPJ [John Paul Jones Arena], they go crazy when it happens, and they have no idea what that does to us on the floor. It's crazy, man. It's crazy.

As everybody knows, I wasn't a great shooter, but I had to find ways to be able to be a threat out there. So, the coaches worked with me before and after practice on different shots, like going outside of the lane and looping the ball up, which Coach Bennett calls the "giant killer."

I remember when he taught me that, and I got it down pat with both hands, right and left. He said, "I don't care who you are. It could be Tacko Fall – they're not blocking it." The way you're releasing it like a hook shot, but it's a layup, [and] you're outside the lane... it's just the giant killer – that's the perfect shot.

I was like, *I must be special if he's teaching me this because he said that was his go-to move when he played.* So, to learn that, the floaters, [and] different type of finishes when I got into the paint – he allowed my offensive game to be decent enough for people to respect it.

We worked on the jump shot; it's just something I wasn't really comfortable with. Maybe like catch, one dribble, two dribble, pull up, yeah, but just catching it and poppin' from three – that just wasn't my type of game.

But to tip my hat to them, the coaches did work with me on my shooting. It just never translated into the games – only the floaters, and the giant killers, and the different type of finishes. But we did work on my offensive game. I don't want people out there thinking, "You wasted four years just doing defense." No, we worked, you just have a role on the team, and you play that role to the best of your ability.

I'm like, *Dang man, you can easily take me out and put somebody in who can shoot. But you saw something in me that could help the team win.* It was, "Alright, if we do this, we'll have a better chance at *this*." So, they actually took the time to [say], "Let's work on your floaters. Nobody can stop you from getting into the paint, but you need a shot to get off in order to be successful."

I don't think other coaches in the country are trying to do that.

They're recruiting kids that already have the tools equipped with them. Here at UVA, they're adding value to what they already have. And it's truly amazing, man, the stuff that goes on behind closed doors with the program.

They definitely do things that make us better players. You can see it! From Mike Tobey to Malcolm Brogdon to Joe Harris, nobody knew who those guys were coming out of high school. Now, look at them. I think Mike Tobey is overseas [playing professionally]. Malcolm Brogdon: [NBA] Rookie of the Year. Joe Harris: Three-Point [NBA] Champion. He always finds those hidden gems that everybody overlooks, and he turns them into great basketball players.

It's guys that got overlooked, got a chance, came in, worked their ass off, got better because of the coaches and because of [themselves], and achieved success. I don't see any other coach doing that besides Coach Bennett. He's not getting these five-star, McDonald's All-American, one-and-done guys. I mean, it might be now in the next couple of years, but before this year or last year, no, it wasn't! He's getting these guys that [are] three-stars, maybe four-[stars] at the most – not McDonald's All-Americans; guys that nobody really heard of – and he's bringing them in, and he's turning them into great players.

I think that needs to be put on notice because he's been doing it for years. I get so excited because I've seen it with my own eyes. I've seen the development of Malcolm Brogdon. I've seen the development of Joe Harris. I've seen this! And it's just like, *Wow, these are some really good coaches – great coaches.*

Man, Mike Scott! He worked his ass off, don't get me wrong, he worked his ass off that fifth year. But with the coaches' help, it's like, *Dang, they gave him the tools to be good [and] what to work on.*

He worked on it day in and day out, and now, he's having a long career in the NBA. It's crazy. Even with the Assane Sene: the coaches got their hands on him. His catching became better his last year, his finishing became better, [and] his free throws! These are things that are going unnoticed. He might not have played a long career after UVA, but during his last few years at UVA, he strengthened his weaknesses. Coach Bennett and those guys have the blueprint. They know how to strengthen people's weaknesses.

I think as a program, we do the things that these blue-chip programs don't really take pride in: playing the heck out of that defensive end, trying to strengthen our weaknesses, and trying to be better from the neck up.

Coach Bennett teaches decision-making drills. I'm like, *Dude, I know how to pass the ball!* But then, I get in the game, and I have like 3-4 turnovers, and it's like, *Alright, I need those decision-making drills.*

What other coach out there is doing that in practice? Passing of the toss back so that your passes are crisp. I'm pretty sure all these other big programs are just going in there and putting up shots, going through plays, competing, of course, getting better that way, but we're actually doing the little things [and] fine-tuning the little things so we can last longer.

It's just different. Coach Bennett's a different type of breed, man. I'm not just saying that because I played for the guy. His basketball mind is... intact. He's a genius when it comes to basketball, and what he can do with the talent he has... ohhh man. It's fun to watch.

Joe: That second year, we played really well. I can't remember exactly what our record was, but we started off the year unbelievably hot. We were 17-3, 18-3, something like that.

Johnny Carpenter: Back when trending on Twitter wasn't even a cool thing, [Mike] was one of the first people to be trending on Twitter for his second half at Duke his senior year. That was wild – he didn't miss a shot.

People don't give him enough credit for how hard he worked. We saw him work going into that final year. He knew what he needed to do. The number of NBA threes from feet set to stepping into a shot… he was just grinding, and that came along with the culture. Everyone being of one accord, [and] everyone being about getting better every day and finding ways to improve.

Joe: And then we had a lot of injuries throughout ACC play. Malcolm was getting hurt, Sammy was a little banged up, Assane got hurt – all basically going into the end of the year.

Jontel: We were playing Maryland [in the last game of the regular season]. It was their senior night, and it was a close game. We had to win that game because we didn't know whether we were a team on the bubble [of the NCAA Tournament] or not.

And [Coach Bennett] called this one play [up 2 with about 30 seconds left in overtime]. I forgot what it's called. I want to say Through-Split. I have the ball in my hand, and the big man comes and sets a ball screen for me to come off, but I reject.

Now, when I reject, I have two or three options: I can hit the big guy over my shoulder, I can hit the guy in the three-point corner by our bench, or I can just lay it up. We practiced that all the time.

When he called that play, nobody was in the stands; it just felt like it was me and four other UVA players. The first option wasn't there, the second option wasn't there, the only option was [to] lay the ball up, and I laid it up!

It was like, *Dang, we practiced it.*

We win the game, and we end up going to the Tournament.

Joe: I think we still ended up finishing around fourth in the ACC [and] made [our] first NCAA Tournament, but we sort of limped our way into it. We didn't have a healthy roster at all. We didn't even play with Assane or Malcolm in our NCAA Tournament game.

And, oh yeah, I forgot I broke my hand literally in the middle of the season, too, so I played the second half of ACC play with a broken hand. So, what had started off with what looked like a lot of promise, we still played well, but it just wasn't quite what it could have been, barring a lot of the injuries and stuff that we had.

Angus Mitchell: As we were on the way to the Tournament, Darion [Atkins] wore this Nike shirt that said, "Lazy but Talented," and then Williford saw him, and he was like, "Coach Bennett cannot see you wearing that shirt. You have to go back and change right now." Williford was always watching out for Darion.

Before the Tournament game against Florida, we had a special show from Dick Bennett. He performed a super impassioned rendition of "Casey at the Bat" [by Ernest Lawrence Thayer]. That was hilarious. It was a legendary performance. It was serious but also comedic – he knew it was absurd.

Akil: I remember before that game being shook. I don't really get too nervous – that might have been the most nervous I've ever been. Then that Florida squad blew us out. We went to Omaha, and they ran us out of the gym. It was done before halftime. We knew at halftime, *Ah shit – this is bad.*

But it fueled the heck out of us.

Summer 2012

Part One: Nolte's Recruitment

articulated by:
Evan Nolte

Evan Nolte: I was a late bloomer in high school in terms of people being interested in recruiting me, and Coach Bennett and the staff were one of the first people – basically my freshman year. [In] my junior and senior year, I had a lot more offers, and bigger schools came after me, [but] UVA started when I was a freshman, when I was under the radar.

I talked to Coach Bennett on the phone after the first time he saw me play on the bus ride back with my team, and I remember being in the back, and that's when he offered me a scholarship, which was cool. Honestly, I didn't really like the whole recruiting process because I thought a lot of coaches – mainly assistant coaches my first two years of high school – it was kind of a lot of bullshit, and it felt very disingenuous.

For me, my older brother played basketball for two years at [another school] and had a bad experience. My parents wanted to make sure I was going somewhere with quality people – people who meant what they said. The whole entire time, Virginia stood out.

It's not like there were other schools who were doing anything two-faced or anything. Ron Sanchez, now [the head coach] at UNC-Charlotte, he's the one who recruited me initially. Just the overall environment – not only just talking to them on the phone in the allotted times that they could call us, but when I went to visit there, compared to all the other schools, there was something about how genuine the entire staff was – not just the coaches or Coach Bennett, but everybody that surrounded the program. It seemed like everybody was a quality person.

You could tell they meant what they said, whatever they were saying. And the players, too – when I went to visit UVA, compared to the other schools, I felt very comfortable with the type of guys Coach Bennett had. At the time, there were still people there that Coach Bennett didn't recruit, but there was something different about how you could tell that there were quality people everywhere surrounding the program.

I learned from my brother: playing basketball at the college level, you spend more time with your coaches and teammates than you do any other person by a long shot, like ten-fold. So, that's gonna help shape your experience because you're going to be around this type of people. The type of players that were there – whether it be Joe, Akil, Thomas Rogers, Jontel Evans, all those guys – when I would visit, it was like, *Man, these dudes really like each other.*

Usually, when you play on a basketball team, there are these cliques, or people butt heads, but when I would visit a couple times, I was like, *These dudes are cool.* And the other places I would go, there were a bunch of different egos and other bullshit that you expected, but with UVA, I think it really comes down to the type of people.

Obviously, Coach Bennett makes a bunch of decisions, but there are other people there that help make the decisions for who we should hire for Video Coordinator or who we should hire for administrators sending out letters to recruits, and I think they genuinely want people that are quality people. I don't know how else to say it.

I could tell there was a different vibe at UVA. They made it to the Tournament that year [before I got there] against Florida and got demolished, but I think they emphasize the type of people that they want in their program – and it's not just players. That really stuck out to me.

I'm not a religious person at all, but there are a lot of people in the UVA program who are deeply rooted in faith, and there were some other coaches that I talked to from other schools who acted like they were and they weren't, and [with some UVA coaches,] you could definitely tell that God is their life, which sounds so deep or whatever. And seeing how the coaches interacted with the players in a practice, or how the players treat each other in an open gym [that] I would watch – I don't know why – it was just a different feel from the beginning.

I got there, and I'd never been on a team where everybody got along so well, and I don't know exactly why that was, to be honest. I think a part of it is UVA is such a good academic school, so whether or not it was number one or number four, getting a good education was on *a* priority list for everyone that went there.

So, I think that all ties into the type of people they look to recruit: guys that really do want to be part of something bigger – their egos are not getting in the way. All four years, that was something that was shocking to me: how the older guys really cared about the younger guys, which – obviously, I haven't played for another team – is pretty rare. And I've heard from the guys that were fourth years when I got there how they were treated as freshmen. So, I think there's a certain type of quality of people that they look for that are also attracted to UVA and the style of play.

The most common question I get when people come up to me and talk about UVA is, "Is Coach Bennett really as good as he seems?"

I'm like, "Yeah man, anything you see on TV interviews, that's legitimately how he is," and I think that's pretty rare. That's one hundred percent where it starts, the kind of people they recruit, and they look for more than just talent and athleticism.

Because for myself, I was like the worst defender in all of high school. Literally, AAU was a disaster for me because I couldn't guard anyone in one-on-one play. I was a fucking disaster at defense. I feel like I was more of a heady player who understood a lot more of the game than my body could catch up with athletically, so I think they care more about things outside of just talent and athleticism, and [they] look at the family situation, in terms of the support that you're getting and what type of guy you are, and I really think that's the core of the whole thing.

You can tell from Coach Bennett's first recruiting class to now on the team, they're guys that are quality – they care about something bigger than themselves. And there are guys that transfer who think they can do it better themselves, and for some people it worked out, and for most of them, I don't think it can be considered a success for transferring.

That's one of the things I remember about Coach Bennett recruiting me: "There's no guaranteed minutes or starting. You have to come in here and earn it." That's something I really liked because that's what I think is the healthiest situation for a team to compete on a daily basis, and you are what you've done.

I think there's probably a different answer now just because of how much success the program has had since I was recruited there, but another question I get asked is, "Did you know you were going to be playing this type of defense?"

When I was getting recruited, there was not a mention of defense – no one knew that it was a defensive system. I didn't know that for sure. And you end up realizing that in order to compete with these teams like the Kentucky's, the Duke's, [and] the North Carolina's, you can't outscore them, so if you try to outscore them, you're going to lose.

I realized pretty early on, within the first year, *Holy shit, [with] the guys we have on our team, we aren't gonna beat the other people one-on-one, and we're not going to beat them on fast breaks running down the court. We're going to beat them by playing together as a team on defense, we're all gonna be fucking attached by a string,* and that takes a special type of player [and] a special mindset to not waiver and do something on your own or try to be the man, basically.

It takes a collective effort, and that's what's special about all the guys: we collectively beat all those teams. I don't know what the record is now over the past five or six years in the ACC – it's not even close. So, having people who are willing to be something bigger than yourself, you can't do what UVA has done if you have players who don't put their egos to the side.

It was hard for some people, so they transferred. You look at guys like Marial Shayok – and he didn't have a big ego, he's an incredible dude, I love Marial – it wasn't the right system for him, and he goes to Iowa State and has a breakout year. So, you have successes outside of that, and you're not going to hit the target from a recruiting standpoint one hundred percent of the time, but I think the leaders on the team was a big part of it when I got there: Joe, Akil, [and] Jontel.

Those guys, when you're coming into a college team, you're like, *Holy shit, I can't believe this is this much work, I can't believe how good everyone is,* but you have the leaders on your team who are so humble, and down to earth, and hard-working.

You have one time to make a first impression, so our first experience of college basketball was those guys leading the team, which had a huge impact on people like Justin. Malcolm sat out my first year, but he was someone who had one of the most disciplined, crazy work ethics I've ever seen.

So, when those guys are at the top right when you get there, that's what you look up to, and that's what you try to be like the rest of your career. That had an everlasting impact for years to come because then people grow up into those roles like Malcolm and Justin after Joe and Akil left, and you have the next class that comes in and sees those guys, and you have the people in the middle like Tobey, myself, Justin's part of that crew, but that's the only team we've known: these humble, hardworking guys that really don't care about anything other than playing together and winning.

Development

articulated by:
Mike Curtis

Mike Curtis: For me, as an alum, I am very thankful for the opportunity to be here and be here with Tony Bennett. I don't think there was probably a better person to take over this program, and I'm just fortunate to be part of the equation as it relates to what we've been able to do. At the end of the day, it's his ability to identify talent [and] to identify character, and then I think that I've been able to do my part in terms of the physical preparation.

But at the same time, if he doesn't bring in as good-quality, high-moral kids as he's brought in it, I wouldn't be as effective as I am. It all goes back to the top.

My dream and my aspiration when I came back here was, "I want to go win a National Championship," and that was something that I probably articulated more than most of the guys on our staff did early on because I didn't want to be afraid of it.

I didn't want to have our kids not think in those terms, in terms of what our aspirations were as a program. It's something that has driven me for a long time. I've had friends and colleagues that have been able to achieve that, and that was one of the things that, *You know what? That's what I want to do here.*

Fortunately enough, our leadership, in terms of Tony, created an environment that made it possible for us to get to that and have the amount of success that we've had thus far.

Given our environment and the type of athletes that we recruit, we're not going to have guys that are here for a year or two years. And just in my journey, obviously, I've had some opportunities to work in professional sport.

When Tony called and asked me to come back to Virginia, I

had already ventured back into intercollegiate athletics. Upon my return there, one of the things that I had learned in my time in the NBA was there were certain guys we evaluated that went through the draft process, and in many ways, you could see that they were ticking time bombs in terms of just their basic movement competency. You knew that with a drastic increase in volume of games and exposure, some of those deficiencies and asymmetries were probably going to yield some type of injury.

When I went back to college, one of the things that was part of my mindset was to make sure that I was creating a process and a training system that was not going to lend itself to some of those things that I observed in professional sport, which was to take my time and make sure that foundationally, these guys had the tools to play the sport, which is movement.

Obviously, there are some things that underpin the demands of the sport as it relates to force, and velocity, and things of that nature, but at the end of the day, they don't play this sport with a barbell or dumbbells attached to their bodies. They need to be able to move and move efficiently in order to complete those tasks that are specific to basketball.

So, coming back into this environment, I wanted to make sure that is what we started with: making sure that from a movement competency standpoint, they were where they needed to be to reduce our injury risk. But in addition to that, obviously, the demands from an energetic standpoint – like conditioning [and] things of that nature – early on, those are your limitations.

If you can play, you can play. I think one of the biggest things that we joked about when I did work in the NBA was during Kevin Durant's draft period, where he couldn't bench press 185 [pounds] one time. But in the grand scheme of things, did that particular measure in regards to strength have anything to do with his ability to play basketball?

No, there was no correlation there. But we knew he was an efficient mover. You could see the way that he was able to take this seven-foot frame and move about small spaces and big spaces in order to complete the task, or specific demands, for basketball. So, foundationally, that's where we should always start.

We have the luxury of having diagnostic tools. I've kind of evolved over the course of time, in terms of using technology and other things, to be able to triangulate on where we need to focus our time. But those things are secondary to establishing movement abilities first. That's been foundational to what we've done since I've been here.

When you get into Year 2 [or] Year 3, we address things that are secondary to that – force and velocity deficits – to try to bridge the gap. Early on, you're going to see there's an increased output in terms of the things that we value: being able to jump higher, being able to exhibit more acceleration and speed, [and] the ability to change direction. You're going to increase those things by increasing efficiency of the athlete, and at the same time, reducing injury risk that is associated with someone who doesn't move well. So, that becomes our first priority.

Once we've done that, then we can add more horsepower to the engine and to the frame. I say this to a lot of our recruits: "If you have a Pinto or a Prius Chassis, and my primary objective early on is to put a Lamborghini engine in that frame, I'm going to break it apart."

So, our goal is to do some work on the structural elements and some of those things that are potentially rate-limiters from that perspective to handle the horsepower that we want to put into you later on. So, that lends itself to more of a slower progression, per se, but early on, I think it allows these guys to focus on what's most important, which is staying on the court, working on your skill, [and] being able to practice and play with their teammates so there's a camaraderie that is built, instead of trying to expedite this process and increasing injury risk, which then takes you off the court.

For us, if we don't have the highest level of athletes, I think Tony does an amazing job of identifying IQ, EQ, and underlying skill. I think our deficits a lot of times fall in the genetic potential

– athletically – of our athletes. So, if I can just make sure that they are able to stay on the court, we will shorten that gap.

Some of those schools get guys who are probably better athletes but may not have the same IQ, EQ, and underlying skill set that some of our guys have the potential [for]. If we can keep them on the court, if we can keep them working at a high rate to work on their skill set, and along the way, keep bringing up those physical capacities, we end up having a pretty good product at the end.

We haven't eliminated [injuries]. Those things do come up. But I think per our training, we expedite recovery of those things when they do come up. I will first and foremost give credit to Ethan Saliba, who has been a mentor of mine since I was a student-athlete myself and in the Sports Medicine program [at UVA]. I've learned a lot from him in terms of trying to construct a training process for us that takes into account all the variables that relate to increasing risk of injury.

Early on in our time here, as with most of the programs, you go through this initial standardization of culture and trying to install and implement certain things that sometimes lends itself to more work and workload than these athletes can tolerate. And I think we still went through that process here.

You have to respect history, you have to learn from those things, and I think we did. And that speaks to Coach Bennett, myself, and everyone else who was part of our athlete support teams. We did have some hiccups early on.

My thing was, *You know what? There are ways for us to quantify and objectively look at some of these things that are potentially propagating factors for injuries.* And I kind of made a stand and said, "Hey TB, we've got to do a better job of looking at these things because they're affecting our availability [and] they're affecting our ability to stay on the court."

Very early on in our time here, we decided that we were going to invest in technology, [and] we were going to invest in athlete monitoring and utilize that to better serve in creating our training process both from a physical preparation standpoint but also what we did from a technical and tactical standpoint, in terms of [Tony's] practices, the durations, and things of that nature.

So, those things have created a process for us that has created an environment that lends itself to a reduction in those injuries. And we have great kids, too. Listen, when we go over Key Performance Indicators, and we talk about behavioral things that need to support what we're doing, for the most part, our kids listen. I'm not going to take all the credit for that – a lot of that has to do with the kids.

When we say, "Look, you have this much workload this week or this day. It's important that you get your eight-to-ten hours of sleep, you hydrate, and you eat these things." And those guys have been pretty compliant [with] those things. So, that lends itself to those outcomes as well because we're in a partnership together.

We've been fortunate in that way. And like I said, we learned a lot from our early time here, and moved forward from those things, and adjusted our practices and our approaches to training in such a way that I think it has reduced our incidents of injury.

Summer 2012

Part Two

articulated by:
Rob Vozenilek
Angus Mitchell
Akil Mitchell

Rob Vozenilek: We needed to replace like six guys that had left, so [there was] a huge class coming in, [and I] spoke to Coach Bennett. Ryan [Wright] wasn't going to play again, and Angus wasn't going to play again. I was really the only one who wanted to move forward. But I think at that time, no one had really made a decision.

So, he said, for the summer, they were going to focus on the guys that were coming in. It sucked. I didn't think it was fair, really, but I was never guaranteed anything as a walk-on, especially one that had tried out.

I worked out that whole summer at St. Chris [St. Christopher's School] and came back ready to try out in the fall. I think that might have been my best tryout, but they didn't take anyone out of it. They were going to rely on the fifteen guys they had and then managers like Maleek [Frazier] and Johnny.

So, that was a weird year. I didn't really want to be a manager. Looking back on it, I probably should have because I probably could have gotten a lot more experience that would have helped me after school if I wanted to stay in basketball – that was initially what I wanted to do.

I could have been learning the different film softwares, and Synergy, and things that helped Johnny and Marcus [Conrad] and these guys go get jobs. Being from Richmond, and being in the Hall [fraternity], and just having a bunch of other friends at UVA, it was nice to just kind of be a college student for a year. I mean, that first semester was certainly my lowest GPA, and, you know, I had a ton of fun.

As we got back into the spring, I had to refocus my efforts. I had kept in touch with Coach Williford and some guys just over the course of the year. I would see people get hurt, and I'd be like, "Hey, if you need anybody..." So, I stayed in touch with the coaches throughout the course of the year, but it was nice to kind of get away.

Angus Mitchell: As for deciding to only play one year, it just ended up being a huge time commitment, obviously, and I had no realistic path to playing. I talked to the coaches after the season. I was like, "Look, this is a ton of time. We won like 22 games. I think we would have won 22 games with or without me."

Ritchie McKay was like, "I don't know about that."

And I was like, *Ehhh, I feel pretty confident about that*. "I think it just makes sense for me to focus on school next year."

I felt bad about quitting. I really liked the people. I did think the walk-ons were helpful. Anyway, that's why I quit. But all in all, it was a great experience.

Akil Mitchell: That was an interesting summer, actually. We did two trips abroad that summer, or I did at least. We did the team trip abroad, but right before that, I went on an Athletes in Action trip. So, I got to travel a little bit.

I don't know what it was about... I had just gone through a breakup or something. I remember being on that trip like, *Alright, this is going into third-year; it's kind of time to step up. This is my time. Mike's gone. I'm an upperclassman now, like, I have to do it.*

That was my mentality for that whole season.

<u>*Year 4*</u>

(2012-2013)

articulated by:
Akil Mitchell
Joe Harris
Jason Williford
Johnny Carpenter
Evan Nolte
Thomas Rogers
Ritchie McKay

Akil Mitchell: Tom and I lived our third year in a little box apartment. It was maybe 400 square feet... maybe. We couldn't shower in there. The bathroom was so bad that you couldn't shower because I couldn't stand up without hitting my head.

I would shower at the gym every day, and come home, and sleep. I don't think I ever showered in there. The carpet smelled terrible because [someone] threw up one night in there, and it just never came out.

That was the most fun season we had, other than winning the ACC Championship. We just had a blast, man. We had a ball. We were right across the street from GrandMarc [Apartments].

Joe was having an incredible year, Jontel was having a good year, and it was just fun. It was like work at that point: you just get into a rhythm.

The class schedule kind of makes sense. You know where you're going, you know who everybody is, [and] everybody knows who you are. If I need to stay up until four o'clock in the morning to get something done, cool. I got it now.

Joe Harris: We were able to kind of ride the momentum from that second year to third year, [and] continue to get better players. That's when Justin Anderson and that recruiting class came in:

Mike Tobey [and] Evan Nolte. It was the best recruiting class that Coach Bennett had had to date. They were all highly touted players. They came in and contributed a lot as freshmen.

Akil: Justin, you can see the potential that he's got. Darion [Atkins], you can see the potential. You know it's coming. We all knew it was coming. We just had to figure out how to get over the hump. And that year, we were *this* close, man. We were *this* close.

Joe: It was just unfortunate, though, because we didn't have Malcolm. If Malcolm would have been able to play my third year, I think we would have been even better.

Akil: Just like Mike [had done], you can see [Malcolm] doing the rehab every day, you can see him getting the shots when he's allowed to, [and] you can see how focused he is. I don't know how he did it, honestly.

He was there when we were practicing. You could see him on the side on the bike, you can see him doing his work, but then I'd come in, and he'd be like, "Yeah man, I just got up some shots."

I'm like, "Malcolm, it's six o'clock in the morning. What're you talking about?"

He's like, "Yeah, I got up some shots. I'm gonna come back in before the game."

Before games, he's sweating. He's working out. It got to a point where I think he had to have special shoes made. If you go back and look, he had one pair of Kobe's in like six different colors because those are the only shoes that would support his feet from the amount of work he was putting in. He was an animal that year, and it fueled all of us over and over again because we knew when he came back, *Yeah, he's going to be good.*

Jason Williford: I still think Malcolm Brogdon is one of the most committed and hardest workers we've ever had. The dude was a machine. From the time he broke his foot here, to rehab and his commitment to getting back on the floor, and his work ethic – that's what a lot of guys following him have seen.

I think he has shown that through hard work, anything is possible. He wasn't the most vertical athlete, not the quickest athlete, probably had one of the funniest releases on his jump shot, but he willed himself to be who he is today, and that guy is borderline an NBA All-Star who's now making a ton of money on his second contract, and it is a result of a lot of hard work, dedication, and discipline.

So, London [Perrantes], and Devon [Hall], and Ty, and Kyle, and De'Andre, and whoever to follow definitely have benefited from the work ethic that guys [like Malcolm and Mike] have put in.

Johnny Carpenter: Malcolm gets injured, right? And then even when he's injured – this is back when me and my brother Mikey were student managers – Malcolm would come in, [and] he literally couldn't put any weight on his foot, so they had this little scooter constructed for him where he had his left leg down (if his right foot was the injured foot), so, his knee is basically bent back behind him in this little scooter.

Malcolm's work ethic literally didn't change an ounce. The only thing that changed was the wheel and the boot. We're helping Malcolm into the shower, and Malcolm's like, "This isn't going to stop me," in the same way that it didn't stop Ty [in his NBA rookie season].

Malcolm, that January, was cleared to play. One, their Scout Team was really freaking good at the time with him and Anthony Gill, but two, Malc was so freaking driven. We'd go in the morning because in his head, even though now he's free to play, he was like, *This still isn't going to change who I am. Getting injured isn't going to change who I am. Coming back from injury is not going to change who I am. I'm still gonna be this crazy freaking worker.*

We'd go in at like 5:30 [a.m.] with Coach Curtis, who was helping Malcolm with some basketball stuff and on-court conditioning. When he got back to working with Coach Curtis, I was like, "Do you guys need help in there?"

So, we'd get there at 5:00 a.m., we'd work out, then Malcolm would do his morning workout [with Coach Curtis], then Malcolm was starting to do an extra, third workout at night.

Coach Curtis found out about it and was like, "Bro, you need to slow down. You're putting in too much time. We can't have another injury."

Malcolm was trying to combat him on it, so Malcolm said, "Alright, Johnny, this is what we're going to do: get up around 3:30 a.m. and pick me up instead."

I was like, "What do you mean?"

He's like, "Coach Curtis is going to check the afternoon slots. Coach Curtis isn't going to check if we get one workout in the morning. So, we're gonna go in the morning [and] get shots up before he gets to the gym around 5:30 a.m."

We'd knock out a quick hour workout and just drive and wait until Coach Curtis was coming in. Once we knew it was safe to show up around 5:00 a.m., we'd go back in. So, Malcolm was still getting that third workout in.

Jason: Johnny can attest because Johnny rebounded. He chased balls all over the gym for Malcolm. It wouldn't surprise me if he got a fourth one in at like 10:00-11:00 p.m. that same night after going to class. He was just that dedicated.

Evan Nolte: That first year, I played a ton. I played more then than any year. When there are one or two guys that are off in terms of not scoring, [or you're] not together as a team on defense or offense, you get some bad losses.

One of the first ones was George Mason. The margin of error in college basketball is so slim that you don't really understand it until you get punched in the mouth by someone you definitely should not have lost to.

Thomas Rogers: We go up to Wisconsin for the ACC/Big Ten Challenge. Obviously, Wisconsin is a special place for Tony and his dad. So, we go up there for shootaround, and at this point, we're still trying to make a name for ourselves and establish our program, and that was when Wisconsin was very good. We kind of looked at them as, "This is what we want to be."

After the shootaround, we go to center court, and Tony's like, "Beneath our feet, my dad had them carve the Five Pillars underneath the court. This program, Wisconsin, this court, was built on those Five Pillars."

Basically, "Let's show them what it's about." That was a powerful moment for our program because that's what it's all about.

And we won that game.

Ritchie McKay: Because of how quickly VCU, Richmond, and Old Dominion were growing, the Governor at the time in Virginia had this mandate to bring them into the fold, and we did this tournament in Richmond at the Coliseum. We were kind of told, "You need to do this."

We played Old Dominion, who was struggling, and we lose to them right before Christmas, and we stunk. I said in the locker room after that, "Man, there goes our NCAA Tournament."

We had gone the previous year. I was really into the analytics and rankings – Sagrin, RPI, Ken Pom, etc. – that's a horrible loss. I remember driving home from Richmond and telling my wife, "This loss is catastrophic to our Tourney chances."

Akil: We hadn't figured out how to win every game yet. We beat NC State and then dropped [Georgia Tech]; beat Duke and then dropped Boston College. We were still kind of inconsistent, still may be down a couple of pieces that would've made us a real contender, but you could see the pieces starting to come in. That was the exciting part: I knew we still had so much more potential.

Johnny: It was a year that we were actually excited about, but then through injuries and stuff and some horrible buzzer-beater losses – like Florida State got us the buzzer – we ended up not making the Tournament.

Ritchie: We were a #1 seed in the NIT. We lived on that bubble.

Akil: We got snubbed, bro. We were supposed to make the Tournament that year. We definitely got snubbed. And I remember reporters coming in and asking... everybody knows me, but I don't really hold my tongue a lot, and I was pretty pissed. I was upset that we didn't make the Tournament.

I was like, "I don't want to play in the NIT. I want to play in the Tournament. I'm not really here for second place."

Coach Bennett didn't like that (laughs). He really didn't like that, and he came in after, and he's like, "Well, we've got guys telling the media that they don't want to play, so you know what? Just go home. Everybody just go home."

We were frozen, like, "So, we're done for the day? You're sure we get the day off?"

And he was like, "Yeah, just go home."

I'm like, *Alright, I might start talking shit more often!*

We made the Tournament my second year with Mike, and that was part of the motivation for why I was so upset the next year. We touched it. We knew what the competition was, and I wanted to play against the best. I didn't want to go face Iowa in the [Third] Round of the NIT. I wanted to go to The Garden [Madison Square Garden]. I wanted to be on the stage, and I knew that our guys could compete at that level if we had a chance.

We ended up making a little run in the NIT, but again, [we] just couldn't stay consistent enough to get over the hump. But like I said, it was another year that we knew that the next year we were going to be good. That whole year was building confidence towards something bigger.

Ritchie: After that season, when we lost to Iowa in the game to go to New York, I remember thinking, *I don't know if we can do this.*

Joe: We still had a good team. We finished fourth in the ACC again. We had the bad loss to ODU, and we lost to George Mason.

They were both bad losses that killed us from getting in the Tournament. If we didn't have even one of those losses, we would have made it into the Tournament and been able to have a chance to at least get some sort of national recognition.

All along the way, we were slowly building up and getting a lot better. Our record got better every year, but we still weren't nationally recognized. I think people within the ACC were starting to take notice, and they realized that there were better players coming in, how difficult it was to play against us, and how much better guys were getting while they were in the program.

That's one thing: Coach Bennett and the rest of the staff, when I was there, they took guys like me who were good players coming out of high school, but we were not these super heralded prospects. Their development was so good that we just improved a lot every single year.

Summer 2013

Part One: London's Recruitment

articulated by:
London Perrantes

London Perrantes: For me, it started off in high school with them recruiting me for a little bit. Maybe a couple of weeks after talking to them when they were recruiting me, Coach McKay called me and said that they weren't going to recruit me anymore because Devon Hall had just committed there and re-classified into my class. He was a point guard in high school, so they thought that we couldn't play together and that we were two in the same. So, they told me that they were going to stop recruiting me.

I was hurt. I was hurt a little bit because for me, it was a big thing. It's an ACC school. That was a huge thing for me. It's always been my dream to play against the Duke's and the North Carolina's or be at one of those schools. So, having that at first, and then them kind of stepping back – it hurt for sure, but you think about it [as], *This just wasn't meant to be.*

Maybe a couple weeks later, I guess Coach McKay had been out at the same tournament that I was playing in, and then I guess [he] told Coach Bennett that we [could] play together. So, they ended up coming back to my last AAU tournament of my career in Vegas.

I remember walking out of my hotel room talking to Coach Bennett, and that's when he offered me a scholarship. They were the only school that had told me that they were going to stop recruiting me and then came back into the picture.

I didn't necessarily have too many offers or official visits lined up. I had three visits: Virginia, Arizona State, and Illinois – three completely different programs [and] three completely different conferences. Those were the three officials that I set up going into my senior year. I took my first official visit to Virginia, and that was really it.

I went with both my parents. Devon ended up showing up to my official visit with his family – just that feeling that there was no hatred, or shadiness, or anything like, *Oh, he doesn't want me to come here.* That played a big part in it: the personality that Dev had. And even his family welcomed me with open arms, regardless.

That ended up being cool: getting that vibe [from Devon] and getting the vibe from the players that were there. I was able to be around, and play a little bit in an open gym, and just feel everybody's personality. Everybody welcomed me with open arms – that was a selling point, too.

Obviously, the school's education was another big selling point, but realistically, when I knew I wanted to commit was when Coach Bennett had a little barbecue at his house with all of us. My family [was there], [and] I think some of the guys on the team came over [who] were taking me around the campus.

Coach Bennett took me into his office, and we watched film on my high school and AAU stuff. Other places that I'd been on official/unofficial visits, they had boosted this crazy highlight tape, which was cool, but Coach Bennett kind of pointed out shit he thought I needed to work on and pointed out, "If you're going to come here, you can't do this."

If I was to come here and play for him, I'd have to do this, this, this, and this, and, "If you want to play at the next level, you have to be better here."

And him being an NBA player [and] an NBA point guard, that all played a huge part. Hearing that was like, *He's already looking at what I need to get better at to make it to the next level [and] to be a contributor at this level here now.*

He is definitely one of the best with X's and O's. Just being a point guard, you have to learn so much and know so many different things. As a point guard, you've got to know all five positions of every single play: you've got to know what they're doing, and you've got to know what the defense is doing and be able to talk to all your teammates. As a point guard, mentally, you have to have a high IQ and be able to do a lot of different things.

That goes with the point guards that he brought in, really. Shoot, Ty, myself, Kihei [Clark], all of us have that IQ [to] be able to take what he's thinking about or what he's seeing and then bring it out to the floor. So, that PG mindset is definitely used for him in coaching.

I wanted to commit when I was there, but my mom was like, "Oh, you need to wait until we get home and wait a couple of days," and then I just waited a couple of days and committed to Virginia, and then played my senior year kind of freely. That was a fun year.

[I] went there for our first summer, where me and Dev felt like we got thrown into the fire like crazy. I would say it was a struggle for the first bit of it because of the Pack Line, and learning that was super hard. As soon as you step on campus, that's the hardest thing you have to do: learn the Pack Line.

It's different for different people. It's tough. It's something that you have to get ingrained in your head. It's not necessarily a normal defense like most people play. It just comes with repetition. Obviously, some people get it quicker than others.

The game is different when you're playing against other people that don't know what the Pack Line is. When you're going up in practice, everybody knows how to play against the defense you're playing, and then you go up against guys that have never seen it before, and it's completely different. So, learning that – that first summer was tough.

Think about the guards that we had my freshman year: Joe Harris, Malcolm, [and] Justin. We had a lot of big guards, so coming into it and having to guard them and get our feet underneath us at the same time was... me and Dev used to go back to the dorm room and look at each other like, *Are we good enough to do this? Are we built for this? Because this shit is hard.*

So, I think me and Dev really bonded our freshman year summer just going through the trenches with each other. It was just us two [in that recruiting class], so it was learning, and putting our backs together, and fighting just so we didn't give up. Devon was obviously a big part for me, and I think myself for him as well.

Managing

articulated by:
Grant Kersey
Kevin Oberlies
Will Gent
Ben Buell
Johnny Carpenter
Barry Parkhill
Joe Harris

Grant Kersey: As soon as I made the decision to come to UVA, I knew I wanted to be some part of the basketball program. One of my high school friends was actually a fourth-year manager. We'd play summer ball together, and he suggested that I try out for the position – he put me in contact with Ronnie.

Of course, I had dreams of always trying out to be a walk-on, but I knew my chances were stronger for the manager position. I didn't want to risk being turned down as a walk-on my first year and not being part of the program. So, I put all my focus into trying to be a manager, and luckily it worked out.

Kevin Oberlies: When people ask me about my time there, the word I use is "program." They really treat it like a program – everybody's involved. They treat everybody there with the same amount of respect, whether you were a guy like me or whether you were Coach Bennett himself. That's special.

I wasn't there for the first three years [of Coach Bennett's tenure], and I'm sure it was a little bit different. The fact that Ronnie has to say no to certain managers – that doesn't happen at other places. You have to hand out flyers on campuses just to get people to be your managers. That's crazy. And that probably took a long time.

All those guys, they make you feel like you're part of the team. I wasn't necessarily best-friend level, but everyone made you feel like a part of the program. Anthony Gill was definitely one of those guys – what a nice guy. They're all nice guys. I really don't have anything bad to say about any of them.

Will Gent: I have a bunch of manager friends from different schools in this industry, but for us, it was pretty simple. It wasn't a closed process, but it wasn't necessarily advertised. You kind of had to reach out. And for my year, there was really one simple interview process.

We have ten as a group at Virginia, which I think is about normal. They always select two-to-three, [and] my year they selected two. From there, the managers welcome you in and tell you, "Here's kind of what we do," in this really short onboarding period – [you] get in the mix really early.

For me, I found out about what being a manager was, and I was excited because I played in high school like a lot of [managers] do, and it didn't really feel quite right for my basketball journey to be over. I had a real strong passion for coaching, and at the time, I thought that would be a dream job. I wouldn't actually get to pursue it, but the management experience would at least extend that career, and I'd be around like-minded individuals – ended up turning into a lot more than that, obviously.

I can't speak for other schools, but [at] Virginia, it's sort of what you want the experience to be. There's a collective amount of work that needs to get done, whether it's helping the video coordinator get film ready, or just setting up practices, [or] things during practice, like wiping up sweat, filling Gatorade coolers, having a whiteboard ready for Coach – just anything and everything in between.

In my interviews for jobs, what I would say about managing is every day is unexpected. There's always a new task. It's really just being extra hands and voices available when needed. We divided and conquered, and you gravitate towards what you're good at or what you're interested in, maybe. A lot of my work was on the floor rebounding in drills, and then I'd say even more so helping guys individually outside of practice.

Ben Buell: I grew up a huge UVA fan. My dad went to UVA. I grew up going to football games [and] basketball games. The statement, "A dream come true," I think is overused, but in this instance, it really, really, truly was a dream come true. To be around this program that I looked up to and was interested in for so long, and to really be a part of it and learn from these people, I'll forever be indebted to Coach Bennett and to Ronnie Wideman, who's our Director of Basketball Operations, who was my direct supervisor.

I reached out to Ronnie the summer going into my first year at UVA. There are some interviews. He said, "Email me back once you get on Grounds." There was a group interview process with some people in the office.

I remember talking a lot about my experience [at Collegiate School] with [Alex] Peavey [and] the similar CCC 7 approach that he brought: Character, Compassion, Community, the Seventh Generation, and I thought that was very similar to these Five Pillars that Coach Bennett espouses. I thought they – Ronnie in particular – liked that I brought that commitment and understanding that everybody has their part to play. That's, I think, the big part about being a manager: recognizing that no task is too small and taking pride in what you do, even if it's not the most glamorous thing.

Kevin: I was lucky as a manager to find my place in there. Just a quick background: most managers come in their first year. There are only a few people that didn't do that. During my second year, I was just playing pickup ball, and Johnny Carpenter – who's in my top five favorite people of all time, just so nice – he used to beat the crap out of me at Slaughter [Recreation Center], that red gym by first-year dorms.

I specifically remember: he beat me so bad one game that I

hated him. I saw this dude around campus, and I was like, *God, I hate that guy,* but then he's such a nice guy. This is why I didn't like him: on the court, he's so nice to you. He'll talk trash by being nice.

It's one of the most effective strategies ever. He'll get under your skin by tapping you on the back and being like, "Yo, nice shot," after he drops like twenty buckets on you.

So, for some reason, I guess I stood out. [In my] second year, I was on the women's practice team, which was fun, and I got to know Johnny better. I guess I played him [my] first year and hated him, and then got to know him better [my] second year, but it was actually Luke Ford.

Luke Ford always kept in touch with me for two years, and then he invited me to come on [as a manager] as he was departing. I guess this was 2014 summer. I sat down with Ronnie, and [it was] just very organic. Ronnie is just a great, great guy.

So, I was lucky in that way, and I never stopped appreciating the fact that it was unusual to get into the program later. The reason I use "program" is because some of my best friends came from that managing crowd, and everybody feels involved. They always invite managers to have meals, which is just cool. It just makes you want to feel involved. It doesn't hurt that a few of the managers were used in practice and felt that usefulness.

Will: It's weird how you kind of get roped into guys. There's a joke as managers that you don't want the players to get your numbers because as soon as they get it, they're going to hit you up to rebound. I thought I was getting honored with the opportunity to rebound for Malcolm two weeks in. I didn't realize until years later that the guy who gave him my number was actually tricking me into running miles and miles because Malcolm is a workhorse.

So, I got latched on to him, and that was an amazing experience. Actually, we're working together again now with the [Indiana] Pacers, which is super cool. But yeah, for me, it was mostly a lot of rebounding, and they want you to balance [managing] with your schoolwork. If I could go back and do it again, I would have done less school and more managing, but you make it work.

[Malcolm is a] pretty silent killer during the workout. That's not really his personality off the court, I would say. He is quiet, but when you know him, he jokes around a lot, but he's very focused, very diligent, [and] very regimented. He knows what he wants to do going into the workout. He has a plan.

I think what made us vibe the best is... I mean, it's not that skilled of a task to feed back balls, but I think in a workout like that, there's sort of an energy and a vibe that you want to match and make sure you're sweating as much as he is to let him know that you care and that you're invested.

We overlapped for two years, his fourth and fifth year, my first two years. Then he went to the [Milwaukee] Bucks, and then, when it was my turn to try to get into the NBA, he signed with Indiana, and there was an opening. So, that worked out more than I expected it would.

Grant: We would work out guys whenever, every day. I mean, more in the offseason because we're not practicing as much, but for hours, you're just in there. You get close with the guys, too, in the gym, just helping them work out [and] do their drills.

You finish a workout and just talk and hang out with the guys. They are always appreciative. I feel like I've heard of some other schools where they don't really take care of the managers, but here, it's the complete opposite. Some people can just get caught up with the players, but here is the complete opposite. Coach Bennett will always say he has zero tolerance if you disrespect a manager.

I didn't know what to expect. I thought, *Oh, yeah. I'll be a manager. I'll pass the guys on Grounds, I'll say what's up, and it'd be cool.*

Then, Kyle and I got to know each other off the court, and we decided to be roommates. We lived together my second and third year after dorms and before he left [for the NBA]. The guys on the team all became like my best friends. I still keep in touch with them, and I'm thankful for these relationships.

We did everything together: going out to eat, playing cards, watching movies – anything. The entire experience was more than I could have imagined and so much better than I ever expected. Everybody really is the same – it was a truly humbling experience.

They'd want to go shoot, and I'd go work them out. Nobody was weird about it. It wasn't like, "Oh, you have to do this." It was an equal commitment. Everybody buys in to their role, and it really did make us better off the court and on the court.

Johnny Carpenter: When you go through the history of players and managers, it's been the players that had the crazy elite work ethics: you think of Malcolm, who brought on Marial [Shayok] and Devon Hall, then Devon brought on Ty and De'Andre. But the weird thing was: when the managers would see these players work, [managers] would be rebounding so hard.

Will's [Gent] first year was '14-'15, and Will and I are similar in that we want to do everything we can to help the players on the court. Will said his first day, he's rebounding like crazy and going after it, [and] Malcolm said to AG [Anthony Gill] and London, "This guy's the new Johnny," because of the hard rebounding.

Will was like, "I have to beat this guy!" Will and I are great friends.

It's just a unique parallel to see the managers and how their careers are all shaping up. They're going into the sports field. The managers all have dreams to coach or to work in sports, but ultimately it comes down to: can we help the players reach their dreams? It's a beautiful symbiotic relationship in a lot of ways. It's neat to see.

Grant: Coaches during practice, they say, "Oh, I know people at this school or this school, this has a GA [Graduate Assistant] spot." Every coach is always super willing to help us out for life after basketball – or life after college, I should say, because a lot of the managers stay in the basketball field.

Barry Parkhill: I can guarantee you: Tony would say everybody involved in the program, they're all equal. They just are. The players get the recognition, but managers are so valuable.

The one thing that's really cool in watching so many practices over the years is Ronnie Wideman – I would think – someday will be an Athletic Director. That kid is unbelievably efficient. The guy's unbelievable. I think he does a lot of the at least initial selection.

They look at kids that are in school that played high school basketball because a lot of the managers go on the practice floor – they're cannon fodder. They're getting the snot beat out of them every day, and they just do it, and they probably love every minute of it.

That's really cool that they look for kids like that along with kids that are willing to sacrifice time. I think the kids that do it love it.

Joe Harris: Coach Bennett's goal is not to have guys playing everywhere or working everywhere, but he's going to help you out in whatever you want to do – that's the thing. Obviously, if you're part of the program, you probably want to be involved in basketball in some capacity.

I've said it about us as players, but the same thing goes for those guys that are managers: if I ever wanted to hire anybody that wanted an entry-level job into the NBA, in terms of a video coordinator, a front office role, whatever it might be, the guys that are recommended from Coach Bennett would probably be the first on my list because you know what you're going to get.

Everybody that has ever been a part of his program, they're all built and wired the same way, regardless of if you're a player or a manager.

Will: I think the best part for me as a manager, what made me feel so appreciated, was those outside-of-practice rebounding sessions. Again, people make fun of me for always being there for Malcolm, and I still get made fun of for it to this day by some of the managers.

Well, I can say we're good friends, but [it's] pretty much what I describe as a great working relationship: he gets that I care, and just the authentic, "Thank you," he would give me at the end of the workout – I felt very appreciated.

No one did a better job of that than Ty. Ty was always very thankful [and] showed the appreciation. I mean, our year and my career ends the way it does [with UMBC], but then the next year, I felt more attached than ever to the program when I was outside of it.

Summer 2013

Part Two

articulated by:
Rob Vozenilek
Akil Mitchell

Rob Vozenilek: As we went back into that summer in between my second and third year, [the] same thing again: [I was] at St. Chris playing with that team, working out there, and getting ready, and then back into a tryout for the third time my third year. And that's when Jeff [Jones], Maleek [Frazier], and I made the team, and Maleek made that conversion from being a manager to a player. I don't really fault the coaches for it, but at times, I just felt like I was grouped in with them – and Maleek as well. I just felt like I'd already been on the team.

The reason I went back was I had a small taste of the program. We had made the Tournament for the first time [my first year], and we kind of all knew something special was happening. We knew that there was a lot of good talent coming in, and we thought that our system would eventually start to break people.

Akil Mitchell: Going into summer was the first time I'd ever thought about playing pro. It didn't even cross my mind. I was like, *I'll go to work or something.*

It didn't cross my mind, honestly.

Coach McKay called me to the side, like, "You know you're gonna do this. You're going to play professionally."

I'm like, "Uhh, shit. Hmm... that sounds cool... I can do that. Okay, yeah, let's do that."

So, I went out to Vegas – I went to a couple of camps, actually. I went to a few Nike camps that summer and played really well against some really good players.

On the last day of the last camp out in Vegas, I popped my

hand, got my finger caught with an elbow, and broke it. [I] called Ethan [Saliba], [and] Ethan's like, "Alright, don't move. Don't do anything. Just relax. We'll get in tomorrow."

But! It was the last day of the camp, so they were paying for guys to go play paintball. I hadn't done anything the whole time, so I was like, *Alright, I don't think it's broken. I'll just go play paintball.*

So, I was out with Mitch McGary, [and] I think Aaron Craft was out there. We're out playing paintball, shooting each other with paintball guns, and I had just broken my hand – definitely made it worse. I'm shooting with my right hand, so every time the gun jolts, I'm definitely fucking something up in there.

So, I get back, and Ethan's like, "What the hell did you do?!"

He was ready to kill me, for sure.

I had surgery that summer, and mentally, that really set me back. It was [my] first time really dealing with injury. Again, I was so excited for the season, but now, *I can't get the work in that I want to.* I was kind of in a funk going into the beginning of the year.

I think Joe was coming off an injury, too – he did something to his foot. So, we were kind of rolling into [our] fourth year not the way that we should have, but again, we still knew we would be good. Having guys coming back off of injury, and it was probably a bit of arrogance, too, just thinking that it [would] go a lot smoother. But we were on everybody's radar at that point – we were getting everybody's best shot every night.

It's a different beast being the underdog versus the guys that everybody's gunning for, and it punched everybody in the mouth.

Year 5

(2013-2014)

articulated by:
Joe Harris
London Perrantes
Devon Hall
Thomas Rogers
Akil Mitchell
Johnny Carpenter
Rob Vozenilek
Evan Nolte
Ritchie McKay
Jason Williford

Joe Harris: Going into [my] fourth year, you bring in more recruits – London Perrantes [and] Devon Hall – Malcolm is healthy, everybody's already kind of in the system. You have really high expectations going into the season.

London Perrantes: That year was crazy. Devon ended up finding out he was going to redshirt right before our first game. Living in the same room as him throughout the whole year, I was a little nervous that there would be some tension between us or outside influence on him saying, "Oh, you're better than him. You should be playing, blah blah blah," but never was that the case.

That was just his path, and he knew that since he had reclassified, it would be better for him to be getting work in with college dudes instead of being at a high school. He kind of took it all as, *This was supposed to happen.*

Devon Hall: It would've been easy for me to have some type of animosity towards him. We lived together for all of our college life. I wanted him to be successful. He was a better point guard – it's that simple. He came in, and he was much more patient and prepared.

I was a young gun. I wanted to play fast. I wanted to go to work, shoot some shots, [and] make the flashy stuff, but I had to calm my game down and relax. He was just so much more prepared, and I saw it, and it hurt because I wanted to play.

And yes, there was a piece of me that was like, *Man, I wish I was in that spot,* but I wanted him to be successful because we ended up creating a bond – that's like my brother. I'd take a bullet for him. Most of the time, when I talk to him, we don't even talk about basketball. And he led that ship – if I'm being one hundred percent.

London: Me and Dev are still super, super close. Like I said, the stuff that we have been through together – and he has that personality that kind of made it work for both of us. It goes along with the kind of guys Coach Bennett recruits.

That right there is another big thing: he always recruits guys that are a team-first type of person. That all goes back to Coach Bennett recruiting the guys that he wants.

Thomas Rogers: You know the song Juke Box Hero [by Foreigner]? So, a lot of us had never heard of that song, which is probably not surprising. It talks about the guitarist outside the stadium – he wants a shot at the title fight ([Tony] loves that saying). He talked about the passion that guy has for performing and doing what he loves in front of other people – easy translation there.

Juke Box Hero is, uh, obviously a little outside the wheelhouse of most eighteen-to-twenty-two-year-old college basketball players, but we had shirts that said JBH. It was just the passion. He played the music video for us in the film room one day. At first, you're kinda laughing, *Tony's back at it again,* but it's inspiring.

It's like the *Rudy* thing: I've heard Kobe Bryant say, "What if I had the kind of heart that Rudy had? What if someone as talented as me loved the game and played as hard as Rudy did?"

It was kinda that. We're first in the ACC: *If our passion is a lot better than everyone else, and oh, by the way, we're just as talented or more talented than everybody, we're probably gonna be pretty good.*

Joe: We started off the year well, but not as good as we had all thought we were going to. I think guys were a little stressed out just in terms of the outside perception of how we had been playing – we'd struggled in some games. We struggled against Wisconsin in the ACC/Big Ten Challenge.

That past offseason, we had a lot of hype because Akil and I had been doing a lot of different stuff all summer – like USA Basketball and scouted camps – where we knew that we were good enough to maybe have a chance to play professionally. So, it was kind of a weird dynamic where guys were maybe overthinking about their own production versus anything else more so than we had prior. We were starting to get a taste of the recognition a little bit, you know?

Akil Mitchell: We had a tough schedule, too. I remember it was Wisconsin early, VCU early – veteran teams that knew how to win. So, early on, we kind of had to figure it out and again, just couldn't quite get over the hump.

Thomas: Some of our early season troubles were figuring out our identity and maybe a little bit confidence-related because we had never before been where we wanted to go.

So, we lose at Wisconsin Green Bay, who was a good team and should've made the Tournament that year, probably, but we were experimenting with Malcolm at point guard, Justin starting, and London coming off the bench, and for whatever reason, it just worked better to start London.

London: If you look at the three guards that started at the beginning of the year: three NBA guards in Justin, Malcolm, and Joe. And Malcolm wasn't necessarily a point guard at that time –

he wasn't playing point guard like he is now. So, that mesh of all three of them being scorers [and] being able to get their own buckets on their own [was tough].

I think that with me going into that role – playing the point guard and being able to get everybody involved – it was a way better flow for Joe and for Malcolm, and then having Justin come off the bench and be that sixth man.

Devon: Justin is one of my closest friends now, but when I first met Justin, I hated him with a passion. I knew him since I was a young gun and I was like fifteen, but I hated him with a passion.

He was so loud. He was super obnoxious – he's still both loud and obnoxious. But I thought he was arrogant. I thought he was super overconfident.

So, we dealt a ton, and we [butted heads] – but as brothers. Even now, if we don't agree on something, we're going at it, but at the end of the day, it's like, *That's my dawg.*

I remember dapping him up last time we had an argument. He's like, "It don't matter. You're still my brother, but I don't agree with it."

I dealt with him a ton, and he showed me the ropes a ton. Malcolm as well, man – learning how to put in work. His industrious work ethic was what I tried to model. I wanted to get better and better and better, and he showed me how to do that.

AG [Anthony Gill], too – he kind of gets thrown out [of] the mix. How good of a person he is on and off the court; he helped create that culture that's there. And he's a dog on the court – a *problem.* AG definitely had a huge impact on that culture: his energy every single day [and] his positivity every single day was on another level. *He* was on another level.

Joe: We struggled early on. We lost to Wisconsin Green Bay, and we lost at Tennessee.

Thomas: We got waxed by Tennessee on the road – one of the more painful losses.

Devon: Got smacked – 30-clip.

Thomas: And I was ready. I was like, *Tony's gonna be so pissed.* First off, they shot like sixty percent [from the field] and made some tough shots, and we did watch the film. They had a point guard, who was fine [but] not great, though – he made a half-court runner going into halftime after we'd cut it to [19].

After the game, Tony was like – not in a giving-up way, in a you-guys-need-to-think-about-this [way] – "I'm not going to yell and scream; you guys feel this, too."

He gave us the day off the next day.

Joe: After we lost the Tennessee game, we were all kind of at odds with each other. We're a really close group of guys. We were friends off of the court, and we got along really well when we played, but people were just pissed because of how we had started.

Johnny Carpenter: People forget that Coach Bennett was on the hot seat that season. After that Tennessee loss, he was on the legitimate hot seat. And what happens? The star player comes in and says, "What do we need to do to turn this around?"

Joe: I remember going to Coach Bennett's [home] basically right after we had the game and talking about, "What can we do differently to get everybody on the same page?"

He changed some different stuff himself, and we also started having some more players-only meetings where we sat down, and we basically came to the conclusion that the way that we play, guys are not going to be able to put up gaudy stats.

We were like, "This isn't where we're going to be making our mark and getting attention from the NBA. Guys that are playing for Coach Bennett, we're scoring in the 50's. Nobody's going to be averaging 20 a game."

We put all that stuff to the side, and we said, "As long as we win, that's when people notice. As long as we win games, nobody cares about who gets the recognition. We're all going to eat. We're all going to have a chance at the end of the day to play further, and we shouldn't be worrying about what each of us is doing individually from the stats perspective."

That combined with some of the change-ups that Coach Bennett made after that Tennessee game – we just went off from there. We started having so much fun playing together and not caring about who scored this night or that [night]. It was such a collective effort all the time.

I think I led the team in scoring, and I averaged like 12 points a game. Everybody sacrificed for the better of the team, and we ended up doing extremely well, and it catapulted everything else for Virginia Basketball.

But even for Malcolm and those guys [after us], too, I think it gave them the platform and the realization of, *Okay, this is how you play for Coach Bennett. As long as you have success, everybody takes note.*

Devon: And that's what it is, man. When you win, everybody eats. That's how we tried to carry it. And that's what was most important, I think, for everybody. People wanted to play in the NBA, but winning was so much more important.

Coach Bennett always said, "This is going to be hard. This is not easy. This is going to be hard, but you're going to have to do it. In order to win and stop people, you're going to do it."

I think buying in was a big problem for a lot of people that wanted to get out, or wanted to play more minutes, or wanted to score. And there wasn't a lot of points going around.

Maybe Malcolm – he would average 18 his last year. He was scoring at a high level, but I mean, other than that... like my senior year, the highest scorer was probably Kyle. He averaged like 12 points. I averaged 11.7 or something like that.

It's not a bunch of points going around. If you want to win, it's going to be the hard way.

Akil: That wasn't a pretty trip, but we just decided to put everybody's ego to the side. It was kind of like, "Look, man, this is what we got to do. Let's do it, and let's do it together."

I mean, those guys are brothers now – all of them. If you call anybody from that team, they'll answer. They'll do anything for you. And it's because we shared a moment where it was like, "Alright, we're doing this together," and we accomplished it.

That gives me goosebumps thinking about it.

London: Like Joe said, some guys had to take a humble pill and learn, *If we're going to try to win, we've got to do it a certain way.*

And sometimes, you do need to get knocked in the mouth. Sometimes you need one game to... shit, I'd say that game changed the program.

If that game didn't happen, we wouldn't have figured that out, and figured out what we needed to do, and then gone on that run. That game really changed the program in terms of how we started to play and how we bought in to Coach Bennett.

From then on, every year, everybody was just bought in, and you can see what happens now. That was a big game – a big pivotal point for us. It was brutal, though. It was a brutal ass-whoopin', but I guess it was needed, for sure.

Thomas: Sometimes you need stuff like that to get your attention, and [Tony] got our attention by *not* trying to get our attention. The film session was rough, but giving us the day off – we all thought about it.

I think some guys had some personal things, like, *I should be starting, I should be scoring x-amount a game.* Justin was a highly recruited guy, and he was probably a top-three player on that team, but because Joe and Malcolm were also on that team, that's tough.

Coming off the bench was everything. That bench was ridiculous: Justin, AG, Darion – that's three NBA or A-level Europe guys.

I think we were afraid of [Tennessee] happening again. I was,

I know. Obviously, the guys that played more, you can't think about it like that, but I think you have to be locked in every second of every game: *If I let my guard down, it's gonna happen again.*

The Tennessee game was scarring. We came in there confident, and that's different from being just locked in: *This can change anytime.*

That's kind of Tony's mantra, too: "Never too high; never too low."

We just came together at the right time. ACC play is the right time to come together.

Rob Vozenilek: A lot of people look at that Tennessee game, but it was [at] Florida State right after the Tennessee game: Joe goes out with a concussion 2 minutes in, I think that was London's career high at that point, Malcolm had a huge game, and from there we won [three] in a row.

At some point, there was a thirteen-game win streak that ended with the Syracuse game. And there was just so much confidence that came from going down to Florida State – on the road – and pulling out that win without our best player. It was a huge game for us.

Thomas: Florida State was really good, as they always are, and they were pretty similar to [Tennessee], in retrospect: Jordan McCrae and Josh Richardson for Tennessee are now NBA guys – really good. I don't think Florida State had anyone quite on that level, but they were long and athletic, and they can turn you over and make tough shots. We were scared. We were afraid, and we just dominated them from start to finish. It really is just a mental game.

We played at NC State: beat the living shit out of NC State. We were actually up like 27-5. I think we won by [31].

NC State was a tough place to play. They were good and may have had T.J. Warren – he was a lottery pick – or Kat Barber. Either way, they were good.

So, that was a Saturday game, then we played Monday at Duke. Cameron [Indoor Stadium] will humble you. We came in there confidently, but kinda the same mentality. We shot like thirty percent [from the field] the first 35 minutes of the game (and that game is on YouTube).

We had a couple big plays: Justin gets an and-1 tip-in, hits a three, [and] Joe gets a steal and layup. We were down 11 with 4 minutes left, and we took the lead with 30 seconds left. You don't win games accidentally in Cameron – you just don't.

Rasheed Sulaimon hits the luckiest shot of his life: hits the back of the rim, and goes up in the air above the shot clock, and drops in with 5 seconds left, and they win. We were feeling better about ourselves but still worse about ourselves.

We were confident, but we were angry. Then we won [thirteen] straight games in the ACC, and everyone was like, "Oh, it's the unbalanced schedule. They only played Duke and Carolina once."

Carolina sucked that year. We beat them by 15 at home. But in the ACC, people don't believe you until you've done it for… it's like a chicken and the egg:

"We just got good this year."

"Yeah? How long you been doing it?"

"Well, we just got good this year. We're a good team."

"No, you're gonna choke like you always do."

Evan Nolte: The year before, Miami had Shane Larkin, they had a crazy record, they won the ACC (the whole thing), they might not have even lost, but I remember going into that next year thinking, *Man, we're gonna do this next year.*

We ran the table that year. I don't know what it was – we were flowing. You could see they *hated* playing against us.

There's always a time in a game when you can see the other team roll over. It's usually [in the] second half. I think we beat NC State by like 30 at their place, but there wasn't a single time when I thought, *Oh, this is how we need to play.* It was kind of over time, game after game, and slowly, the whole team realized, *Okay, this is how we need to play*, and, *Oh, we can be the best team in the entire country.* So, that was pretty cool.

The first year or two, there was someone who – when the coaches were meeting [at halftime] – would go up to the whiteboard and write down a few things we thought we needed to do better in the second half, but there was definitely a sense of self-governance in practice and also during halftime.

There was a lot of encouragement. If someone was having a rough first half, people would pick him up a little bit and say something, or maybe a guy that everyone is aware thinks he should be playing more went in, and missed a shot, and got taken out, and was kinda down on himself. I think it goes all the way back to the camaraderie of the type of players and how we all really love each other. There were very few feuds.

Thomas: It'd be like five minutes where we're talking to each other. A lot of it's adrenaline, non-sensical stuff – yelling stuff that doesn't make sense – then you level set and think about it.

We got to a point my sophomore or junior year where Doug Browman would get up and write three things we needed to focus on for the second half on the board, which simplifies it. It's, "Alright, that's what we gotta do. We don't need to worry about if some guy is gonna hit like 4 fadeaway threes in a row. Contest shots; tip your cap."

At Georgia Tech, Georgia Tech was not good, and we were losing. It was halftime, and they were hanging around [and winning 30-29]. We didn't even have a halftime speech. I remember I said, "We don't give up [30] points to Georgia Tech at half," and that was the sentiment: "What are we doing? We don't do this. This is not us."

So, sometimes, Tony would come in, and we'd be like, "Coach, we're good. Let's go."

Akil: So, it's a lot easier to go on a run when you're in your fourth year and you're not really going to school. Honestly, I was chillin'.

I could've graduated early, but I had a couple credits left here and there. So, it was: wake up, go to the gym, come home, [and] play video games for a couple hours. It's a lot more of a professional life. It was way more focused: watching film, talking to guys about our next opponent, and then just going out and doing it.

There was really no talk of like, "What's going to happen next year?" Like, no.

We're locked in; we know what we need to do; we're doing it – that level of focus was with everybody. It was a whole lot of fun. You really got to see some guys really step up. AG, a guy that I'd known for a long time, was playing some of his best basketball. You could see Justin kind of blossom as a defender. Evan is shooting the ball. It was just a lot of fun.

Ritchie McKay: Year 5 was the change. It was a turnaround in terms of belief from everybody in our program. And Tone did something that was so amazing – copied it at Liberty, like I have many things.

We win the ACC Regular Season Championship at Syracuse, and we flew home that night, and it's 1:00 [a.m.]. One of the custodians there – who served mightily – got a ladder. Ronnie got it organized because Ronnie does everything.

The ladder was set up, and we circled around, and we cut the nets. Nobody else in the gym, no fanfare, and it was the culmination.

There's an old African proverb that [Tony's] dad and he always referred to: "If you want to go fast, go alone. If you want to go far, go together." He talked about togetherness, how there's such great strength in our unity, and man, it was a beautiful moment.

I still have a piece of that net. It was a marker in my life about building something special and not skipping steps in that process.

Ironically, the next year, we won it again against Syracuse at home, and we cut it in front of all those people, and all those people at JPJ that night, they validated us: *We share in this moment with you.*

At Liberty, we won the Atlantic Sun Conference Regular Season Championship [in 2018-2019] – or shared it – and we cut the nets when we got home in front of no one. This past season [2019-2020], we won the ASUN [Regular Season] Championship – tied for first – [and] cut the nets again privately, but [then we] won the [ASUN Tournament] Championship, and cut the nets in front of our fans.

You know what I thought?

Man, this is God allowing us a picture of, "See, if you just trust me, what you thought you may never touch or do again, I'm letting you see what an authentic trust in me and the process can do for you."

So, for me, it was a great reminder of: if you stick to that process and the details, great things can happen.

Akil: Then you get into the ACC Tournament, and at that point, it was like, *Alright, we cut down a net. That's a lot of fun, but we got more work to do.* That was kind of the one thing – all four years – we just couldn't figure out.

I remember getting to Greensboro and telling my parents, "We're going to win this," and that was the last time I talked to them until after the [ACC] Tournament. I didn't leave the room.

I still don't remember a whole lot from that week. I just remember playing, going home, sitting in an ice tub, sleeping, waking up the next day, [and] playing again. It's amazing.

After we beat Duke, I saw my family and everybody. I remember getting on the bus after [and] I just turned my phone off. I was like, *I'm exhausted.* That was the most exhausted I've ever been: "I'm sure we'll get a #1 seed, and if we don't, I don't care because we got it done. We got that trophy. I'm happy. Call me when it's time to start getting ready for the [NCAA] Tournament because I'm going to sleep. I'll be there, but right now, I need rest."

Rob: For the ACC Tournament, we didn't sit on the bench. There was this whole snafu. James Coleman, who was a punter on the football team and lived with my brother, Alec, wrote an article for The Cav [Cavalier] Daily about how our academic guy [Director of Academics], T.J. Grams, was sitting on the bench while [some of the] players were sitting in the stands.

The coaches and Ronnie came up to us and tried to make sure we were alright. I always wanted to be like, "No, I think it's complete and utter bullshit."

I mean, it's an ACC thing. It's an NCAA thing. Jay Bilas retweeted it, and it kind of blew up. That's why it caught their attention and became a bigger ordeal. But I mean, it was somewhat above them as well.

There's a funny story of this guy, Jack Wooten, who was on the 2009 Carolina team – he was a walk-on. With like 30 seconds left – Carolina's up 8 – he goes into the locker room, puts on his uniform, and then runs out and celebrates with his team because he wanted to be out there, and he was in the stands because there weren't enough seats on the bench.

I'll give [the coaches] credit: everyone travels now, everyone sits on the bench, [and] guys are getting scholarships.

London: We ended up winning the ACC Championship, which was cool. For me, being a freshman, it was huge: my first ACC Tournament in Greensboro, stuff that you see all the time as a kid, then winning that my first year – that was big time.

The year before was another big year where they barely missed the Tournament, but getting that ACC Championship, it kinda sparked that Virginia run that we're on right now.

So, yeah, looking back at it, that was a super fun time [and] a super fun year. The ups and downs from the Tennessee game to winning an ACC Championship, it was a lot of fun.

Akil: Again, it was that feeling from a couple of years before. We're playing against the best [in the NCAA Tournament]. As a competitor – all of us were competitive; all of us still are competitive – that drove us even more.

Who'd we draw... UNC Wilmington? It was ugly. If you watch,

in the first half, it was kind of close to begin with. We kind of struggled to match up [and] had to shake off some nerves, and we ended up blowing it open in the second half.

Joe: We were able to get the #1 seed. The week of the Sweet Sixteen, everybody started to see Virginia as sort of a Blue Blood program.

When we were first there, nobody cared about the basketball team. It's kind of funny because now, it's obviously so difficult to get tickets – even for the students. When we were there, they used to have us go and do these meetings with the Hoo Crew to try and get more fan engagement from the students. We would get fans at the big games, but we would maybe get like eight-to-ten thousand people at the games that whole first year that I was there.

And so, it's kind of funny to see how much it's transformed, but all of that comes with success. Once you start playing well, all the other stuff sort of falls in line.

We basically went from normal guys on Grounds to people actually recognizing who you were. We were not in the same ballpark as the guys now because now, kids go to school, and they recognize Virginia as a premier basketball program. It could almost be considered a basketball school.

When we were there, Coach Bennett would tell us all the time, "It's not going to transform overnight."

Even when we came in, his whole message to us was that it was about building something special at Virginia, and being a part of something bigger than yourself, but also knowing, "This might take three or four years to get where it needs to go. But I promise you, if you just stick with me, stick with the process, it'll all pay dividends in the end."

Evan: Our first year in the NCAA Tournament was an incredible experience just seeing how people in Charlottesville and the community were so hyped up, and they got fully behind Coach Bennett. It's kinda been a linear progression since my second year when we won the [ACC] Regular Season and ACC Tournament for the first time in however long. Since then, yeah, it's been awesome.

I could definitely feel the community and alumni support grow significantly from year to year. JPJ got louder, and people were a lot more passionate as years went on and we got better.

I started to realize my second year, when we were starting to get better, people would start showing up earlier and earlier, and during warm-ups, the Hoo Crew would be there earlier and earlier, and there'd be a lot more of them. People are pretty quiet right when the doors open, but you can definitely tell, *Oh wow, people literally want to wait outside for however long just so they can get a better seat because they're so bought in.*

Jason Williford: I think our fan base deserves a good team. I think the students deserve that experience. Because what I remember from my four years as a player: I remember U-Hall being loud. I remember it being a crazy atmosphere.

And it wasn't every game, but my experience was, *This was fun.* It was great to be a part of some good teams and some really good home wins when I played here at University Hall.

When we first got here [as a staff], I mean, we could've given away a couple thousand tickets. No one came to the games, but again, winning cures all of that, and that's probably [found in] most fanbases throughout the country. But I think what's happened is people have gotten behind what we built and are excited for the product, and winning is fun.

Obviously, Cameron is one of the best places to play, and it gets loud, and the students are on top of you. I've never been to Phog Allen [Allen Fieldhouse at Kansas], but I hear it's the same – a much bigger version.

But every assistant coach in the league – and we all talk when we're on the road recruiting – they all talk about how loud our place gets and how intimidating it can be. I love that. That's what JPJ in Charlottesville should be, and when it gets loud, it definitely gets loud.

So, you know, it's fun to now be right up there with one of the best arenas in the league as far as fan experience, [and] as far as game day experience, and we want to keep it there. That's where it should be.

I vividly remember: maybe our second year, we had an afternoon game on a Saturday. One of the players needed to go to a study group right after the game, so I drop him off at Alderman Library. There were more kids on Grounds and coming to and from the library than were at our game, which might have been like a 1:00 p.m. game. I'm like, *Why don't these kids come to the game?*

And I hope it's now the opposite, where the kids are all lined up coming to the game, or on The Corner somewhere watching, and not just going to the library. At least for the two hours that we're playing, they're locked in. So, that's a good thing.

I want Virginia to be thought of as a Blue Blood. I want Virginia to be thought of as: they're as good as anybody in the country, and they do it the right way, and you can have it all here.

Expectations are good. Now, they just got to keep them in check.

London: Even the NCAA Tournament was amazing being able to play in Madison Square Garden in one of the best games that I've ever played in. One of the toughest games [and] craziest atmospheres that I've ever played in was against Michigan State in Madison Square Garden.

Whenever we played a team that plays that physical way, we knew it was going to be a dogfight because that's how we played. We knew that both teams just weren't going to back down. Those games were always the days where we were so toast. We'd need like two-to-three days off the next day. Those games were so much bumping, and grinding, and bruising.

Looking back at it, obviously, we wish we would have won that game. A couple of things here and there – AG not rolling his ankle would've been huge for us – but it was an amazing experience for us. I think we should have won, but I mean, it is what it is. That was a great year and a great energy to end it, being in Madison Square Garden.

Johnny: It's all about being an underdog. Even though we won the Title [in 2019], we feel like we're the underdog. We feel like people are just saying, "Oh, you got lucky, you don't deserve it," all that crap.

Well, we were so unlucky with random illnesses. AG rolled his ankle against Michigan State; otherwise, UVA would've won that game and probably would've won the Tournament. I love the '18-19 guys, but the '13-14 guys, hands down, I'm taking them over any team in the Tony Bennett era: depth, skill, pros – that squad was unreal.

'14-15, Justin's pinky.

'15-16, we just blew mud down our leg [against Syracuse].

'16-17, Isaiah [Wilkins's] mystery illness. People sleep on that. Isaiah's one of the best plus-minus guys over his four years in UVA history. From year one, he was unbelievable. He lost like 45 pounds over two weeks with this mystery illness. We didn't have a chance without him. He was so good defensively.

'17-18, De'Andre broke his wrist, and the one year we're perfectly healthy [in '18-19], everything goes well.

It's been unique because we have a system. Coach Bennett says, "First comes discipline, then comes freedom," and you have to earn that right. Do things the right way, then you'll earn the freedom within the system.

Joe is one of the guys who put UVA back on the map with that Sweet Sixteen run. Those guys tasted how bad it was. They had that nasty taste of, *We don't want to be this bad. We want to compete,* then they tasted how good it was to be good.

Malcolm was on those teams, too. London was a part of the '13-14 team that turned it around, but he didn't really face the adversity of the 2012-2013 season. He came into UVA as an unheralded recruit, not a great recruit, but we loved his feel – one of the elite minds of college basketball history as a player.

'16-17 was an average season. Yeah, there were injuries, but we didn't have guys who had been through true adversity like Ty, Kyle, and Dre [De'Andre Hunter]. Those guys had all committed to a team that had been ranked #1 in the country. They were back on the map, and it was about taking a good team to a great place.

That next season ['17-18], we all thought we were taking a step down, and everybody counted us out – that was the best season in school history prior to this [2019] season: dominated, #1 ranking in the country, ACC Tournament Champs, wrecking teams with unbelievable chemistry and unity, but still not a ton of guys who had been through the adversity stuff.

Then you get the immovable chip, the chip that will be on our shoulder forever [UMBC in '17-18]. And even though we won the National Title [in '18-19], there's still a chip because people will be looking at it with a grain of salt.

This year ['19-20] is gonna be a team that will go through growing pains, and face adversity, and go through the, "Ah, this ain't the same Virginia." They're gonna face it. And in a couple years, we may be back in it.

Education

articulated by:

T.J. Grams

T.J. Grams: Coach Bennett, obviously, it all starts and ends with him. The culture that he's created is why we're all here – not just the players, but all the professional staff, too. For me, in this position, to have a coach like that, in a place like this, with the type of students he recruits, very rarely are any of our guys super elite academically, but they're very engaged in that process.

They're very comfortable having both sides of that student and athlete existence. They certainly want to go to the NBA, and they want to put time into their game, but they understand that part of that expectation is to engage in the classroom, and raise their hand, and show up on time, and do all that little stuff. As much success as we've had on the floor, which has been remarkable in the time that Coach has been here, we've [also] had a lot of really great success stories [in academics].

What's unique about the way we do it is there's a lot of development, and handholding, and micromanaging, and skill-building early on, but we're not making any decisions for anybody. It's a very proactive student experience. They're making their decisions. We're not watering down their schedules. They're exploring things that they want to.

We've had guys pursue the Comm School and take Calculus, and Pre-med, and all that kind of stuff. Because of that, our team GPA isn't the best. Whenever we go to Louisville, they list all their All-ACC Academic Selections, and everybody turns on me, like, "How does Louisville have seven of these guys? What's going on with our guys?" Like, context is important here – [strength of schedule].

But there's a value to the way Coach supports what we do because of that. Some of the best stories that we've had over the years are how Coach has moved practice time to support our guys academically. By the time Malcolm got to his fifth year, he's in a Batten graduate program [Frank Batten School of Leadership and Public Policy]. Well, there aren't eight different sections of a class when you're in graduate school. There's one, and it's from 3:00-6:00 p.m., and that's when you practice.

So, the year that Malc was the ACC Player of the Year, there was one or two days a week that he either got to practice late or left practice early to go to class, and there's not another coach in the league or probably the country that would let the Conference Player of the Year do that.

The reverse side of that is the great example of Mamadi [Diakite]. The fact that Mamadi has a UVA degree is a great testament to the University's community. I certainly take a lot of pride in the fact that he graduated, and I had a lot to do with it because that's what my role is, but from the coaches, to even his teammates, faculty members on Grounds, advisors, tutors, and all that kind of stuff, his starting point was so low that for him to make it through but also develop as a part of that is really remarkable. Again, it really says a lot about the UVA community.

His first year, his spoken English was okay, but his written English was really low, and he struggled in his first-year writing class, even though it was designed for ESL students. So, his second semester, he took a not-for-credit ESL developmental class that was again during practice, and Coach let him skip practice – I want to say at least one day a week, maybe it was two, even – to go to this class that he wasn't getting credit for.

For Tony to have that foresight, and for him to listen to me and us really talk through that and say, "Well, let's look at this developmentally down the road: is this going to help him earn his degree and grow?"

Tony makes those connections from a basketball standpoint, too: "Is this going to help ensure his eligibility?"

There's not another coach that would say, "Alright, come in in this first year [and] don't worry about basketball. Matter of fact, skip practice one day a week to take this class that you're not getting any credit for."

The other statistic that I know Tony is really, really proud of – it was one of the really early times as he and Carla [Williams] were building their relationship. They were at a VAF [Virginia Athletics Foundation] Fundraiser or something like that, and they were talking about something, and he leaned over to her and said, "We've graduated one hundred percent of our guys that have exhausted four years of eligibility," and her jaw dropped.

That doesn't happen. I mean, we've certainly had guys transfer and quit the team, so when you do those federal numbers and the stats come out, we're not quite at a hundred [percent], but it's really comforting to sit across from a recruit and say, "Well, if you're here four years, I guarantee you're going to get a degree."

In the decade that I've worked with Coach, there hasn't been a player that hasn't gotten a degree after four years.

Actually, last night I was talking with Justin Anderson. He's actually enrolled in classes this summer. Since everything's online, he's like, "Silver lining to a pandemic: now I can take these classes." So, he's working towards his [degree], too.

Justin was the first one [to go back to school after leaving for the NBA prior to earning a degree]. He's a little further removed, and I think his basketball career is shifting in a little bit of a different direction. Kyle talked to me this summer, and I don't know if Kyle will. The fact that he reached out, he probably will. I would think Ty will. Ty and I have talked about it, but none of those guys that just left after last year have started anything yet.

De'Andre, I don't know. I mean, he's in a different level contract-wise [and] basketball-wise. He probably won't need to ever, but he's certainly in good standing, and a smart enough kid, and a talented student – the opportunity is there. We've worked with some other guys in the past, too, that I didn't work with while they were in school, but a couple of guys in past years have finished up as well.

Again, it starts with Coach and his evaluation process, and he's seeking out really high-quality kids. We've got guys that come from great families, and their character is so high – far from perfect, obviously, but high-quality. It says a lot about the UVA experience.

UVA has this weird dual-identity: sometimes we're a state school, and sometimes we're kind of a liberal arts curriculum, smaller, almost like a private school in how we operate. Same thing in how we support our students. Sometimes we're really hands-off, and by design, the structure is, "Well, you got into UVA, you're a talented student – you have to kind of figure it out."

In athletics, we're very much the opposite of that by design – we're hands-on. So, we kind of teeter back and forth, and it's a really hard balance to find: "How are you going to navigate this on your own? How do you find your own voice?"

One of the things that I carry with me a lot: Akil Mitchell came back... since Carla had been here. He sat on a panel to talk about race and sports or something like that. I went and listened to the panel, and he referenced our relationship without using my name, but he talked about how there was somebody who believed in him and encouraged him to seek out his voice.

Akil's a great example of a success story in our program and somebody that really navigated UVA to the beat of his own drum, where he tried a really challenging academic path and struggled. He's a smart guy and a hard worker, but sometimes Calculus gets all of us on some level.

He decided, "You know what? I can accomplish what I want in a different direction." So, he pivoted, and he ended up with an internship in the [UVA] President's Office. [In] his fourth year, we won the league, he was an All-League Defensive Player, and in between games and practices, he's sitting in the Board of Visitors meetings taking notes – what a cool experience.

It's a great way to show that our guys kind of have these dual roles – some more than others, and that's natural. Again, we try not to herd cattle too much. We really try to listen and find that balance between supporting them and letting them have some cushion where they need to and grow into it.

It's a delicate balance. I don't mind skinned knees; we don't want any broken bones. You're going to learn something from falling down and skinning your knee, but if I don't advise somebody to change Calculus, Chemistry, Econ – if that's [their] first semester – I'm setting them up for failure as much as I'm manipulating the schedule. It's really an interesting balance in our field: to take a developmental approach, and really listen to them, and try to push where we can, but also let them kind of feel their way through it.

Basketball is a bigger part of the experience for some guys, and they don't want to challenge themselves academically in the same way, and that's okay. You know, I get it. Every student has their own experience, and I just try to walk that path with them as best I can.

Usually, our incoming first-year class starts class in the second [summer] session. It's not pushing too much. Right away, it's, "Get your feet wet, get a feel for the landscape, get a feel for what basketball means at this level, [and] get a feel for how you're going to interact with your faculty members."

Our curriculum is set up to be pretty user-friendly for our students: "You're this blank slate when you come in. Don't feel like you have to take any specific set of courses. Take a couple that you liked in high school and you know you'd like again. Take another one that you thought sounds cool, and you've never had a chance to take it."

Sometimes, it's more important to figure out what you don't want to study as much as what you do want to study, and then taking something that's an elective that's a little bit lighter to find some balance in there. We talk a little bit about majors, and if they know that, we'll start down that road.

Justin and Mamadi are probably the two biggest personalities that we've had since Tony's been here. [Justin] wanted to do media. He's an in-front-of-the-camera kind of guy. I remember talking with him and his dad when he decommitted from Maryland and was on this not-super-secret, covert recruiting visit. Not a lot of people knew that he was on Grounds.

So, we're sitting here talking about these different programs. He didn't choose UVA because of the Media Studies program, but we talked about it, and it was, "How do we fit all these pieces of the puzzle together? How does your interest fit into basketball? How can they complement each other for after basketball as well?"

He's a Media Studies major. He's got two Media Studies classes that he took this summer. So, some of those conversations start in high school. We've got a handful of guys this year, the guys who are third-years, who have done a lot of exploring, and we try to vet that out a little bit, too. We're more evolved with that now as we've done some different career planning with our guys.

We try to personalize it as much as we can. Again, the priority early is: have some success and kind of ease into it a little bit. The fun part away from the basketball side for me – the advising/academic part that I like the best – is not necessarily following the plan that's laid out. It doesn't have to be Chemistry, Calculus, and Econ in that first semester.

This even goes back to before I worked with athletes: the fun part is working with a student that wanted to double major, and study abroad, and then minor in Art History: "Let's figure out how we can fit all that stuff together. We'll take this class this semester, and we'll get ahead of the sequence."

Devon graduated in three [years] and got a Master's degree. Jack [Salt] has a Master's degree. Jay [Huff] is in a Master's program now. Jay is actually a great example, too. Jay came in, and his faith is a really big part of his identity, and he wanted to be a youth minister. So, what do we do with that?

He found this program in Curry [School of Education]: Youth and Social Innovation. It's not a teaching program, but it's about youth development and creating programs to work with kids. So, he did that, and then we fit in a [Religious Studies] double major – that's perfect. Again, because he had a fifth year, now he's in a graduate program. He's maxed out his UVA experience.

Those are the ones where it feels really good, but then there are some guys that you have to drag to the finish line, too, and you're happy about those guys because it's a qualifier for the rest of their lives that they already have that degree and that qualification.

It's so hard for faculty and the general student population to really grasp what the student-athlete experience is, especially in football and basketball. You are high profile, you stand out, and again, it's a delicate balance of those dual identities. I apologize if I'm geeking out a little bit – I'm writing my dissertation on that.

Isaiah, Malcolm, and Akil are probably the best examples of guys that [thought] basketball was a part of who they are; it's not the only part of who they are. They were very comfortable in their own skin. They were comfortable going up and having those conversations [with professors].

So, it was easier to coach those guys up a little bit. And that's my bias – that's what I was like as a student. I was a fine student, but I was a grinder, and I was in office hours, go up before and after and ask a question, and all those things. That's the bias I bring to how I interact with students.

We really spend a lot of time talking about that. I think people don't understand it's actually pretty intimidating for student-athletes to go up to a faculty member. I tell [players] the story all the time: my first year, I failed a Botany test or something like that. I wasn't going to major in it, but it fulfilled a requirement. The teacher had written the book. His picture was on the back of the book, and I had to go up and talk to this guy – I didn't want him to think I didn't take it seriously or was screwing around.

We talk through that a little bit. Everybody is almost more intimidated to talk to student-athletes and interact with them, but we can personalize it a little bit and say, "Look, I get that this is hard. Let's just get over the hump," and I try to facilitate that as best I can.

We do a lot of outreach with faculty members where we bring them in. I bring a faculty member to every home game. When our pregame schedule was a little different, we used to have them come to shootaround, and then they'd sit [and] eat the pregame meal with the team. So, if it was somebody that had a class with a teacher, they'd sit with their teacher two hours before the game, or if it was an administrator that I was building a relationship with, they'd sit with the coaches.

We're really laid back as a program. I like to sit there with Tony, or Jason, or Ron Sanchez, or whoever like two hours before the Carolina game or the Duke game to see how they're interacting and how genuine it is.

From a student standpoint, just by bringing the faculty member into their environment, it makes it a little easier to interact. If I have a guy who I know doesn't raise their hand, or if I'm getting feedback from faculty members of, "Oh, he's sitting off to the side, [and] he's got his hood up," [students] are just less likely to do that kind of stuff if [they] have that personal interaction. We bring teachers into practice just to watch, we bring them to games, [and] I've walked guys over to office hours before to kind of break the ice a little bit.

When Justin was a freshman, he was so intimidated to go and talk to the teachers. I was like, "Alright. Well, you know, I've emailed with them a bunch. I'll walk in there with you. That's okay." I sat there and kind of facilitated the conversation the first time, and then every week after that, they hit the ground running.

I think the teachers really respond to that. [At] a lot of other schools, I think more responsibilities may be put on somebody in my position to manage all the details of things, but that's such a valuable skill to build that, so I'll coach the guys up.

Again, it's really natural for some guys, and other guys are just intimidated by it. And that's part of the UVA stigma, too, right? I've worked at Notre Dame, Duke, and UVA, and there are some students that are so intimidated being there that we need to make sure they have a feel for their own sense of belonging and they know that there's value that they add to the class. So, we really try to talk through that, and that's part of your identity also.

I did my master's thesis on Athletic Identity Development, and it was pretty surface-level. I didn't have quite the perspective I do now – I was right out of undergrad. I knew I wanted to get into athletics.

I started a higher-ed program in Curry probably four years

ago, and I've been chipping away. As an employee, I have this professional development money, and I kind of plateaued a little bit professionally – I'd been in the same position for a long time – and my interest is to shift to more of the administrative side.

I love working with students and the connections with them, and the impact is really significant, and it's fun. And who knows, I could be wrong, and at some point, I'll be like, *Oh, I really miss working with students,* and go back, but who knows where this thing will take me.

As I've been waiting for opportunities for myself, I was like, *Alright, I need to reward myself for being so patient.* The only thing it's costing me is sweat equity: sitting up at the kitchen table until midnight, reading, and taking classes.

If I was going to do this, I needed to do something that I was passionate about or had some perspective on. It's like saying, "I've got some yard work to do this weekend," and then digging a ditch. It's not like, "I'm going to rake the leaves or cut the grass." It's really heavy lifting, and it's such a long process.

Thankfully, there's a couple of faculty members in Curry that do work on athletic identity. And I've certainly experienced it myself because I'm in this field because of the sports. I'm a basketball guy. I coached, and my dad was a coach. I've just been around it, and as much as I value the educational side of it, I'm not working in the Dean's Office. I'm here because at 3:00 p.m. for my job, I get to go to the gym. I readily admit that, and it's great.

Malc, and Akil, and Isaiah are such great examples of this. There's an identity theory that talks about identity foreclosure, and it happens with student-athletes where you reinforce so much as an elite athlete from the time you're nine, ten, eleven [years-old] that it's so competitive and you can't give any part of your mindset – let alone time or energy – toward any other pursuits or any other identities, even. Whether it's where your values fit socially, or religion, or race, or sexual orientation, you have to think only as an athlete.

Those three guys I've given as examples, they understood that the only way to be successful as an athlete is not to be just that one person. It's not a zero-sum mentality, right? Because you're socially active, because you're a strong student, it's not going to take away from your basketball experience.

My research is studying the impact that coaches have on students' identity development. I feel like I'm too close to our program, so I'm not going to interview and study our guys, but to use our program as an example, it's the culture that Tony creates.

He'd be the first to admit he's a basketball guy to start, and as much success as we've had academically, and great stories, and wonderful kids, it's basketball first. That's the priority. And I get that – again, that's why I'm here – but just the fact that those conversations happen, and we do have that kind of culture, does that foster more or less identity foreclosure in these students?

Duke is pretty unique. I worked there [and] I drank the Kool-Aid for a long time. Coach K [Mike Krzyzewski] is great. He is on point with all kinds of stuff. He has very clearly made this shift in the last decade, but he graduated kids, and he found that balance.

For the type of student that we recruit [at UVA], I think [the academics] do help the basketball because it's a richer experience. There's more balance. If you have a bad game, or miss a shot, or something like that, you're able to function in society. There's a maturity to that.

We can use UMBC as a great example for that. The way Tony handled that, and the way we talked about it inside the program, it forces you to recognize what's unconditional in your life – that's the way Tony talked about it in the media.

If you have these multiple identities or if you value your family, or faith, or academics, or whatever your passions are, if you have more than just basketball, that balance comes into play when things are hard. I think it allows you to be a little fresher when you're playing because you don't wear yourself out in the same way. You draw energy from other areas of your life.

But boy, that's not the norm nationwide. I'm biased from my own experiences, but I was a three-sport athlete in high school that was also on student council and the newspaper. Again, that's how I worked it, and that's the type of environment I've sought out to be a part of as a professional. I think I found a good niche for myself here.

When I was at Duke, I think of some of those really high-profile guys, and even for [those] one or two years [they attended Duke], there was value to getting up, and going to class, and living in a dorm with other students. As soon as they enter the NBA, that bubble becomes so much tighter. There is value to going through that experience.

It seems like the needle has shifted in a different direction. You see some of the facilities like the housing facilities that Kansas or Kentucky has for their players, and there's not quite the same experience there. I think you lose a little bit in that because you have to be able to interact with other people – development comes from that as well.

Joe's wonderful. If you were to ask me, I'd say Joe is the most important player in Tony's tenure. From Malcolm, to Kyle, to Dre [De'Andre Hunter], to Kihei [Clark] and Mamadi throwing one in at the buzzer, Joe set the standard. There are still things that happen in our program today that were established just because of who Joe was and how he interacts.

He did that by the time he and Akil left, and it ended up going down to Darion, and Malcolm, and Justin, and London, and then that got passed to the next group. That's where programs get really good over time: when that culture is so strong.

Joe wasn't a great student, but he understood what was expected of him as being a part of this University and this program. He didn't pursue as much as Malc [academically]. He and Jay are probably similar talent-wise academically: very engaged students, their grades are fine, [and] there were never eligibility issues.

Jay was somewhat more specific. He knew what he wanted to do. Joe didn't necessarily, and we found an academic plan that fit his interests, but he had a good balance. Basketball was not the only part of who he was.

The program started taking off, and he was the face of it. It was hard for him to walk around Grounds a little bit towards the end, too, because he was such a popular player, but he was such the Everyman of UVA. He went to class, and he walked through Newcomb [Hall] at lunch, and he got Chick-fil-A, and he sat there and ate.

That's a really valuable part of the experience for our guys in our program at this place. It's not the direction college athletics is heading because everything is so siloed. I get it: you want to support them, and nutrition is important, but they would never leave JPJ if they didn't have to.

So, I actually took that philosophy and flipped it on its head. I would do study hall in the libraries or in the lounge of Comm school just to get them out on Grounds and spend time among their peers. Otherwise, they'd be on Grounds for fifty minutes or seventy-five minutes in class, and then they'd be in JPJ. They could study in JPJ, and eat in JPJ, and all that kind of stuff. So, there's some value to that.

There are so many people on Grounds that are supportive of our program, and that's something that I'm happy to try to promote. Tony is such a hot commodity, and he gets called for jobs. I don't think he would ever leave for another college job. I think at some point, maybe he'd go to the NBA or something like that. Who knows? Having played there, and he's such a competitor.

I think where coaches get disenfranchised at a university is when they feel like they're battling internally, whether it's an Athletic Director, an admissions office, or majors, or this or that. There are so many people in every single department across the Grounds that have supported our guys, and I think our guys have warmed to that type of support because they are good stewards [and] they engage in the classroom.

Malcolm is getting ready for the NBA Draft as a fifth-year student, and he has to complete his internship, or externship, or fieldwork, or whatever it was. Amanda Crombie, the administrator, and a couple of his faculty members were like, "Alright, well, how can we do this so that there's a standard that you have to meet?"

We seek out the faculty's suggestions of, "Tell us where it needs to be, and then we'll do the legwork to make sure it fits."

There's so much support for the program. I'm biased, but I think it's warranted because our guys come in and do a good job. Tony really values that. Obviously, he's had so much support athletically, but he's not the type of guy that wants to be the highest-paid coach. That's not what motivates him or what's going to keep him happy here.

It's, "Can we reward the staff? Can reward the students? How are we interacting? Are we butting heads with people? Do we feel like we're holding up our end the bargain, too?" And I think he feels really supported there.

Rachel Most is the Associate Dean that our guys work with. I've worked with Rachel for a decade, and she's known all of these guys, and she really worked very closely with Jontel because he was an Anthropology major.

And not just academically, but from a cultural standpoint, Mamadi didn't understand the value of his teachers expecting him to show up on time. We were talking one time he said, "Well, my dad won't go to an appointment until he knows the other person's there." That's just what the culture is [in Conakry, Guinea]. It took him a long time to understand that.

We've been really fortunate: really good guys to be around, and great men that they've evolved into, and the people that Tony attracts from sports info, to sports med, to the assistant coaches. It's been the greatest blessing for me to be a part of it. It's impacted me personally and professionally in such a profound way. That I get to have an impact on it – it's a great environment for me to work in.

Student-Athlete

articulated by:
Isaiah Wilkins
Jack Salt
T.J. Grams

Isaiah Wilkins: It's expected you go to class. They send class checkers out randomly to see if you're there. After you're proving that you're there, they'll leave you alone.

But they're watching you, and if you don't go to class – unless you text. If you text them and say, "Hey, I'm running late today, but I'm headed to class, I'll be there three minutes," as long as you don't make a habit of that, it's all good.

And if you do the work and you show that you're capable, T.J., who's [our] Academic Coordinator, who's awesome, he'll work with you and help you get things done.

Also, you start to make it a competition. You take classes with some of your teammates – everything is a competition. I think that helps it, too.

When you go to the Tournament, you miss twelve classes. You're gone for so long. You miss Wednesday, Thursday, Friday, you come back Sunday, [and] you're there Monday, Tuesday. You have to have a good relationship with your teachers.

And that's the first thing that T.J. told us: "Hey, go in there, introduce yourself, and sit where she can see you, and don't be an idiot for like a month, and you should have a good enough relationship to be like, 'Hey, I'm going to miss class. Can I have the work before?' or, 'I'm going to miss class, what can I do to keep up? Can I go to office hours?'"

I think it all contributes. If you don't have any classroom headaches, you can focus on basketball. If you don't have any missed assignments, or if you go to class, I just think it helps so much. You can just focus on basketball, and that should be the goal: to try to win the Championship, which they did, so they must've been going to class.

They're also big on pushing you. They work practice around your class schedule. If you're interested in something, they've never held you back.

While Malcolm was doing his Master's, we changed the practice schedule so he could do it. And everybody who does a fifth year – Jack did it, Devon did it – we had to tweak practice a little bit, but if you're interested in it, they'll tell you, "Go for it, just make sure that you're not wasting anybody's time."

Some guys take extra classes. Out of state [tuition] is... $50k? You might as well get everything you can out of it – squeeze it dry.

Jack Salt: If you don't go to class, you don't practice. I just think all that stuff trickles down. I mean, if you don't go to class, it trickles down – I think – to basketball. Obviously, I'm not saying you go to every single class. Sometimes you get in really late at night, and I'd be tired in the morning.

But I think the coaches and the staff do a great job of instilling the importance of education and that once you get done with basketball, you need that education to fall back on.

[For] most guys, it's good to have a degree to fall back on and start their post-professional career. So, yeah, they do a really good job of making sure we get the grades. We handle it.

A lot of the credit goes to T.J. Grams on that one because T.J. is amazing at what he does. I'm really close with T.J. T.J.'s my twin – we have the same birthday. We also both love pineapple. I gave that to him on his birthday, and he gave that to me on my birthday.

T.J. Grams: We've kind of got a special bond. I would always tease him because I'd be sitting there at breakfast – and obviously, we'd let the players go first; it's all about them – and these guys eat so much food, and he would just hoard the pineapple. I'm like, "Come on, what are you doing?" So, it got legs a little bit over the years.

Jack: When we're on the road, he always waits for me to go first for the pineapple because he knows I love my pineapple. A lot of love for my Virginia family.

Athlete

articulated by:
Will Gent
Mike Curtis
Jason Williford
Rob Vozenilek
Will Sherrill
Johnny Carpenter
Joe Harris

Will Gent: Coach Curtis is amazing: knows what he's doing [and] knows what's in the best interest of the players. Coming from high school, I'd never seen anything like it: the players fighting with the strength coach and the coach telling the players not to work as hard as they are. I mean, it's not really that – it's working smarter – but that's what the image looks like.

I'll never forget Malcolm was in one of those situations, monitoring his workload. And Coach Curtis was like, "Alright, get off the court."

It's a daily routine where he says, "Get off," and [Malcolm] keeps shooting, but eventually they get off.

It was the middle of the season, and Malcolm is very regimented: if he's not hitting his shots, or in his mind, he's got to make a certain number, he's not leaving the floor 'til he does it. Then there's the most intense version of this argument where Coach Curtis is like demanding him to step off the floor. Maybe I'm embellishing it in my mind, but I remember players and staff kind of circling around watching – almost like a high school fight you see in the movies.

Malcolm is just telling him, "I am not getting off this floor."

Coach Curtis tries to take the ball from him, and then [Malcolm] says, "Look, [if] you take this ball, Will and I are going to that basket, and we're shooting over there."

He was throwing me under the bus – throwing me in the fire. I'm like, "Look, keep me out of this, Malcolm. I get it, but like, Coach Curtis is a scary guy."

Malcolm kept shooting. He won the battle. I remember Coach Curtis being upset, but it was a bit of a compromise. Malcolm is respectful, and he's told me, actually, that the person who he's got the best relationship with is Coach Curtis.

So, it was a heated relationship between good friends and people who mutually respected each other. Malcolm wrapped it up, but I do remember that being pretty intense.

Mike Curtis: I mean, it's a good problem to have. I'd much rather have that than have the opposite. It's just good. It's good because what it does: it lends itself to education.

For these guys, one of the messages that I've always had is, "You need to be your own advocate once you leave here in terms of your health and the process that you go through in terms of physical preparation. And if you're empowered enough to be educated on what it is that is going on with your body and you can articulate that to a performance or medical staff member, you're head and shoulders above those other athletes."

A lot of people joke with me when I talk to these guys and I talk in anatomical terms. When I coach, I dumb it down a little bit, but when we're having conversations related to what's going on with them in recovery, I speak in terms that I hope they will be able to absorb so that they can articulate those to the people who are taking care of them when they leave.

[With] those types of guys, it's easier. It's enjoyable to go through that process with them because like I said, you want to empower them when they leave here, and they hopefully have the opportunity to go play professional sport.

So, if something is going on, Ty Jerome can say, "This thing is going on with me," and use the proper anatomical terminology. Instead of saying, "This thing," they can say, "I know *this* is bugging me." It helps the next person who's taking care of them to be more efficient and have an understanding of diagnosis and treatment for that individual athlete.

Those guys, they're treats when it comes to that. So, yes, education is the product from them being as zealous as they are in terms of their preparation, which speaks to where they are now. No one projected any of those guys being where they are now, and them having an understanding of their journey and their process as it relates to the physical things that they need, they were students in that process, which I think helps in terms of where they've ultimately ended up.

Jason Williford: Mike's done the same thing: he had to shut Malcolm down, [and] he had to shut Ty Jerome down. Those guys just lived in the gym and wanted to improve themselves immensely. There's a fine line between overkill and being smart, and you've got to get right up to that line, but you can't cross it.

Those guys would push Mike every day: "Can I get another one in? Can I get another one in?"

And, you know, that's what the great ones do.

Will Gent: Coach Curtis is always on top of the latest stuff. Ronnie would be the first one to admit that he makes fun of him. You look at some of the warm-ups they're doing, it's like, *What are they doing?* They're like rubbing their stomachs, and he knows what he's doing.

From hearing from managers in the past as well as with my experience, something I think Coach Bennett does a terrific job of is: he's very, very open and listens to Coach Curtis. He's like, "Mike, how much time do I have?" And there's the occasional time where he'll be like, "Sorry, Coach Curtis, but these guys gotta do it right," like once in a blue moon.

Rob Vozenilek: If they were guarding us in an action, and it should have been done five minutes ago, and they still weren't getting back in transition, or someone got beat to the outside, anything like that, if he wanted to keep going, he felt the need to always yell towards Coach Curtis and let him know that he was sorry.

Will Gent: Before I got there, I can't remember how long the practices were, but I remember each of my years, they got shorter. You hear in the NBA that load management is sort of the big thing. In college, obviously, it's a different animal because you play [fewer] games and you need to practice more. But Coach Curtis is – from everything I've heard, just watching him, and the respect the guys have for him – just top-line.

Rob: The first four weeks of everybody's training is bodyweight only. Coach Curtis is doing a ton of different functional movements, screening, and seeing how your body works. He's never trying to make you do an exercise that is going to put stress anywhere on your body.

A lot of it's his training, [and] a lot of it is just year-over-year of learning from the past year [and] seeing what type of injuries guys might have had. We don't run – really ever. A suicide doesn't exist at Virginia. I mean, we do some running at the end of practice. Everyone would go up and shoot two free throws. If you missed the first, it was [a] half-court, full-court [sprint]. If you missed the second, it was just half-court or something like that.

Everything moved on to the bike. All of our conditioning was done on the bike because Malcolm broke his foot, which I think was somewhat stress-related, and Joe had something maybe his first or second year that was stress-related. AG did, [too]. A lot of guys were having stress-related foot and shin injuries.

We weren't really running a whole lot before that, but it really emphasized that all of our conditioning should just be on the bike or on the court in practice. So, going one-on-one full-court, going two-on-two full-court, three-on-three full-court, those were how we built up our conditioning – playing in transition during practice as opposed to just going out and running suicides.

In terms of in the weight room, Coach Curtis is incredible. Everyone speaks so highly of him. He cares a ton about everyone's body. He cares a ton about sizing up other guys that we're playing against.

My first year, we were playing Baylor, and Quincy Acy was... I mean, we didn't have anybody like him. Coach Curtis had been there for like three years. I think Joe and them were sophomores – [five] of [that recruiting class] were there; two had already left. So, that was their first class of guys. And the closest guy we had to [Quincy Acy] was like Solomon Tat. I still remember Quincy Acy blocked a shot twice on the same possession, and Coach Curtis was like, "I need one of those guys. Like I *need* him."

He was always sizing up dudes on other teams. His ability to just be so focused on building the right muscle and building strength that was functional – you needed guys to be able to move. You can't go out there and be some muscle-bound dude. You needed the ability [to move].

Will Sherrill: Mike Curtis is a genius. He unlocks strength and athleticism in guys even that come into the program being super athletic. So, another year with him is incredibly beneficial.

You see guys in the NBA who leave college after a year, and between their first and second year in the league [NBA], they make a leap. That's the same thing as sitting out a year in college, but when you sit out, you're doing the entire practice that the team does, you're working out with Coach Curtis six days a week, and you're also getting an hour, hour and a half of individual workouts [with] an assistant coach all the time. There's no need to rest your legs because you're not playing the game, so you are purely working on your individual skills, and that time is well spent.

I wish I could have stayed an extra year and played, but player development is one of the coaching staff's strongest suits. It's a great part of the model that they've built.

When you look at the guys that sat out, a lot of them, whether it's Mamadi Diakite, when he was a freshman: super skinny, pretty young – same with the De'Andre Hunter. Then you look at some older guys like Mike [Scott], who are sitting out later in their careers.

The coaching staff is very strong in player development. That's probably their strongest suit. Tactics and Pack Line and all that's great, too, but guys get a lot better every single year. And I think you've seen that in guys: how they developed from freshman to senior year. Guys get a lot better every year.

And yeah, you get to learn, and you get to learn the Pack Line and that stuff, and that always helps, but that's a little bit separate. I think it's more so getting another year of just focusing on you, and you get another year from a strength and athleticism standpoint to work with Mike Curtis, and that is tremendous because he really is a genius.

He is very intense about GPS tracking and not stressing the bodies too much – everything like that. He's doing his job. Mike's also one of the most high-strung dudes of all time. It's hard to get a smile out of Mike – happens only after they win and only if he's happy with the win.

He just gets the most out of your body. He used to tell me all the time, "You can't fight genetics," which, obviously, I knew full well, but it's just maximizing your ability to play basketball better. That's jumping higher, being faster with your movements, being more stable in your core, being stronger, being in the right amount of cardio shape, [and] not being tired – it's holistic.

It's everything, but at its core, he gets dudes a lot stronger, a lot quicker, and a lot more athletic, and he turns that into usable athleticism. A lot of dudes can jump from the free-throw line or whatever, but, "Can you use that in a game?"

Rob: Those first four weeks, it was isometric bodyweight exercises – probably four of the hardest weight training weeks you could go through. It was three-to-four days a week, and the workouts were so difficult. You do six-to-eight pull-ups that you're holding at the top and at the bottom for five seconds. Push-ups, the same way, and having to hold each of those – it's not fun. Walk-ons were doing them at like 6:00 or 7:00 a.m. with the weight coach GA [Graduate Assistant].

[Coach Curtis] cares so much about guys' bodies, making sure they're right, making sure they're healthy – everything. Coach Curtis and Ethan, they're the ones that are scripting practice. Coach Bennett meets with them every single day before practice and after practice trying to understand where guys' bodies are.

[Coach Curtis is] tracking. It started out with just a heart rate monitor, and then it went to the Catapult system, which is that chip that guys wear in that bra on their back. The NBA has it, and tons of college programs have it now where guys are being tracked, and it's tracking your movement across the whole court. They're doing it during games.

Johnny Carpenter: Our practices are not pushing the time limits or wasting time, "Oh yeah, water break," and guys walking. It is machine-like precision. There is no wasted minute of practice. Coach Curtis is a mad scientist when it comes to that.

Coach Bennett communicates with Coach Curtis every day about how long they should go. Coach Curtis has been tracking drills based on wear and tear on the body *by drill*. That's nuts – it's quantifiable data.

Coach Bennett takes his advice, "Alright, this is going to be more of a rest day or a mental day." If we have two games in three days, it's a little more mental practice. I think the NCAA mandates one day off per week, but we're so efficient with our time that we get what we need to get done, done, then the guys go home and rest.

It's not just one huge rest time, but it's built-in. Over time, with advancements in technology and a bigger budget, you can say, "You know what? Instead of being on a regular bus, we're gonna go on a sleeper bus over the past couple years for certain bus trips for guys' legs." Massage technology boosted within the past five years, so more massages for student-athletes. Rest and recovery are huge, and we just monitor it so much.

That's also something that's learned: "Hey, we went on a foreign tour this year," – every four years we go on a foreign tour – "what happens in terms of our bodies? How long are we going? Is that season too long? Should we structure and choose tournaments that have fewer games in them so that when we go to Atlantis," – it's a lot, it's three games – "do we want to go for a tournament with two games? Do we want to go with Maui if it's that far away?"

It's all calculated, it's extremely efficient, hyper-focused, [and] communicated from the top all the way down. It's precise communication, and our Ops guy, Ronnie, does a phenomenal job communicating with our guys. All the off-the-court stuff, the apartment stuff, everything like that: he's on top of it.

Our Academic Coordinator, T.J. Grams, does a phenomenal job organizing their academics and communicating with Coach, with Ronnie, [and] with the players. It's so detailed all the way through in every area.

There was an English cycling coach [Sir Dave Brailsford] that Coach Bennett read about who said something like, "You gotta get one percent better."

So, we try to find ways to get one percent better: "Let's watch film during practice! Let's change where we watch film because attention span studies show that if you watch it in certain places, players start associating it with *blank*, and if it's too dark, players are going to sleep. Hey, let's watch it in the arena on a flat-screen. Let's make sure the clips are… instead of an eight-minute edit, let's pick two examples of each, and it's a one-minute edit, and guys are engaged, and we're on to practice."

It's just very efficient – everything, down to every detail. Even Coach Curtis's workouts, the Academic Coordinator's study hall schedule… the guys are so focused and get all their work done so efficiently that there is time to rest and time to recover. We implore guys to take care of their bodies. As much as we suggest it, the guys end up adapting to it on their own.

There's a culture of accountability where if someone broke a team rule, yes, there's team punishment or whatever conditioning-wise, but then the player has to go in front of the team, and a senior makes that guy run. That's not staff-imposed; that's player-imposed.

Guys want to get better, they hone their craft, they want to take care of their bodies, they care about the team and themselves, but they care: "I'm gonna go get my treatments. I'm gonna go get my NormaTec thing." I still don't know what that thing is – something about extra blood flow. Extra stretching, cherry juice for sleeping better – [it's] every little thing.

Over time, guys started buying in to that, and they do it on their own now. So, as much as we suggest it, we're never forcing them to do anything. It's a culture of empowerment. Guys feel empowered to get better, and it's a holistic approach.

Mike: It's funny, on this other screen that I have over here with my three screens, I have spreadsheets and statistical software open on this other side. There's a plethora of data that we're collecting via Catapult [and] via subjective measures – the data is awesome.

But there's another side to that that also has to complement that, and that's the qualitative stuff that has to take place, in terms of me asking questions, and interactions, and my relationships with these guys.

So, I can look at trends, which is part of the sports science short approach. You've got a longer, longitudinal thing [where] we do a lot of stuff retrospectively. But if I'm looking at trends that start to look like we are ramping workload or not getting enough recovery, those things spark conversations with our athletes.

Once again, it goes back to the trust: "How are you feeling? What's sore? Are you adhering to our KPIs?" Those things in conjunction with the data help me articulate to Tony what's going on environmentally. From that, we make decisions on how long a practice should be [and] what the content of that practice should be. My biggest thing is not to tell Tony what he can't do.

My biggest thing is to say, "Can we tweak this here? Can we move this around? Can we reduce this and still meet the objectives that you have from a technical and tactical standpoint so that we are inching ourselves to what you ultimately want us to get to, in terms of their readiness from a skill standpoint?"

But for me, it's, "What adjustments do I need to make on the back end of that?" which is the training aspect. Do I need to cut something out of our weight training sessions to make sure that they are able to recover from everything that we've done in that week [or] in that month? And it's the art and the science.

A lot of people get caught up in the data, and the data does drive much of our decisions, but we deal with human beings, and that means we have to also take into account what's going on with them outside of the numbers and quantitative stuff that I look at. Because these kids have classes, they have academic stress – that's part of coming to Virginia. There are certain things that you have to endure from a social [and] academic stress standpoint that I also have to take into account.

And that's part of what I'm studying as well: looking at those things and trying to look at what other compounding factors are part of this equation, in terms of making sure that what we're doing and those inputs that are going in on a daily basis equate to a high level of readiness for us when the lights go on and it's game day.

I don't know if I talked around the science because I didn't want to get too much in the weeds with that, but I think the most important thing is understanding that it's a blend of both of those things that ends up being part of what is deliverable for me, in terms of those conversations with Tony.

A lot of people like to do things with reports and visuals and things of that nature, and for us, in our scenario, I can do that, but Tony and I are most effective when we're just talking through what I've already interpreted. The last thing that I want to do is give him a two-to-three-page report with graphs and other stuff, and he have to process that along with the basketball, and the practices, and everything else that he's doing from a basketball standpoint.

He's a machine when it comes to looking at practice and looking at basketball statistics. I want him to be able to focus on that and me be able to just provide the thirty-thousand-foot view as it relates to the sports science so that he can better make decisions from a basketball standpoint, and that's how we go about that process.

Most of the time, it is conversational. And when I see yellow flags or red flags pop up in the data, then maybe it's a little bit longer conversation. But my goal as a strength and conditioning coach and a person who delves into sports science is not to create roadblocks; it's to create pathways for us to be able to meet our end goals and objectives.

Jason: [Mike] is one of the best guys in the country. He's our secret weapon, no doubt, but he has to sometimes talk in layman's terms because I have no idea [what he's talking about]. It's so scientific. I mean, he's using all of these big medical words, and that's his background.

He takes tremendous pride in what he does. He was a Kinesiology major, and he's got a little bit of a medical background and his fitness and strength and conditioning training. He knows what he's doing, and those guys love him.

A testament of that work is the number of guys that have gone on to either play in the NBA or overseas who all come back in the summers just to spend a couple of weeks with Mike to make sure they're doing some of the right stuff. Anything corrective that they need to do – he's there to kind of point them in the right direction and give them updated guidance and lifting manuals that they can take with them. Whenever you've got guys coming back, that means you're doing something right, and those guys all come back in the summer.

Those NBA guys get a little spoiled. Once you get to the NBA, you can have your own guy. You don't necessarily have to listen to the strength coach of the team. If you've got a good guy, they let you use that guy. Ty is one of many that utilizes Mike to this day.

Mike: Yeah, I try to supplement those guys and a lot of their programs. I'm not pushy on those things. If they asked me for help, I'll do that.

I try to respect the organizations and the people that they're working with, but at the same time, I've spent four years with these guys, and I have some knowledge of their bodies and where their deficits are, probably a little bit stronger understanding of those things than some of the people who they work with in a professional setting, just because maybe they've only had one-to-two years of exposure to them.

In addition to that, the quantity of time that I've spent [with them] is greater than what you typically find in a professional setting. So, if I can supplement anything in terms of my knowledge of those kids' bodies (or men, now), I try to help, but like I said, with respect to the organizations that they are part of currently. I try to help whenever I can.

Rob: We've been fortunate to have Coach Curtis this whole time. I think if he wasn't an alum of UVA, he would've been gone by now. Another walk-on! He played back with [Jason] Williford and them in the early '90s.

He cared about us. He knew our weight coach from St. Chris, who was then at UVA for wrestling. So, he knew that I had a ton of experience coming out of high school with weightlifting. We all had our own workouts.

Everyone was doing something that was particular to their body, and I did overhead snatch. I think me and Darion Atkins might have been the only guys that were doing snatch. Maybe Justin? A lot of people were doing deadlift because of their back and not wanting to put any load on their back. No one was doing back squat.

The few of us that were doing snatch were doing front squat – again, to protect guys' backs based on how they moved and based on these really weird exercises like the Functional Movement Screen. You're doing some insane things to see how your body works, like if your core is strong enough to do certain things, and again, it's all fully unloaded.

It's just these weird, weird exercises: stepping over a hurdle, putting your heel down, [and] coming back up with a plastic bar on your back and then overhead. And they're filming all of it. From there, I guess it's a software program that just either spits out exercises or different things to avoid. He's good at what he does.

Look at the transformation that guys like Darion Atkins made from freshman to senior year. Look at what De'Andre did in two years. Look at a guy like Joe Harris – I mean, Joe Harris doesn't know how strong he is. There were times when he would dunk on someone, and we were like, "What was that?"

It looked horrible, but it's because Joe was strong as hell and had become so much more athletic over the course of his four years. There are dozens of guys. Look at what Devon Hall did over the course of time he was there. Isaiah was tiny when he got there. It wasn't just about putting weight on; it was about putting weight on and being able to move with that weight.

Whether it was breakfast or dinner on the road, [Coach Curtis] was always walking around [and] giving everyone a look when he looks at their plate. A lot of it is jokingly being an ass.

Most of the guys all had [protein] shakes after practice if they were trying to put on weight. Especially for the guys that were trying to put on weight, he had them recording what they were eating over the course of the day.

It was always trying to be healthy with what we were eating. It wasn't like the football team with linemen who are getting a pizza every night during camp or getting two Chick-fil-A chicken sandwiches. It was nothing like that.

It was the same meals over and over again on the road. We always knew what to expect. We'd have the same exact offering of stuff on the road. I think we had Chipotle before games, and then if we ever had anything on the weekends, I think we would get wraps from Zazu's – sometimes Bodo's. He was always pretty dialed into what the guys were eating.

It was generally focused on a few guys: the Jack Salt's, the [Mike] Tobey's, the Darion's, the Isaiah's, and then the freshmen. Those were the guys that he was really focused on in terms of what they were eating.

Guys like London, and AG, and Malcolm, he didn't really have to worry about. Malcolm could not be a more boring individual in terms of his habits.

AG made up this story one time, and they all lived together: he walked out in the middle of the night one time and turned on the light – Malcolm was on the counter eating an onion. And he claims the story is true. We all know it's false, but we like to make something out of it because he's just a boring dude.

Joe Harris: I think there's not much validity there. AG likes to add fuel to the fire. And I think he's a funny guy, and I know that he got away with telling the media a lot of different stuff, but it was more out of just riling people up and causing a stir.

Summer 2014

articulated by:
Jack Salt
Marial Shayok
Isaiah Wilkins

Jack Salt: Well, let's get it started. I went over to a Nike camp in Asia, and I played well, and Coach Bennett found out about me through that. Also, one of the best players ever to come out of New Zealand, Kirk Penney, was really close with Coach Bennett, so that was a bond that definitely helped me.

So, I ended up going on a visit to Charlottesville. I loved it. At the end of my visit, I committed. It was the only visit I went on. That was the best school that was recruiting me, and I thought to myself, *I don't want to look back on my life and say I didn't push myself to the highest level.*

I'm comfortable with my decision that I made to go there, and I think it's worked out for the best for me. I'm really happy with how everything has turned out.

I came over to Charlottesville early because I wanted to play for my National Team [New Zealand]. I came to early summer school. [In] the first practice, I got there, and I was like, *Wow. These guys are amazing.*

I saw Anthony Gill, Darion Atkins, Mike Tobey, Isaiah Wilkins (he was my age), and Evan Nolte was there. Just watching them practice – with [NCAA] compliance, I couldn't play yet. Honestly, I was like, *Damn, I don't know if I can play with these guys* – just watching them play [and] how athletic they were.

I tried to learn from Isaiah Wilkins a lot. He's a guy that I look up to, and he's one of my best friends. [Isaiah] and Darion – obviously, I'm a little bit biased – they might be the best defenders I've ever seen; just the way they read the game.

That's a credit to the coaches because of how they teach defense, but I think they already had stuff you can't teach. Those two were just really amazing defenders. I tried to learn as much as I could from those guys, but mainly Isaiah because he came in with me [in the same recruiting class]. I learned a lot from Isaiah.

And then I carried that throughout the rest of my time. I had a similar role throughout the team my last three years. [My] last two years, I had more of a leadership role. I tried to help the team any way I could and be someone that was getting it done in the classroom, in the weight room, and in practice.

I eventually got to practice with them, and I just got a bit of confidence. I knew I was probably going to redshirt. I had those conversations with Coach Bennett, and I was fine with redshirting. Actually, I was looking forward to it because I knew the level that I was at was far off these guys, so I needed time to get better.

I have a really good relationship with Coach Curtis, so I was able to work out with him every day. Mark Vershaw helped out sometimes with practice, and he was a really good bigs coach.

I got to do the extra workouts with the coaches, so I loved it. For me, it was just a time to work and have no pressure to play – just really work on getting myself ready. So, my redshirt year, I loved.

I credit a lot of my success to Mike Curtis and Ethan Saliba. Those two are just an amazing team. Coach Curtis, he's just phenomenal. I've been with a lot of different strength coaches around New Zealand [and] around America, and nobody really compares to him and also Ethan. The way they work together and the communication they have between them and Coach Bennett – it works out so well.

Coming into UVA, I was skinny, but I had baby fat on me. I was just a little kid. I was coming in there as this puppy-eyed New Zealand kid, and I had a long way to go. I was humbled very often in practice by Anthony Gill, Mike, and Darion, and I fell in love with the weight room.

Coach Curtis was amazing. He knows what he's talking about.

He researches what he does, and he's a big reason why in my post-career after basketball, I'd love to get into strength and conditioning. I can't say enough about Coach Curtis and Ethan Saliba and what both those guys have done for me.

The defense sometimes takes a little while to learn. When you come into practice as a freshman, you get killed. You've got three or four coaches, one on each sideline, and they're just yelling at you, and you've got the players that have been there for a while, and they're just killing you because they know how to do every drill. You really get thrown in the fire, but I mean, that's the best way to learn. You're constantly uncomfortable to practice.

Even the older guys – and I don't mean this in a bad way at all – you're treated like you don't know how to do it. It's constantly: perfection. When it comes to the game, you're executing pretty well, but then you'll look at it with the coaches, and they'll say, "Oh, this is where we went wrong." There's just always room to improve, which is awesome.

The level of play that is held by the coaches for offense and defense, it's so high that it takes most guys a while to get used to it. By the time that third year [in the system] comes, I guess some of them are used to it. They're just playing confidently and well.

For me, I was lucky because growing up in New Zealand, I was actually always the worst player on my basketball team. And I somehow just worked hard, and I made whatever the starting five was, but it also helped that I grew to 6'10". I won't be oblivious to that fact. Being 6'10" also does help in that.

I had no problem with being the worst guy on the team when I got there – when I say it like that, I don't mean it in a bad way, but I was getting punished in practice every day, and I was fine with that because that's how I made it up through basketball when I was younger. I was just the young, small kid, and I'd get pushed around, and I would never back down, and eventually, I grew, I got bigger, and I made my way onto the team.

I had no problem with that. Obviously, at times it was tough: playing against these guys that are so skilled [and] athletic and having five coaches just constantly on you. But for me, it was the ultimate environment to learn and get better.

I mean, the coaches do a great job of humbling you at all times, and so do the players. The players and the coaches... you're constantly being put out of your comfort zone, and you can tell who can take it and who can't. It's pretty evident at practice, and that's a credit to the kind of players that the coaches pick up because if you've got a guy that can do no wrong, he's not the kind of player that would do well at UVA.

You get told a lot that you're wrong, and that's just how it is. That's how a team does well: if players can hold themselves accountable, and they're okay with other people holding them accountable, I think that's how you get the best team success, and I think that was pretty evident through Coach Bennett's last six years at UVA.

Marial Shayok: For me, it was different because I didn't commit to UVA initially. I actually had committed to Marquette. I went on a visit prior to my senior year. I remember London was a freshman, [and] Justin was there. [UVA] kind of came in late in the recruiting process.

Coach Bennett recruited me kind of hard, so I went on the visit, but I think I just wanted to go to Marquette with the style of play. I didn't do my research. I didn't know much about UVA other than the ACC had some talented players.

So, I turned it down to go to Marquette with Buzz Williams. My whole senior year, I was going to Marquette, and then Buzz went to Virginia Tech, so I got out of that signing.

I didn't want to rebuild. I wanted to go to the Tournament. In high school, I was probably naive. I definitely didn't do the research I probably should have done choosing schools.

I was one of the better players in high school, so obviously, the confidence is there. I was just like, *Wherever I go, I want to just go play, kill, and try to get to the league [NBA].*

Back then, wherever I went, it didn't matter. But it definitely does matter. Style of play definitely does matter, obviously. I didn't know that at like seventeen-to-eighteen [years-old].

I remember once I got done signing, Coach Bennett called me up, and I was like, *I already went on a visit there.* I wasn't much into top-five schools. I wasn't into coaches texting you the same thing every day [or] calling you every day. I wasn't into that.

So, I was like, *I already went to a UVA visit. I liked them, and they just went to the Sweet Sixteen with Joe Harris. We're going to get to the Tournament; they're a really good team.*

Coach Bennett was like, "You're going to be able to help fill in that Joe Harris role."

For me, it sounded good – not knowing Justin is going to have the year he's going to have. I didn't even do my research on who was on the team. All I knew was Malcolm was on team, they lost Joe Harris, and I was extremely confident, so I was like, *Whatever.*

I signed there, and as soon as we got there, we played pickup the first two days of our summer program. I remember I was killing. I'm like, *Man, I'm gonna play for sure.*

Then that weekend passed, and that Monday, I found out I had to get surgery to remove a cyst or something like that on my knee. So, my whole summer was gone.

By the time fall came, I was playing catch up. I was down – it was my first time not being able to play basketball in my life.

Isaiah Wilkins: They recruited me [in] my junior year of high school. They were going to look at another guy and ended up seeing me. I went to the same high school as Malcolm Brogdon [Greater Atlanta Christian School]. So, I knew somewhat what [recruiting] was about. My high school coach was still really close to the coaches. It was one of my first high major offers, and I knew right away that it was going to be [Virginia] or University of Miami, most likely.

I went up there on a visit. We drove up from Georgia because my granddad couldn't fly because he wasn't a legal guardian. So, we drove up together.

I was probably mentally committed in the first couple hours. It was just a big family deal. Justin Anderson, AG, and Malc were my hosts. It was incredible. I just fell in love with the whole team family concept straight off.

We went to Paint the Town Orange. They put me in an orange shirt, and I was like, *Man, this is awesome.*

My visit was two or three days, and on the third day, I went down to Coach Bennett's basement, and he was like, "Are you ready to commit? We like you, but obviously, this is a pretty crazy time, so we just need to know where you're at."

I was like, "Yeah, I'm ready to be here. I'll commit right now," so, that's what happened. My granddad said it was cool, my mom said it was cool, and it was over. It was over pretty quickly, actually.

We were in his basement, and all the team was upstairs just hanging out. I didn't say anything when I went back upstairs – I think I was still excited and kind of shocked. I think AG said, "Did you commit?"

I was like, "Yeah."

They were like, "You're not gonna say anything?!"

So, I went up early [my first summer] because I just wanted to get up there and wanted to get going. I went up early, and I met B.J. [Stith], who was my roommate my first year, and we hit it off immediately. We were having a good time. The first days of our summer thing is the Kids Camp. So, we're at the Kids Camp having a good time [and] taking it all in.

The next week, we started, and I don't think I've had a worse summer – as far as basketball – in my entire life. Every day, I would go back to the dorm with B.J., Marial, and Jack, in pain, and had scored zero points, and got scored on every single time.

It was to the point where I was like, *If they don't redshirt me, I'm going to be extremely, extremely surprised.* I'm not exaggerating: I think I scored one time. I scored once, and Coach Bennett came up to me after that practice and was like, "You had a really good day today."

I think it was like a lucky reverse layup.

[I] hit the weights [that summer] because I'd never lifted weights before. Meanwhile, Jack is already kind of physical and strong. So, I'm like, *Okay, he's doing something right.* Marial was probably the best out of us because he was playing insane, and B.J. was even doing alright. It was a tough summer – on top of school.

We were going from like 8:00 a.m. to 1:00 p.m. for class, and then go to practice, and then at night do your homework. It was a pretty long day. I remember on the weekends – I don't really sleep in – but those days, I was sleeping until like 1:00 p.m. when we didn't have anything.

The four first-years, we were all terrified of MC [Mike Curtis]. So, it was trying to learn everything as quickly as we can and try to keep up. He was good with us. He was patient. We didn't do any crazy lifting. I don't think we lifted anything that wasn't our body weight for the first summer: all your movements, learning how to control your body, hip mobility, and all that stuff. He had me eating and drinking protein shakes and Gatorade like all day just to try to put on some weight so the summer wouldn't be as bad.

So, we started meeting target weights and target goals. My body felt really good. I felt like I was getting stronger every day. He was really good with us – him and Ethan. Because right after [practice], we needed to go get the ice tub and see Ethan and get patched up after DA [Darion Atkins] wrecked my whole chest. It was amazing there. MC was great.

I had to be getting close to 5-6,000 calories every day – just trying to bulk up a little bit. At some point, it was like, *This is disgusting. I don't even enjoy this.* Two burritos from Chipotle – they had to be burritos, not bowls, stuff like that. At that point, I liked that, but it was the protein shakes and the muscle Gatorade bars that were nasty. But it worked – I put on a lot of weight.

At some point, it starts to click. I'm not scoring still, but I'm picking up the defense. I watched a lot of film on Akil, and that started to make sense to me about how that could be me.

Jack ends up redshirting, and we're like, *Okay,* so that's kind of off our minds. Then you start putting things together bit by bit. By then, the first game is there.

Year 6

(2014-2015)

articulated by:
Isaiah Wilkins
Will Gent
Jack Salt
Marial Shayok
London Perrantes

Isaiah Wilkins: I actually played in it. I think somebody was suspended, and then a couple other guys are in foul trouble, and I'm in the game, like, absolutely panicking. The whole time in the game, I'm panicking. But I think I had an alright first game at JMU.

After that, it was just figuring out the little things, like how to prepare my mind. I knew I wasn't going to play every game, but sometimes I would randomly get called and be like, *Oh, I have to go in.*

I would be on the bench joking with Jack or somebody like that. Jack knows he's not getting in because he redshirted.

So, I'm on the bench messing with Jack, and then Coach Bennett's like, "Go."

I'm like, "Go where?"

He was like, "Go in. I need you to guard this guy."

Will Gent: [That was] my first game ever: I drove up separately to JMU, and I got to take the team bus to the game, and we are getting a police escort.

I'm telling my parents, "I mean, you won't believe what's happening to your son right now. I'm getting a police escort. I'm flying on private planes." It's like you get thrown into a whole world that you just never thought was even possible for you.

[On] my first day on the job, [I was] making Gatorade. Coach

Curtis is a very intimidating guy but very nice. I was in the ice cooler, and I was going to let him by to get something, and he's like, "No, no, do your thing,"

I'm just pouring in ice – it'd take ten seconds – but it's my first day, and I was like, "Oh, Coach, it may take a while."

I'll never forget: he just stared at me and said, "It might take a while?"

I was so flummoxed. I forget if I grabbed the ice or if I just left the scene.

Then my second practice, I hit Malcolm in the neck or the face with the ball, so you only do that once. I think Justin yelled, "Malcolm don't like that!" I was freaking out.

There are definitely those practices where you're like, *Ouch, that was a bad one,* especially my first year.

There was one drill. We were doing this cutting and shooting drill, and B.J. Stith had some happy feet or something. He'd always throw in one extra cut, and he was supposed to be sprinting left, he was sprinting right, and my ball was firing out at sixty miles an hour, and the ball just goes all the way down the wrong side of the court. Coach Bennett happened to be like right there, and I did it twice. That was my worst practice.

Isaiah: My first year was the year after they won the ACC Tournament for the first time in a long time. I didn't really play that much, but I got to observe the guys who I looked up to (and still do) and how they went about their craft.

There was obviously a major drop-off between the way Malcolm, and AG, and DA [Darion Atkins] are preparing and the way that I prepared. It was different. To learn that – every year, we took a step up, and it just became more and more the norm.

Jack Salt: I mean, just the role models that I had at UVA – that's where I learned the most. When I first got there, it was DA, it was AG, [and] it was Malcolm. When I got older, you've got Devon and Isaiah.

So, those guys I learned the most from: the way they operated, the way they handled school (most of them), [and] the way they worked out. It made it easy for me to just learn and grow. It was a really good environment for me to be the best version of myself: when you have guys that are just amazing leaders and amazing people with good values.

The way I grew as a person at UVA, I could have never thought I would be the person I am right now – the way I deal with things. That's a credit to everyone else that was before me and everyone else that helped me along the way.

I think I'm just really present. When I was younger, I was always thinking, *Oh, what's next? What's next?* – always in the [future] – and sometimes, I'm still like that right now. I mean, I am twenty-four, so hopefully, I've got a little while to go in my life.

I'm very grateful for the opportunities I've had, and I'm excited for the next however many years I've got. I just think me being very present and just enjoying the moment is something I got to learn very well while I was at UVA.

Marial Shayok: I was just watching. I wasn't really into weight room stuff back then, so I really didn't want to do the weight room stuff. I just wanted to get back on the court and play. I didn't really know how to work for real. I thought I did, but I didn't. I was just waiting to get healthy and play.

I think it was October [when] I was cleared to go, and the season starts in November, so I had a month to really prove I could play. I think I did well: practicing hard [and] playing well in practice. That first year, the starting lineup was London, Malcolm, Justin, AG, and Darion.

I figured I wasn't going to start, and I'd come to terms with that a long time ago, but I was like, *Alright. I can just be the sixth man on this team, and I'm only a freshman, anyway. These guys are all freaking about to be pros. Let's just get it going.*

We start 19-0, and I'm like, *Man, this college stuff is easy.*

London Perrantes: We played at Harvard, and they scored like 9 points in the first half [39-8 at halftime; 76-27 final]. Some of the stuff that we were doing was unheard of.

It was just unreal to be a part of it, and for it to be so second nature for us, and for us to be like, *This is what we're supposed to do.* That mindset of, *If we were going to win, we're going to strap you up. You're not going to outscore us. Even if we're not as good offensively, you're still not going to outscore us.*

[8] points in the first half of a Division I college basketball game [against] a Harvard team that made it to the Tournament that year, if I'm not mistaken [#13 seed, lost 65-67 to UNC in the First Round].

Marial: We didn't lose a game until January [31] to Duke. I'm playing well. I'm the first man off the bench – me and Tobey. I'm playing well [and] playing hard, we're winning every game, [and] everything was cool.

Practices are only like 30 minutes because it's a veteran team. At the time, I wasn't really into the after-practice shots like I am now. To an extent, I still didn't know how to work. I was good enough to play, but I wasn't doing – when I look back at it – what I wish I did.

I was growing through [the] experience of playing, but I could have been sharpening my skills at the time, too. I mean, I was eighteen – I didn't really know.

Once we lost to Duke, we were still the #2 team in the country after Kentucky. That was the same year Kentucky didn't lose until the Finals.

London: I mean, realistically, Justin being hurt was really what messed [us up]. We were on such a roll, such a rhythm. [Justin] was in such a rhythm, such a roll. Malcolm was in such a rhythm. Everybody kind of stepped it up a level from the year before – having that year underneath our belt, [and] AG having that year underneath his belt after transferring.

Justin being hurt [was tough] – not necessarily in the regular season but when he came back. Even when he was gone, we were still rolling, but the fact that he came back, it was kind of hard for us because he wasn't himself – he wasn't the Justin from before he broke his finger. So, trying to figure out a way to play with him, it was hard. We didn't have enough time. [He came back] right at the beginning of the ACC Tournament, so that was tough.

It's like starting the season over again, you know? Because he couldn't practice with us. And [he broke the pinky] on his shooting hand – that was tough.

When we were playing [without him], who started for us? Evan might've started in place of Justin, and playing with Evan is completely different than playing with Justin.

As a point guard, you know you have to play a different way when Evan's on the floor than when Justin's on the floor. I think we had a big game at Syracuse where we played well, got a big, on-the-road win, Evan played well – everybody played well.

Marial: We maybe lost four games that season, and every game we lost, we lost the game: up 11 at Duke, we played terribly; went up 1 against Louisville, and their center hits an eighteen-footer for the win.

London: Then the [regular] season ended, and we went straight into the [ACC] Tournament – that's when Justin came back. And it was just tough because you're rolling, you're rolling, you're rolling, and then next thing you know, you've gotta add another NBA-caliber player back into it. I think his injury was the crucial point for that year.

Marial: [We] played terribly against UNC in the ACC Tournament, lose that game, and then started off down 11-0 in the Tournament against Michigan State. So, I was like, *Man, we could've won that year.*

London: We ran into Michigan State again, and I don't think we were ready. We weren't on the same page all together. I mean, Justin was trying to get to the league, especially after the way he started, then breaking his finger, and then trying to prove himself again.

But that was still a fun year. We had a hell of a time up until Justin got hurt. Man, we were rolling – maybe two losses [in the regular season]. That was when Kentucky went undefeated that year.

That was an extremely fun year. It was cool to see that we kind of kept it up: we didn't have a downfall even when Joe left, and everybody still seemed to be bought in. Still being able to prevail, and still being able to do the same thing – that was big time, I feel like.

Practice

Part One

articulated by:
Johnny Carpenter

Johnny Carpenter: Coach Bennett is into every detail. I don't know if there's a head coach who watches more practice film than him. He watches every minute of every drill – even if it's just a shooting or dribbling drill – looking for any area for a guy to improve.

We study practice film pretty much after every practice. After every game, we're studying, we're showing it to the team, we're correcting it on the court with advancements with technology, and we've been able to make really good adjustments, but our guys come in and work.

Certain guys come in and set the standard. Joe was one of the big workers early on in the program, [and] Mike Scott was tenacious. His transformation when he got injured his fourth year and into his fifth year – I mean, that guy changed his body.

Ten years ago, you weren't able to watch practice necessarily live. It was more like after practice, it'd be cut by drill, and all the dead time is removed so that Coach can watch and make his own cuts.

The staff will throw together clips, too, if he wants, and pretty much after every practice, before the next practice, we're watching film. We're going over, "These are the breakdowns," and it gets to the point that, ten years later, we're advanced enough to stream practice on-court and live.

There's a camera feed over a wifi-secure network, and after the play is done, it takes like three seconds for that play to load, but then that play is playing on a seventy-five-inch flat-screen TV. Guys can literally be like, "Oh shoot, there's a breakdown," and they can go as a team or individually – it's correction right there on the spot. Then Coach will also go back and watch film the next day.

Same thing with games: we're analyzing our offense, our defense, we're tracking our system of jumping to the ball: "How many times did a player jump to the ball," or, "How many times did he not? How many times did we have a poor closeout?"

We use numbers and the advanced metrics instead of using, "Oh, great offense is [measured by] points per game."

No! That's stupidity to say that. It's points per possession.

All that stuff about "slow basketball" – I can go on an analytics rant about why that's the worst metric to even quantify because the difference between 150th and 300th [in seconds per possession] is 2.3 seconds or something, and people act like it's, "slow basketball."

Our possessions shrink down the number of offensive possessions overall, but nobody wants to read that – they want to read tweets that say, "slow basketball."

The way we play, it also translates, and over time, who's lasting [in the NBA]? Malcom, Mike, Joe. All of a sudden, these guys are sticking. They're not just making it to the league; they're sticking. You see how much they've actually reached their ceiling versus guys who were ranked way higher [as college recruits and] who went to other schools with reputation, and they're not lasting – they didn't improve as much.

You're starting to see it on another level right now – the whole picture: "We'll worry about the basketball stuff later, let's focus on practice and getting better every day, let's focus on being good people to the community, being good in the classroom, respect, the values, lock in to practice, and then we're gonna be ready for the game."

In a lot of ways, I think Coach was ahead of the ballgame. People kind of give him crap like, "Oh, the way you think is so poor. The way you think is so outdated. It's not modern," all this garbage.

And yet, they're looking at maybe one element, and even the element they're looking at, they're looking through points per game instead of points per possession, which would prove that their point was a complete fallacy to begin with.

Where Coach Bennett was so far ahead of the time is when you get back to stuff like *Talent Code* [by Daniel Coyle] or when you talk about the small-sided games element. That was something that he really built in defensively to our practice: everything was built out of small-sided games.

Then you get into stuff like tactical periodization, which is combining your tactics along with the physical training and planning the workouts with the strength and conditioning performance coach. Coach Bennett was so far ahead of the game with that.

I was actually listening to a podcast [that] was talking about Brad Stevens: "Brad Stevens and Butler practiced 23 minutes today." 23! How can you practice for 23 minutes?

[It] goes through the practice plan, and it's so efficient. [It] was like, "If you do it well, and you do it in a way that's more efficient and [with] more modern methodology, you don't have to practice these crazy long [times]."

[Coach Bennett] spends most of his days during the season planning practice. We're talking, "7 minutes and 35 seconds, we're going to do this. Practice today will be a total of 72 minutes and 30 seconds. This is where our two breaks are for water."

Coach Curtis is one of the secrets to the entire success of the program. How he and Coach Bennett work: Coach Curtis says, "Hey, Tony, we're not going two hours today."

Coach Bennett says, "Alright, let's see if we can cut this out, cut this out..."

It's like, "What can we do to make the most efficient practice, even if it's short and quick?"

If it's 20 minutes, it's a really intense focus, and then we go out and crush the team the next day because we're rested and we're prepared. I think that's something that's huge.

He wants to be super efficient, respectful, and he wants every practice to be quality. All of a sudden, you build up those super consistent daily deposits in your metaphorical bank, and then because of the shared cognition and all the myelin deposits, guys just improve quicker when they go to UVA.

The Pack Line is very much a principle-based defense. It's less scripted; it's much more improv. Here's your x-number of rules: no baseline drives, no post feed from the top, prevent paint touches, force contested jumpers, and if your man has the ball, you're outside the Pack, if your man doesn't have the ball, you're in the gaps. Now, play.

All that instead of, "Now when the ball goes here, you're rotating here, and you..." No. It's not scripted; it's just playing.

Our offense might be a little bit more restricted, but defensively, it's almost like watching an improv comedy show. Instead of it being a script where you're watching a play, it's the genius of when you're watching improv: they're just playing off each other, and they're just taking us down a story – or rap battles, if you will.

For us defensively, it's, *How do we cover for each other?* Our guys become of this one mind.

Then you factor the Pillars into it, too, and there's this belief that they're all in this together, and they have the same goals [and] desires but with different backgrounds and experiences to attain those goals. It all just comes together.

Our practices are so drastically different than other teams' practices. They're so much more efficient. We move from drill to drill. Everything has a competitive element to it. It's all based on small-sided games, which has been proven through books like *Talent Code.*

It's a way of taking a sport, so you can say a small-sided version of soccer is five-on-five. Basketball is more four-on-four, three-on-three. You're creating elements of desirable difficulty, which is, "We're going to really make this harder on you in practice. We're going to make it competitive."

So, you're playing Three-on-Three Close Out. You're playing for a number of stops. You're playing for quality reps, down-and-back [sprints] for the teams that lose, things like that. If you turn the ball over on offense, minus one for your team. But it's all three-on-three.

Why? Because especially defensively, they have to cover these huge distances to close out. We'll still do it four-on-four because there's still more space in four-on-four than in five-on-five.

What happens when you go live: these guys have gotten so used to closing out over these long, long gaps and distances. In the real game, basically, it shrinks the court because there's so many more people on the court now that you're like, *Man, I can definitely close out this gap*.

So, we create elements of desirable difficulty. We might say, "Hey, three-on-three, but you're playing only on this restricted court, and we're constraining the number of dribbles you have."

Then you're starting to habit stack and using all of these buzzwords that came out five, six, seven, eight years after Coach Bennett first got to UVA, and he's been building this every day – a consistent approach with these modern methods.

All of a sudden, when other teams are starting to try to figure out, "What are these new methods? What are these buzzwords? What is tactical periodization?"

Coach Bennett started doing it before he even realized it was a thing.

Offensively and defensively, we look at some stuff by [offensive or defensive] set, we look at lineup combinations, plus-minus per player, per lineup, things like that. Coach is unbelievable, the staff reviews a ton, we prep like crazy for our games, and we want our guys to be as prepared as possible, but so much of that comes down to how focused Coach is.

If he even notices a little thing, he might tell an assistant, "Hey, go tell this player this," or he might just say, "I'm not gonna show this in film, but I want to show this clip to this player," so we'll have that ready to go.

I mean, the efficiency of Coach Bennett… say we're about to do a road trip: so, we practice at JPJ, and from when practice ends, there's an hour before we hop on the bus to go to the airport to fly out.

When practice ends, we set up a laptop plugged into a treadmill for Coach with his code window up so that while he's running, he's able to click through. By the end of that hour, he's covered a chunk of practice.

He's able to go shower, we grab the laptop, make sure [the practice film] is on his flash drive in his bag, he's driving to meet the team at the airport, and by the time we land, practice is ready to go.

He'll give it to me or another assistant and say, "Can you organize these clips," and by the time we get to the hotel for team dinner, the guys drop their bags off, and we're watching film. We come down for dinner, and film is set up for afterwards.

His ability to focus is mind-blowing – *mind-blowing*. He has an ability to hyper-focus in the game, in the moment, and remain calm and so true to who he is, but his mind is unbelievable as well. People talk about his defensive mind, which is elite, but his offensive mind is so frickin' good.

We don't hold back. It's quick corrections. When it's in between the lines, you're full go. Coach is big on "neck-up kids," kids who have feel, kids who aren't afraid to talk, the Ty Jerome's, the Malcolm's.

They talk – and it wasn't just the rah-rah (there was a little bit of that) – but it was a lot of cerebral processing, and leading, encouraging, [and] speaking life to kids and teammates. That was something we were really big on.

It's speaking truth and love, that's one of Coach Bennett's big things: he's not gonna sugarcoat everything, and blow smoke up your butt, and, "Oh you're the greatest thing, you're LeBron James – no *you're* LeBron James." He's not like that.

[Here's an example of] some development plans that I made for our guys' on-the-court season review: "Here's what you did. Here's things that you did well, and here's the data behind it. Your three-point percentage went up seven percent," or, "You shot more threes, and your three-point percentage went down fourteen percent."

It's just one of those honest conversations that I don't believe a lot of teams do, but we're very big on, "We want to tell you the truth. We want to love you to death, and we want to tell you the truth." That's what we do – or try to do. Sometimes the truth hurts, but at least the truth is in love, and kindness, and trying to help the guys get better.

[Coach Bennett] will tell you the absolute truth, but he will encourage you. And that's something that over time, we all got better at: letting guys know we really believe in them individually [and] collectively. It was a unity, a team, and we-over-me. That's how we define the unity aspect of it, but communication is huge.

I don't know how many teams do this, but we love sharing information. We feel like it's our job – if a high school coach wants to come – to say, "Absolutely, come experience practice!"

They're blown away, and they go to other schools, and it's so different.

NBA scouts, they're blown away. They're like, "This is so different."

It's so competitive [and] there's so much noise [with] guys communicating [and] hitting coverages – they're talking to each other so uniquely.

We even had one recruit's mom say that she was blown away by how our guys interact with each other. They loved it. They'd been on other recruiting visits, watched practices, and there's just purpose behind every little thing.

Communication is huge. Coach looks for guys who can talk, and lead, and especially speak the right things – but also speaking encouragement and not being afraid of the truth.

Coach does a great job of empowering. He leads by example [and] by serving in terms of how hard he works. He's in with the team more during the season. The head coach is valuable in recruiting – recruits want to see the head coach.

He tells the players and even recruits coming in, "My job here is to help the guys who are here. I'll go recruit you guys hard when it's recruiting time, but when it comes to the season, I'm locked in, I'm bought in, I'm for you."

I just think of the word "quality" with the program and not in the sense of, "We're a Rolls-Royce." It's like, "When you're on the court, make sure your time on the court is quality. When you're resting, make sure it's quality rest. When you're spending time with your friends and your teammates, make sure you guys aren't doing stupid stuff; make sure it's quality. Make sure it's fun, but make sure it's healthy. Make sure you're not, like, destroying each other's bodies. When you're in the weight room, make sure every rep is quality."

Coach Bennett even says, "Pursue quality."

That's what he wants to do: pursue quality in everything that we do.

Green Machine

articulated by:
Rob Vozenilek
Kevin Oberlies

Rob Vozenilek: My journey was a little different. Tom [Thomas Rogers] was recruited, Doug [Browman] was recruited, there was one guy who was there under Leitao, [Will Sherrill], but with Ryan [Wright] and Angus, [we were] those first tryout walk-ons, and we went through some struggles.

We were wearing blue and orange jerseys while the rest of the team had blue and white. We were like, "What is going on?" We literally couldn't go white. That was almost where the Green Team started – we couldn't go white. We could only be blue and orange, so they were like, "Give them a third pinny. Give them green," and then it spun into this whole Green Machine thing.

Dick Bennett loves the Green Machine. He gave us so much credit – too much credit. I mean, we worked our asses off. I have this hilarious voicemail that Evan [Nolte] left me one night walking home from bars imitating Dick Bennett and the way he talks about the Green Machine – it's spot on.

That group, the Green Machine, it developed but was so close-knit. It was a totally different mindset when you were on that team. We would see it with guys like Darius Thompson when he was redshirting, Devon Hall, Isaiah Wilkins, [and] Darion.

When Darion was playing behind AG and Akil, he spent some time on the Green Team. And B.J. Stith cared more about that than not redshirting. He would just go after guys in practice – Devon, the same way; Darius, the same way. I mean, it was fun.

We had Mark Vershaw, who was a GA [Graduate Assistant] and played at Wisconsin for Coach Bennett in 2000. He was probably the best passing big man certainly I've ever played with and probably ever seen live. I mean, the guy had enough pump fakes to get everyone off of the ground at some point. When Jack was redshirting, it was such a competitive group. Coach McKay was our guy and was always riling us up to go after the guys that were playing.

We'd meet before just about every practice to go through a few sets. It'd be a few actions, and then it'd be mainly finding Devon or Darius in a ball screen with me and Maleek. Maleek was usually just on defense with the blue arms [shorter, less-malleable pool noodles].

Kevin Oberlies: I was fortunate enough to be on the court with some of those guys. I don't want to even try to say that I was up to par with any of them. The blue arms certainly helped a lot.

Rob: I hate those things so much. They got us so many deflections and steals in practice, but we had a lot of smart guys playing at UVA. The longer that guys played against the blue arms, they knew how to play against the blue arms. They would grab the blue arm, and we wouldn't be able to do anything because we're holding a strap inside the blue arm to keep it on. They would grab that blue arm, throw it the other way, [or] hold it. It was almost like a jersey tug that we couldn't do anything about.

Kevin: They literally just hold on to it. I don't blame them. When there are seven-to-eight of us out there with [the blue arms], it gets annoying for them.

Rob: [In] my fourth year, the Green Team was me, Darius, B.J., Vershaw, and Jack. On defense, Caid [Kirven] would get in there, Jeff [Jones] would get in there, [and] Maleek was always in there on defense with the arms. I always had the arms on. We were just always sped up, getting after guys, [and] getting deflections. I mean, it was a ton of fun.

Like I said, Coach McKay was always talking shit, always riling guys up, screaming at every single deflection – exactly what we needed. I've been to a few practices since then, and they're still doing the exact same things. I don't think it's anything that will ever change.

Sometimes one of the redshirt guys would step in for a little bit, but they were usually working out with a coach. It was always Sanchez. So, Sanchez had Devon for a year; then he had Darius; then he had Jack [my] last year.

We would work out with them before practice. We were just full-load the whole time. It was a workout before practice with Darius or Devon – guarding them one-on-one with the blue arms. Then we'd go to practice, and then after, we would play by ourselves just to get some more in.

[For] our after-practice pickup games, it was usually me, Thomas, Caid [Kirven], Jeff, Maleek, and then we'd get a manager in there, Marcus [Conrad], or Johnny, or someone would always come in and play. We'd try to get a three-on-three game after practice two-to-three times a week.

We'd play to 100 by 2's and 3's on the side court. Basically, it's a three-point line, a circle, and a three-point line, so it was just up and down. We'd play to 25, and then you'd switch, so you'd switch three times. It was basically four quarters to 25.

Those got so competitive. Thomas Rogers absolutely killed in those. It was always me versus Maleek, Jeff versus Thomas, and then it would be Caid versus Marcus, usually.

Before games, we would lift. We were always there like three hours before a game. On the road, we would try to lift before. Coach Curtis knew people everywhere.

At Notre Dame, we worked out in the hockey team's facility. I still remember making that walk across the parking lot from there to Purcell Pavilion and my hair freezing on that walk. We had flown in a day early because of a snowstorm in South Bend.

In New York, we were going to random gyms where Coach Curtis had friends who were weight coaches. We'd be at random hotel gyms working out [and] doing all our really technical exercises while there's like an Average Joe on the elliptical.

We would work out before every game, and then for home games, we would then go over, shower, and get dressed. We'd shower before the game. After the game, if we didn't play, we didn't need to shower; we'd just put our clothes right back on. We always had a full load.

Everyone who's on the team now seems like they've been recruited or had some sort of spot coming in. I don't know if that's just a testament to how good we are now or the experience that walk-ons are getting.

The experience the walk-ons get at UVA is so much better than so many other schools. Anthony Gill came from [another school] and said that the walk-ons were dressing in another locker room – like had a separate changing room.

Even more so now, they are just treated exactly like every other player. That's a testament to what we built as walk-ons: me, Maleek, Tom, Angus (I love putting Angus in there), [and] guys like Jeff and Caid over the course of the last six-to-eight years. Now, I think guys are fully integrated into the program. Half of them are getting scholarships just because they're available. I mean, I would have taken a scholarship for a semester and then given it up.

The treatment of the walk-ons is unlike most schools. You're getting all the same care, you're traveling with the rest of the guys, you're getting all the same treatment, and you're getting recognized as part of the Green Team for what you're doing over the course of the year. Every year, there's an article that Jeff White does about the Green Team.

Hopefully, guys – particularly in the Charlottesville, and D.C., and Richmond area – are seeing that. Hopefully, everyone that wants to go to Virginia and be a walk-on knows they'll be recognized, they know they'll be treated well, and they'll be a part of a National Championship program.

Practice

Part Two

articulated by:
Jason Williford
Evan Nolte
Angus Mitchell

Jason Williford: Every summer, we go into, "What can we tweak? Can we make a one percent increase, or can we improve one percent of what we did the year before?" We can make just that small of a percentage of positive change: "Can we improve? Can we be better?" And Tony's always looking to be better.

We tried Kentucky's spread offense, kind of early transition. We tried a defense where we would deny first pass. And we did all of this stuff in the summertime, and as soon as we played the first scrimmage, all of that went out of the window.

We're always trying to do something to keep everybody else guessing what's coming, but defensively, we're never going to change. We're going to be who we are defensively. And I think that's why we're so good, quite honestly. I don't care what we do offensively. If we ever change defensively, we're going to be in trouble.

Evan Nolte: It was tweaked and changed every year. The summers, Coach Bennett had – not drills, per se, because that simplifies it – kind of a new emphasis every summer that we would always do, whether that be a new player development shooting workout, or more emphasis on a defensive aspect because there are more new guys in the program.

Practices during the year were definitely intense. We would basically break down the defense. So, what I mean by that is we would spend small segments of time on, let's say, closing out. Or we do this thing called the post trap where the post comes over to the other one, and the three [of them] play kind of zone defense. So, we would do those in short segments throughout the practice and build up to putting it all together.

There would be pick-and-roll-type situations, and we'd make sure we had the communication right and the right movements, and then we would flip it and do the other side, and then we would [feed] into the post and choke down on him, and then retreat out on a close out if someone's shooting a three if the post kicks out.

We'd do things like one-on-one from the half-court that'd be working on guarding the ball because one of the big things is not letting anyone get past you right away. Coach Bennett is super intense. He doesn't curse you out or anything like that, but he is extremely intense, and he can raise his voice.

On the offensive side, we would do certain cuts and certain screens: if there was a big coming down to screen a wing on the block, we would work on that, and at the end, we would put the offense together or put the defense together, and we would most likely scrimmage or do OD-OD, down-and-back twice, so you'd play offense twice and defense twice.

After that was done, we would dissect what happened in that exchange defensively and offensively, and obviously, there's a huge emphasis on defense – especially with my class coming in because it was huge. It was me, Taylor Barnett, [Mike] Tobey, [and] Justin Anderson, so there was a lot of us, and we spent a lot more time on defense.

[In] my fourth year, it was very much a veteran crew, and we all understood the defense, so it was less about breaking down the defense because we knew it from the past three years. So, the vast majority of our practices were small breakdowns that led up to putting it all together toward the end of the practice, both defensively and offensively.

Angus Mitchell: Another thing is, he used to have the coaches track a lot of non-box-score-related stats. Even though he's not a math guy, I actually think that he's very analytical and goes back to the whole process-over-outcome thing. He's tracking all these process-related stats: instead of looking at rebounds, he's looking at box outs; instead of looking at steals, he's looking at deflections.

I think Tony had a very good model in his head of: *Okay, this is what it takes to add value to this system.* He'd go out, figure out the information that he wanted to track, and then build up from there, and not really pay attention to anything else.

In terms of the way practice was run, it was really efficient. We would do team film quickly for a few minutes. It'd be three good things [and] three bad things on team-level concepts, and throughout practice, guys would do individual film breakdowns with assistant coaches.

Instead of everyone sitting in the room while a coach goes over something that's only applicable to Joe Harris, Joe would just get pulled over to the sideline when he subbed out or when he was having a natural break, and then he would go through his film with another coach.

He's a good teacher, you know? There's not a lot of sitting around like, *Why am I in this meeting?*

Most basketball coaches would probably be surprised at how much time was spent on like really, really basic stuff. We'd do ball handling drills every day, one-on-zero rebounding, just catching the ball at the highest point. We'd do a two-on-one drill every day [and] close out drills.

There's a lot of ball security – that's one that the walk-ons always had to do. So, [rotation players would] work on their ball security, and then there would just be three walk-ons trying to rip the ball out of their hands.

Pregame, we'd always walk through a couple of other teams' sets. That's one of the things walk-ons have to do. If we're playing Maryland or something, we learn Maryland's three basic plays and then walk through those.

You have to be paying attention, but there start to be patterns in it. Or you're like, *Okay, this play is like a high screen and roll.* It's not too demanding.

It's not like Tony was just not paying attention to us, but he definitely delegated that to Ritchie [McKay]. Let's say we're learning Maryland's sets. Tony would be doing something with everyone else – like watching film – and Ritchie would have the walk-on group off on the side learning the plays.

He's a really good boss in general. That's something I did not appreciate when I was on the team. There's nothing remarkable going on, you know? The remarkable thing about Tony is that nothing remarkable is ever happening.

Every day, practice happens, it's efficient, [and] people get their work done. There are no big bumps in the road; there are no setbacks. It's really hard to achieve that, though.

Year 7

(2015-2016)

articulated by:
Kevin Oberlies
Marial Shayok
Devon Hall
Jack Salt
London Perrantes
Johnny Carpenter
Will Gent
Barry Parkhill

Kevin Oberlies: [In] the summer of 2015, I got a little more practice time because I remember Malcolm was away with Team USA. I was not very good, but I could fill in.

Logan and I were pretty good, but he was working a job with Nike, which worked out because now he's with Nike full-time. I just got lucky, and I guess I filled in. That's totally overselling it, but that was a really, really fun summer. I was playing basketball three times a day. It was just fun.

Marial Shayok: Justin went to the league. Justin had an incredible year. Malcolm is coming back. We had three spots open, but the other wing is open.

This is when I'm really starting to work out now. I changed my shot – my mechanics got a lot better. I was doing it just because I had to, but I didn't fall in love with it. I was like 210 [pounds], but compared to my last few seasons in college, I knew how to work. I was just focused on basketball and getting better.

I came back that next year, and I remember Tobey was at the five, Gill's at the four again, Malcolm's senior year [at the two], and London at the one, obviously.

I'm like, *I just want to start*. I felt like I played the most at the wing, so I was like, *Alright, I'm gonna play that three spot,* but then it became me, Devon, and Darius all fighting for that one spot.

Devon Hall: Going into my redshirt sophomore year, I started ACC play, and then I started for the rest of my career there, but when I started, I wasn't thinking about scoring the basketball. Marial was starting before me, and Marial was a way better scorer – and to this day is a way better scorer than I am.

It was like, *Alright, well, I gotta take a sacrifice. I got Malcolm, AG, London, all these guys scoring the ball at a high level. I'll knock down open shots, and I'll defend, and I'll be able to get my minutes. Coach is going to be able to trust me when he puts me on the floor.*

Me and [Marial] were fighting for minutes and splitting minutes, and it was crazy because it would have been really easy for him and me to have animosity. But I knew how good he was. He's so talented, so skilled, and can really, really score the ball, and I was like, *He can do that better than I can.*

I wanted to see him do that at a high level on the court. Obviously, that system might not have been good for him to do that, but I just wanted to see him flourish, and when I got in the game, he wanted to see me flourish.

We talked about it all the time. Before the games, we made jokes like, "How many minutes do you think we're going to play tonight?"

We kept it together, there was no animosity, and it was all love.

Marial: We were so close and cool that it wasn't ever like, *Oh, I hope he doesn't play well.* We all supported each other, but it was to the point that if you had a slow start, you're probably done for the day, which was so frustrating.

Everyone on our team was talented. You can see it now – we're all professionals. Speaking for myself, I was like, *Man, I always envisioned coming to college… I'm struggling in college.*

I could have gone to so many other schools, [and] even though UVA was a really good school, basketball-wise, I was like, *Man, I should still start here.*

You still want to buy in to the team, obviously – and we all did – but we all have our individual goals to get to the league. I was like, *Man, I'm still coming off the bench.* That second season, they started Darius at first, I think.

Jack Salt: My redshirt freshman year, I didn't play much. For some reason, I started a few games – I have no idea why that happened, but whatever Coach thought was best. I played a little bit my first year, but not much.

London Perrantes: Junior year, we lost our second game to GW in a tough game. GW was actually a tough matchup for us. Any four-man that could put the ball on the floor and shoot the ball a little bit gave us a lot of problems.

So, that was a tough game for us at GW – they were rowdy. They went crazy for that game. But like I said, sometimes you need those. We still were kind of feeling good off of that last year. Malcolm was stepping into his big man role, AG was stepping into his senior role, Tobey, everybody was kind of stepping into their senior role, and we were still trying to figure it out.

We had lost Justin, but everybody's role was changing, so we were just trying to get used to that. My role was even changing. Being able to get more balls for me to shoot, not to have to give the ball to Justin, and Malcolm, and Joe, and being able to play within the flow, and being able to be more aggressive was a lot of fun.

And just being more confident in my game. I feel like that sophomore to junior year, I definitely used my summertime. I put in a lot of work [to be] able to come in, and be confident, and know that I was gonna have more opportunities.

Coach Bennett did a great job of helping me instill more confidence in my jump shot. I could always shoot, but for me, my mindset was, *I have other guys – that's what they do.*

Like Justin, that's what he did: he shot the ball. Malcolm, that's what he did: he scored the ball. Joe, he was shooting the ball. So, for me, my mindset was, *I need to make sure everybody else is good. I'm gonna take my shots when they get here.*

And so, junior year, I got a lot more shots [and] stepped into that role a little bit more.

Marial: We lost against GW at GW, and then [Coach Bennett] puts me in the starting lineup to go down to that tournament [in Charleston, South Carolina]. I had a really good tournament: 10, 17, maybe another double-digit game.

I mean, 10 [and] 17 at UVA was like 25, really. So, I'm ballin' now. These are my career highs, and I'm like, *Alright, cool. Let's go.*

Then that whole season: Me, Darius, [and] Devon [split time]. It was hard to get a rhythm. I was a scorer; I wanted to score. Devon is more of a combo guard as far as running the point [and] bringing up the ball. Darius was a point guard, too, so Coach Bennett wanted me coming off the bench most of the year.

London was shooting a lot more. Malcolm's obviously scoring. Malcolm was doing his thing – having a great year.

Johnny Carpenter: Malcolm, that dude was just... you'd just always hear that ball pounding. When I got hired on staff, I remember hearing the ball pounding in the morning, and I'd go down and see Malcolm and Will [Gent].

I was like, *Man, I used to be doing that same thing.*

Kevin: I always knew Malcolm was going to be a good NBA player because he just doesn't stop working. He was always so focused on being better than everybody else on the court, but he did in a quiet way, too, which is great. I always appreciated that.

Coach Bennett – what a great guy. Senior year, so November 2015, everyone wants to be home for Thanksgiving, and we have practices going on, and he invites the whole team – managers included – to the Boar's Head [Resort]. I'll never forget that.

Small stuff like that – everybody feels included at every time. And that's a cool feeling, especially when you're a national powerhouse at that point. It's cool. It's cool being on ESPN, and people are like, "Dude, I saw you on TV." It's not a bad feeling.

London: That junior year, we were very, very good. That Villanova game was fun. We played in The Garden against West Virginia – that was fun. Oh, yeah – I got my appendix taken out my junior year. That was not fun.

But I had to play Madison Square Garden. How could I pass up a game like that? So, I played that a little early – my stomach was still a little jacked up.

I think [the surgery] was like a week before, and it was like right at the very cut-off that they were like, "Okay, you can start to work into playing."

I was talking to my dad: "There is no way I'm missing a Madison Square Garden game, so I'm just going to have to fight through it."

I remember there was a time where I dove on the floor for a loose ball and landed right on my stomach. And I was like, *Awww, yeah, I'm not doing that. I can't do that again. No way.*

At the beginning of the first half, I had like two fouls. I was trying to get my feet underneath me, I'd missed a couple of games, and we were playing against West Virginia, which was a fucking dogfight every single time because they were picking you up at ninety-four feet all game long [and] fouling the shit out of you.

It was already a dogfight, and then I had come in, and I had to get my feet underneath me. So, that first half, I didn't play that well, and then Coach Bennett came into that halftime, [and] he was like, "Alright, if you're gonna play, you need to step it up."

So, after that, I kinda fell into it and started playing freely and not worrying about it. But yeah, playing at Madison Square Garden – you can't turn that down. They're too fun just being out there on that court. Man, I love that court. It's a lot of fun.

Kevin: I always think of the Cal game my senior year right before Christmas. We were down 5 with like 20 seconds. This was incredible.

We ran... it's a closed-door play: so, Malcolm comes through the baseline, and I think it was AG – and I forget who the other guy was who set the pick – they close the door, Malcolm hits a three in the corner right by our bench.

The next play down, we run the same thing, except they know it's coming – and Coach planned this. So, Malcolm comes through the chute, and then whoever sets the pick [for Malcolm] also sets a pick for London coming back. Malcolm gets it, pump fake, one dribble, and then [hits London for a three] – it was perfectly drawn.

We went for the win, too. We were down 2, and we went for the win. It was great. That was a good Cal team, too. That was the Jaylen Brown team.

I don't think Coach Bennett gets enough credit for the late-time calls, but that's a good example. He thinks about this stuff. He loves it. We run the same play over and over again.

London: We played Louisville. Was Terry Rozier still on that team? I'm not sure. [No.] But Louisville is always a fun trip to go to. The [KFC] Yum! Center was always fun. The arena is amazing. It's huge, country, everybody's drunk in there, loud, reckless – it's a lot of fun. It gets super loud in there.

I think my junior year was when Grayson Allen hit that runner-slash-travel jump shot at Duke. That's another game where there was a four-man we had problems with in Brandon Ingram – but he's not a four if we're going to be real about that. That was just something that always gave us problems. That was a good game and a fun game.

Did we win ACC's that year? No. Yeah? No, I think North Carolina did.

The new ACC Tournament in D.C. was a little weird, a little different, [and] we played in Brooklyn my senior year. It's just that Greensboro feel – it's not the same. You don't get that ACC Tourney feel.

But it was cool to be close to UVA. Our crowd was big anywhere we went. It was insane. I talk about it with my dad all the time: once I committed to UVA, I feel like in L.A., now I see Virginia flags everywhere – shirts, hats, everything. So, Virginia was everywhere, which was dope.

[ACC] Tournament time, we lost to North Carolina [in the Championship Game], which was a good game – dogfight. [It] could have gone either way. I feel like towards the end, we kind of got a little cold offensively.

Marial: It was funny. Every year I was at UVA, I always had a little slump. I wanted to start, but by the time the Tournament came, I was like, *Fuck it, let's just play.*

I always had good Tournaments at UVA. We went to the ACC Tournament, went to the finals, [and] lost. I'm playing really well.

London: I mean, we made a deep run – the Elite Eight – and that [ACC Tournament loss] helped us with putting that fire underneath us again, and just making us ready for the Tournament, and wanting to go get back in the gym to get ready.

So, we started off with Hampton, again with the #1 vs. #16 seeds. We were going to be the first #1 to lose. I mean, every time we were the #1, that was always the case. I think the Hampton coach had said something like, "Oh, they're the team to beat because of this matchup."

It never fazed us because it was always something that was always being said. We were always "the weakest." It was weird.

And why was that the case? Just because offensively, we weren't putting up 100 points, or we weren't playing 100-80-point games. It always gave us fuel.

We're just going to keep holding teams to 20 points until you guys finally are like, "This isn't a fluke." It was never something that we took personally, but it adds some fuel to the fire.

We always had the underdog mentality, and I liked that. I always liked that because then you're able to just go out there and play free. People are already talking about how you're going to lose.

In our mind, my freshman year, we played Coastal Carolina. That was a tough ass game. For teams like that, when they don't have anything to lose – it's not easy. They come out firing on all cylinders, saying, "Look, if we win, we're going to go down in history. If they lose... they have a bigger burden on their backs."

My freshman year, everybody was nervous because nobody had been there before – nobody had been the #1 seed going into the Tournament. So, it was all new for us: having that feeling of, *Alright, we're not gonna be that first team that loses to the #16* – although Virginia ended up being that.

But that was always in our mind: *Look, let's just go out here and handle business.* I feel like more often than not, that put a little bit of extra pressure on us – as humans, though, just like regular humans. Anybody would have extra pressure going into something like that.

The Hampton game was a little bit different. I feel like we had that under wraps a lot quicker than Coastal Carolina.

Moving up, playing Butler in the next round was a big matchup for us, and another team that was defensive-minded, and ran sets, and played offensive sets. We knew it was going to be a dogfight, Butler knew it was going to be a dogfight, anybody that knew we were playing against each other knew it was going to be a dogfight.

That was a big test for us. It was a big time; it was a big game. Malcolm played big. We needed everybody for that game.

Marial: I had a little spark against Butler, and we come back and win that game.

London: I thought Iowa State was going to give us a lot more problems [in the Sweet Sixteen] just because of the way that they played: running, gettin' up hella threes, and shooting that run-and-gun style, and then Georges Niang being that four-man who could put the ball on the floor [and] shoot the ball. He ended up having 30 but just because we had everybody else so locked down.

We were like, *Alright, the score is going to be 30-50. That's cool. We'll be alright.*

But yeah, he was a tough matchup for us – again, being that four-man – until we put Malcolm on him, and that kind of took away from that. I thought that was going to be a lot tougher matchup just because of their style of play.

Coach Bennett would always say, "It's a clash of the styles of play. Who's going to break who? We're not going to change the way that we play, we're going to push the way that we play down their throat, and then we're going to make them change the way that they play."

And that's what we made them do: we made them slow it down.

So, that was a fun game in Chicago, and that led up to the Syracuse game – shit, one of the worst things... I still haven't watched that game. It's just frustrating being able to be so close and lose to a team that we played in the ACC, and, shit, I don't think I had ever lost to Syracuse since I had been in the ACC.

Marial: Obviously, we dropped the ball at Syracuse. We'd just come off beating Iowa State (which is funny – I ended up going there). As a team, we're all meshing, like, "Let's go to the Final Four."

That Syracuse game, we start off – we're killing. I have a quiet first half because of [the] bigs. London was hot. I only had one or two shots, so my first half was a slow start.

[In the] second half, we're up about 20 at one point. Usually, I'd come in after the 16:00 mark – I don't come in. But we're still up, so I'm like, *Whatever. We're like 15 minutes away from the Final Four.*

10 minutes left, we're up like 18 still, and I'm still not in. I'm like, *Sheesh. But whatever, we're still up.*

London's hitting threes, everyone on the bench is cheering, and [Syracuse's] Malachi Richardson just gets hot.

I'm like, *Yo, I'm ready to go. Put me in.* We're losing the lead, and we're not scoring at all, so it's like, *Yo, that's what you told me to do: to be the spark, right?*

I wanted to come in and provide that spark, but we lose the lead, and I don't play the whole second half.

[Coach Bennett] goes out with the guys that are on the court, and unfortunately, we lose. We were all like, *Damn. That was Malcolm's last game – all the seniors',* and we were all close.

I'm really close to Malcolm, so I wanted to go out and at least get into the Final Four. It sucked. It was like, *Damn. What do we do now? How did we drop that ball?*

Kevin: That was a sad day for me, man. I really wanted – not for me, for the program – I wanted us to reach that next step, and it made it that much better when we did [in 2019].

But we were better than Syracuse. I think ninety percent of the country will say that same thing.

Will Gent: I admittedly haven't watched the highlights of the Syracuse game, but I remember [Coach Bennett] being very calm during the game. I did watch a couple of highlights when we were scouting them the next year, but outside of that, I haven't. I think it's about time I go back and just get it over with.

Barry Parkhill: He's also got a way about him during the game – I'm talking composure. And he's very competitive – I've seen it on the golf course; I've seen him in practice – but he keeps his composure.

And you look at late-game situations – and normally at a game, I'm watching our guys more than the other team – some coaches are pretty animated. You sometimes wonder, *Are their players really hearing the message?* Tony is composed, and our players play with composure.

The way he handled the Syracuse game with a win going to the Final Four... I felt bad for the players, for the coaches, for Tony, and for our fans. I felt maybe more so for Tony.

I was trying to figure out what I could say to try to make him feel a little bit better. You know what? His postgame press conference made *me* feel better ["Weeping may tarry for the night, but joy comes with the morning" – Psalm 30:5 ESV].

Fast forward to the UMBC game at the postgame [interview] and then winning the National Championship – that's one of the greatest stories in the history of sports.

London: It was tough, but I tell Coach Bennett all the time: those were his learning experiences, in terms of him learning how to get over that hump and learning that maybe sometimes you do need to change it up or have a different way of playing – still keep your fundamental ways, but being able to add something just to get over that hump.

Like everybody else, life is a learning experience, and I think that we were part of Coach Bennett's learning experience. That was a big part of Coach Bennett's learning experience: being able to move forward, and learn, and take what he got from that year and that loss, and instill it in the next couple of years.

Offensively, he added a little bit of free-flowing ball screens alongside with Sides and some of the stuff that we already ran because of the guards that he had: Ty, De'Andre, Kyle. Being able to have the ball in their hands, and being able to have them make plays – which I think would have really benefited me, and while I was there, Malcolm.

He literally learned from that. And I respect it. I don't hold anything against him. I was in there learning at the same time.

So, I do think that opened up the freedom – not necessarily for the top guys – for the main offensive players to be able to create more. Offensively, he was able to find different ways to not only still play the way that he wants to play but also being able to switch it up – just having that versatility.

So, that was a big game in terms of the growth for him and how he was able to move forward and learn from that. So, yeah, that was a tough game, though, just being able to be that close.

That would have been a good Final Four because then we would have played the North Carolina team that we had just lost to in the ACC Championship. I talked to all of the North Carolina dudes, and they were like, "Man, we did not want to see you at all. We were so glad Syracuse won."

And shoot, even at Villanova, just talking to those dudes, they were like, "Yeah, we were happy."

It would have been a good matchup to be playing against North Carolina and playing against Villanova if we would've beat North Carolina – two teams that we had played that year. Did we beat North Carolina my junior year? Yeah, we did. Did we? I don't remember. [Yes.]

We might have, but yeah, just playing two teams that we were familiar with. And that was frustrating just to be so close. I think that was more frustrating than losing in the First Round, to be honest.

I don't even think I watched the Final Four. I was so pissed – well, not necessarily pissed off – but frustrated and sad that we had been so close. I needed that mental break.

Right back to it after that!

Explaining the Evolution of the Offense to a Wrestler

articulated by:
Jason Williford

Jason Williford: This will be easy. [In] our first few years, you probably saw two big guys screening and three guys kind of running in circles coming off the screens, right? That was our... we called it our Motion Offense, our Blocker Mover.

That's what Tony's dad ran when he was [the head coach] at Wisconsin and Washington State. That's what we started out with, and that simply is our two bigs are screening, trying to free shooters, and we play off of that action.

What we evolved to – and London is correct – we went to a little more of a spread ball screen where you saw London using some ball screens more, and then ultimately Ty and Kihei, those guys being able to now use ball screens, particularly in the middle of the floor.

We got guys space, you got the screen-and-rolling to the rim, where we get some of those Jay Huff lobs, Mamadi lobs, or you get Jay and Mamadi picking and popping where they're shooting some of those three-point shots, or you've got one ball handler who can now create and find shooters. So, we sprinkled in both the Motion with our Ball Screen Offense.

After the UMBC game, we needed to have a little more offense and some creativity where our guys could make some individual plays. And yeah, obviously, we missed De'Andre immensely in that game, but his ability to score and play off some isolations is kind of what we evolved to in addition to screening for Kyle, screening for Ty, and getting those guys involved. So, it just became a little more of that – we needed something different to go to.

I thought against UMBC, we didn't have anything else to go to, and so we kept trying to ram our offense down their throats. Shots weren't falling, and we just got tighter and tighter, and that didn't work.

Not having the success against Syracuse late in that game to ultimately go to a Final Four, then getting beat in what was the biggest upset ever in college basketball history, we decided we need to do something a little different. We needed to change, and we utilize more ball screens. I think that's what the game is now.

And we probably play smaller – not traditional with the two bigs. We went more De'Andre or Braxton [Key] as an additional guard on the floor. So, essentially, four guards with one big as opposed to two bigs – and starting to play position-less basketball.

The ball screens along with playing smaller, being able to switch defensively, and doing some other things ultimately is what got us over the hump.

Summer 2016

Part One

articulated by:
Isaiah Wilkins
Jack Salt

Isaiah Wilkins: My second-year summer, I don't know what happened, but I locked myself in my room, I didn't turn the lights on, and I didn't go outside – I didn't do anything. I didn't shower. Jack, and Marial, and Marial's friend –

Jack Salt: Alex. Big Alex!

Isaiah: – brought me food every day. They'd come in my room and just kick it. You know, kind of like it was all normal.

I'm very moody. My mood is like [snaps fingers]: sometimes I'm really excited, I'm over the moon, I'm really playful, and the next two hours, I don't want to hang out, I don't want to talk, I don't want to do anything.

It was hard, and I would explain this to guys coming in – I don't know what the technical term is – but I would tell the freshmen: "I'm really moody. Some days, I'm just going to be in practice, and I'm going to be trippin'. Just pay me no mind. If I'm trippin', and you're kind of confused, and you don't think you can talk to me about it, talk to Jack, and Jack will relay your message. But there's going to be days where I'm just out here in practice, and I'm furious, and I'm just screaming all day."

So, I'm either high, I'm irritated, or I don't really want to talk [and] don't really want to do anything, but they always seemed to get it out of me in practice. Somebody would do something and spark a good practice.

It was tough for sure, but the environment that my teammates, and roommates, and coaches provided when I walked into the gym – it was like it didn't exist.

I don't remember when, but I talked to Ronnie and Coach Bennett about it. Coach Bennett and I had a meeting, and he was like, "How can we help you?" Not like, "How do we get you to play?" Like, actually, "How can we help you?"

Ethan and those guys got me with a therapist. Coach Bennett was asking me, "How do you want to be coached? Do you want me to yell at you? Do you want me to not yell at you?"

I was like, "Just coach me like everybody else. I'm going to come out here, [and] I'm going to exhaust myself. This is the best part of my day."

Then, when I would have my times where I just didn't have much in me, they would help me out that way, too. We were in a Christmas tournament or Thanksgiving tournament, we finished the game, and I told Ronnie, "I can't really come downstairs and eat with you guys."

He had somebody bring some food up to me upstairs. It was insane. I don't think I would have made it if they weren't so helpful and supportive.

That's one of the good things that came out of this: me and Kyle had a lot of conversations, [and] I had a lot of conversations with Jack and people who may not experience it, and just how it's real, right? If you've never experienced something, you just don't really know it exists. So, that's one of the good things that came out of it: I got to have a lot of good conversations with guys.

I'm also a resource for guys: if something ever happens to them, they can hit me up because I still try to stay as close to everybody as I can. I would go back to college right now if I could and just do that again with those guys, for sure.

Jack: I mean, those guys are really my brothers: Isaiah, Marial, Jarred [Reuter], those guys all were my year, and we all looked out for each other, and I tried to look out for everyone on the team. Like right now, I'm going through a time [post-knee surgery], and everyone's looking out for me.

That's just what it is. That's just how we operate, and that's how the team works, and that's why the team is so successful.

<u>Summer 2016</u>

Part Two

articulated by:
Ty Jerome

Ty Jerome: My sophomore year [of high school] in March, [Virginia was] playing in the Sweet Sixteen against Michigan State. I was there in a big, green Michigan State sweatshirt, rooting for Michigan State – picked Michigan State in my bracket.

I probably didn't know anybody on the Virginia team. [I] didn't even know much about Virginia prior to the fact that they won the ACC Championship that year. Other than that, I didn't know much about them.

Coach Bennett and his staff were the first big school to offer me. It happened literally two months after that [Michigan State] game.

I took a visit there [in] late August/early September. They were playing UCLA in football. I took a visit, and it was just everything that I believed in: how everybody was off the court and how close everybody was.

First of all, the Grounds are beautiful. The atmosphere is beautiful. The coaching staff is amazing. Coach Curtis, unreal – that was a big step that I had to take to get to the next level. He still is writing my strength and conditioning programs now. So, it was every single thing.

Coach Bennett played in the NBA for three years as a 6'1", not-the-most-athletic guy. [He] just shot the crap out of the ball and [was] smart and super competitive – reminded me a little bit of me, in a way. I wanted to learn from him how he did it.

All those things, right? Everything I wanted to stand for.

When I got back, I was like, *You know what? Maybe if I wait this out 'til junior year, maybe Duke calls; maybe they don't. Maybe Kentucky calls; maybe they don't. But what better place for me to be at than UVA? There's no point in me waiting.*

Three days later, I committed.

[Our recruiting class] all had a group chat, and we would say things like, "We're going there to win a National Championship." I don't think we knew how hard it was going to be.

When we got to Grounds, it was a rude awakening, like, *Oh shit. Everyone is bigger, faster, stronger; this defense is hard as shit.*

But it was just the same thing: Coach Bennett says, "Keep knocking."

He has a little knocker up, and every time you leave the locker room, you knock on it, and you go up to the court. And it's that same message every day: "Keep going. Keep knocking." And it's work and work and work.

UVA is so special, man, because you don't realize it until you get there and until you embrace yourself in it, but you're a part of something way bigger than you. That National Championship we won started with guys like Joe Harris, London, [and] Devon Hall and Isaiah Wilkins, who graduated losing to UMBC. But they set the foundation. I'm missing a million guys: Malcolm Brogdon, Justin Anderson, I can go on and on, and we understand that without those guys changing the program, we don't win a National Championship.

You just understand that you're a part of something way bigger than yourself, and it's really a family even when you leave. A lot of people say, "Oh, brotherhood this, brotherhood that," but I was on the phone with Malcolm for thirty-five minutes yesterday, and we didn't even play together.

When Joe played Phoenix, and when Brooklyn played us, me and Joe had dinner together, and we didn't play together – stuff like that. UVA, it's an unreal situation. Coach Bennett built it from the ground up, and he's made it such a special place.

I remember our first official visit. Jay, Kyle, and I were already committed. We're sitting in the room with Dre, and Coach Bennett says to us, "Dre, I hope you're going to come here. And if you do, we have already built a foundation. And what I think you guys can do: you could even continue to build it further." At the time, we didn't really know what it meant.

We were like, "Sounds good and all."

Fast forward to winning the National Championship, you look back on moments like that, and it's like, *Oh, we really did it. We took what all those great players before us built and what Coach Bennett has been building for ten years* – and ten years was the year we won it – *and we somehow made it a better place.* That just speaks volumes to everything that came before us.

After that UMBC game is when I sat down, and I talked to people, and I realized, *It's bigger than us; it's bigger than me; it's bigger than individual awards; it's bigger than our team's success. This is a thing that's been going on for nine years, and we have to try to build upon it before we leave.*

Everything they built was, in a way, for us. I still have it in my Notes [on my phone], to be honest. I wrote them down. My biggest goal was to leave UVA a better place from before I got there to when I left:

- ACC regular season champion✓
- ACC tournament champion✓
- final 4✓
- NCAA NATIONAL CHAMPION✓
- Leave UVA a better basketball program than when you came in! For your LEGACY, your family, and coach Bennett!!!!!!!!!!!!!!!!!!!************* ✓✓✓✓✓✓

- NBA✓
- NBA rotational player
- NBA all star
- NBA Champion

When I wrote it down, like I said – like I *keep* saying – I didn't know everything that I meant by it. I didn't know how much it would mean to older players that we won. All I know is, that's the best thing you can do: leave something a better place than when you found it.

I didn't know how good it would feel. I didn't know all the work that Coach Bennett put in behind the scenes.

Faith

articulated by:
Devon Hall
Ben Buell
Isaiah Wilkins
Ty Jerome
Ritchie McKay

Devon Hall: I remember going to UVA – and I've always been a believer in Christ – I didn't necessarily have a great relationship with Christ.

I remember I'd see Coach Bennett, I'd see Anthony Gill, and I'd see Coach McKay, Coach Sanchez, all these guys with like such a peace and happiness about them. And when I first got there, I was so caught up in trying to make sure I was playing, and I didn't have a certain level of peace.

The covering that they had – you could see it. They knew they were covered no matter what. So, I was able to grow in my faith when I got to college. I was like, *Well, I want the same level of peace, and understanding, and covering.* I saw that, and my faith has taken off to another level.

Pretty much, no matter what, no matter if you win, you lose, you get hurt (knock on wood), whatever, you're covered. I mean, you're covered by the blood of Christ – that's how I interpreted it.

Coach Bennett used to always say, "You're covered," but even the guys who might not have had a great faith or didn't know if they believed in God and Christ at all – we are called to love each other as Christians. As Christians, we're supposed to love each other no matter what.

So, I'd never hold that against anyone. Even if somebody said they were a Christian, but they're not going to pray before the games – I mean, that's your choice.

And Coach Bennett did that the right way. He never forced that on anybody. He would say, "I'm going to say a prayer. If anybody feels obliged to step in and pray with me, okay."

He did a great job at not stepping on anyone's toes or making someone feel uncomfortable about his own walk with Christ. We would have optional Bible study if you want to go with Coach Morris, and you didn't have to, but the option was there for guys.

Ben Buell: It's a really difficult line to toe, but [Coach Bennett] does it so well. Faith is obviously a huge part of his life, but I think he defines faith in the context of Virginia Basketball as a more amorphous concept in that you believe – not that you believe in God or believe in something else – but you believe that there's something that's more important than basketball, and there's something more important than winning, and something that's more important than like beating Duke. There's something far more important than that.

Isaiah Wilkins: I kind of try to do things to keep my spirit up, so maybe more spiritual, but outside of that, not so much. I don't go to church or anything like that.

[Coach Bennett is] very respectful of whatever you believe. We say a prayer before the game: he's like, "If you will, bow your head; if you're not into this type of thing, just think a good thought to yourself or about somebody else."

He never forced anything on us or anything like that. Some guys believed, some guys were atheists, some guys were Muslim. It was just like, "Whatever you are, we're here as a family, and we accept you. This is what I believe, and if you want to believe what I believe, cool, but if not, you know, just take your time. Do what works best for you." It was easy.

He says – I think before every game – "Don't forget: you're covered." You can kind of translate that however. I took it as: no matter what happens in this game, no matter what happens in life, win, lose, draw, we have your back.

And I think that goes on forever and ever because I think if I needed something now, I could call him, and he would help me get it done. Him and Ronnie, Jay Willi, Sody [Brad Soderberg], Ethan – it goes through the whole program. I work out with Johnny every single day.

I love going down there. That's why I would drive for two hours. I don't care. I love Johnny, and I love to be in Charlottesville, and I love to be around basketball in Charlottesville. It's awesome. Hopefully, I'll move there one day.

Ty Jerome: So, my faith is actually not super strong – just me personally, the way I grew up, [and] the way I was raised. It's not like, "Oh, if you're faithful, I don't agree with you." It just hasn't been a big presence in my life.

The one thing I respect so much about Coach Bennett is: he's like, "Faith is a big part of me." The Five Pillars come from the Bible. When he prays for the team, he always asks, "Can I pray for you? Do you mind if I pray for you? We're going to pray, but if you don't feel inclined, feel free to sit out."

He's honest about it, he's open about it, and he shows you how big it is in his life and how much it means to him, but he's also respectful of everyone: where everyone comes from, everyone's background, and everyone's religious views. That's all you can ask someone to be, right?

For me, I'm not the opposite. I'm not against praying or being religious; it just hasn't been a cornerstone in my life. But I'm the same way.

Devon Hall, one of my closest friends, prays before every meal we eat together. Every time we eat a meal, he's praying, and I don't, and after, it's the same.

That's what is so special about that program: you've got guys that are super faithful and guys who may still believe in God; it just hasn't been a cornerstone in their life, like Dre and myself. We're not super faithful, but we're surrounded by guys that are. It's pretty cool.

That was actually a special moment after Devon's senior night, so my sophomore year. Everyone went to the baptism – the entire team went. I brought my girlfriend; everyone went; families went. It was a super special moment because you could see how much it meant to Devon. No matter where people stood in their faith, everyone went, and it was a super special moment. No matter what, we're just one big family.

Devon: Yeah, it was dope, man. That was my senior night, senior year (obviously). We went right after the game.

I remember talking to George Morris – and that was who baptized me – he was saying, "You know you can get baptized anytime, anywhere."

I was like, "Let's do it after my senior night."

He was like, "What?"

And [my senior night] might have been like three days later. And that's what I did. My family was there, too. I had family friends there, [and] Coach Bennett was there. Yeah, so it was dope, man.

That was a special moment in my life and for my walk. You're obviously being reborn, so it's like, "Let's start a life trying to be more Christlike."

So, I've just been trying to take those steps.

Ritchie McKay: I think [Tony is] truly authentic in the way he lives. He's not interested in beating you over the head with the Bible or his convictions.

Some people, if they were arrested for being a Christian, they'd be turned loose because of lack of evidence. He's the antithesis of that. His actions speak so loudly that he really doesn't have to say a word.

I think people are attracted to that, and they want to know, "Why are you different?" And if asked the question, that's what I think he's best at sharing: why he believes the way he does. So, I think he has an unbelievable balance in sharing his faith, but I think he's better at living his faith.

Transformational

articulated by:
Will Gent
Devon Hall
Ronnie Wideman

Will Gent: There was a big change [in Coach Bennett], I think. I don't know what sparked it, and I forget who I heard this from, but I definitely noticed it.

Around Malcolm Brogdon's and Anthony Gill's senior year, so my first two years, their last couple of years, I don't think he was as outgoing in his efforts to try to connect to the players. He was always very good to them, and they always viewed him as a mentor figure.

Something happened going into my third year where he started always reaching out to players [and] inviting them to meet and talk. I know he would really talk to the seniors a lot.

There was definitely a much-increased effort to connect to his players. He always put them first but really got to know them off the court as much as he could. I think he felt bad for not doing it more [and] earlier.

Anthony and Malcolm could probably speak better to it, but he's let them know that he felt that he wasn't doing it enough, and so he's made a concerted effort to stay in their lives. I know Malcolm has told me he'll get some texts from Coach, so there's some very good relationship there.

I remember it being a pretty pivotal change, and in the long run, I think it makes him part of the great coach that he is today. We always knew that he had that care, and that love, and that passion, and now, he's sort of bringing it up to the surface more.

Devon Hall: I remember [Coach] had meetings with us, and he would try to figure out, "How can I be better for you guys?"

I remember I told him, "I think you need to invest a bit more in personal relationships."

At first, it's a little awkward because it seems forced, but it ended up being perfectly fine because if you know that you can go to a coach during a game, or sit down, and have a conversation, and talk about anything, it's like, *Alright, cool. Well, I'm okay with him yelling at me while I'm on the floor. I'm not going to take it personally. I know it's for my growth and for this team.*

People don't see the side of Coach Bennett in terms of how he challenges you. He never disrespects you. He'll never disrespect you as a man or when you're a kid or whatever, but he challenges you in a way where you think about it yourself, and you're like, *Man, I have to be better. I have to be better for him, and I have to be better for this team.*

You sit down, and you have to really think about that: *Alright. Well, I made these mistakes in practice. Coach Bennett got on me about that. Tomorrow, I can't make those. If I want to play, if I want to help this team, I can't make those.*

He's able to impact lives. He understands it, too. He can navigate younger kids' lives, and he can instill confidence that can take kids to another level. He always wants to be a better person. He always wants to figure out how he can do better, but he's done a great job at almost perfecting it. He's doing a heck of a job.

Ronnie Wideman: One of the greatest improvements I've seen in him is the player/coach relationship – really being intentional. He read a book called *Inside Out Coaching* by Joe Ehrmann, and it's all about transformational versus transactional coaching.

Most of the time, especially at the elite levels, coaching is just transactional: "I'm giving you a scholarship. My expectation is you to perform at the level that we think you can."

At the NBA level, "We're going to pay you millions of dollars to perform at the level that you're capable of."

It's such a transactional relationship. And this book, *Inside Out Coaching,* is the complete opposite: it's transformational. And that is so in line with what Tony's been about from Day One as a coach, but for whatever reason, a light bulb went off in Tony. This is really after the Elite Eight year, where we got beat by Syracuse in Chicago.

That next summer, he became so much more intentional. Now again, he doesn't have it all figured out – none of us do. I don't think he would say he's great in the area, but he's so much better in the player/coach relationship stuff, and being intentional, and talking to guys about life outside of basketball.

To me, for the players, that kind of goes back to that trust: *Can I trust this guy? Does he care about me as more than just a basketball player?*

Without that, do you get to April 2019? I'm not sure. I don't know. And it's hard to put a value on that stuff, but what I can tell you is: the players respond to it.

Actually, before this approach, Anthony Gill said, "Man, if Tony would just be a little bit more relational, we'd run through a wall for him." And he was right.

To Tony's credit, he was so focused on the X's and O's and trying to have our guys so prepared from a schematic perspective that he almost lost sight of the importance of it. And again, to his credit, that's all he knew. I mean, he played for his dad.

When you play for your father, you know your father loves you. No matter how hard it gets, at the end of the day, you know your dad loves you, but it's different when you're not playing for your dad. Those young men don't know that you love them; even though you do, they don't know that.

When it gets sticky, and you have to get on them in practice and tell them, "Hey, if you're not bought in, there's the door. I'll be here for a while. You guys don't have to be," those players don't know at the end of the day – because it's not their father – that, *This man loves me no matter what.*

So, that's all Tony knew as a player/coach before the NBA,

but more [so] in those times [in early life] when it has some impact.

Tony has really been really good. That's one of the areas I've seen so much growth in him. He has such a big heart. He cares about people and their well-being.

Year 8

(2016-2017)

articulated by:
Marial Shayok
Isaiah Wilkins
Will Gent
London Perrantes
Jack Salt
Jason Williford
Ben Buell

Marial Shayok: I remember talking to my brother: when you look back at it, after all the emotions when we lost [to Syracuse], it's like, "Damn, how do I not play the whole second half? I'm having a good Tournament." I was frustrated: *I'm not trying to go through this another-two-more years.*

As far as off the court, UVA is a really comfortable school. It's definitely one of the best schools in America, and everyone on the team – to this day, we're all cool. So, I was good with the teammates. I had no problems with anyone – even the coaching staff. Coach Bennett was cool; the assistants were all cool. I was like, *Man, I'm really comfortable.*

But basketball-wise, I didn't know how much assurance I was going to have as far as what my role was going to be that year. Malcolm's gone, but London is still there, and I'm already battling with Devon and DT [Darius Thompson] all year. So, *I'm not even going to start as a junior now? Nah, come on now.*

I considered transferring then, and I talked to one of the coaches, and I talked to Coach Bennett, and he was like, "Malcolm's gone. We're gonna need a scorer."

I was like, "Well, that's all I needed to hear." I lost twenty pounds of fat. That summer, I was working – ready to go. I felt great.

I was getting my mind right: *Alright, let's take this next step and come out and be the player I can be with a lot more freedom.*

When I come back, I'm playing well in the summer – a lot more aggressive. As the season starts to approach, they're doing lineups, and he's playing with the lineups a little bit.

As the season approaches, I found myself playing more and more with Ty, Kyle, Jarred [Reuter], and Jack. I was like, *Man, what's going on here?* [Coach Bennett] doesn't say anything to me. I'm like, *What is about to happen right here? Now I probably won't even start. Whatever. Keep playing; keep working.*

Isaiah Wilkins: At that point, I'm a junior, but I feel like I'm one of the higher-ups, big men-wise, defensively. I don't think I ever was able to guard AG. Mike Tobey, I would just foul.

At this point, it's myself, Austin Nichols, Jay, Mamadi, and Jack... I hope I'm not forgetting anybody. Anyway, I can guard those guys. I feel comfortable guarding those guys. I know their moves.

They started to put De'Andre at the four, and I had nothing. I couldn't guard De'Andre in anything. Coach Bennett is kind of looking at me weird because I had done well on [other] guys and in practice, and [De'Andre would] put the ball through his legs but didn't dribble it, and then started dribbling.

By the time I realized what happened, he was dunking the ball – every day. I would hope sometimes that they would put him at the guard so I didn't have to be bothered with De'Andre.

So, we're getting ready to gear up, and Jay, and Ty, and other guys, they're like, "Yeah, they redshirted Dre."

I'm like, "They redshirted *who*?! Are you kidding me? Bro, he's the best player on the team *right now*."

That was insane because he was so, so good. Part of him being so good is his relationship with Ty because I think to this day, they're like best friends. They were always in the gym together, working out, and playing one-on-one. And in video games, it's those two all day.

I think they really made each other better. They got each other to the NBA, probably, because I never saw one without the other. It was pretty crazy, actually. One of them is going to request the trade to be on the other one's team – I'm sure of it.

Will Gent: I think they stopped [the purple Gatorade]. I made it a big deal. I wanted to put my fingerprints on the program (I think all the managers did), and so I called it Purple Fridays. It took off for a couple of years.

And there's the infamous... we would always have blue Gatorade for home games – I forget when we would do orange – and for the first time in like two years, we had a Friday game at home.

So, sarcastically, I go up to London, and I'm like, "London, we got a really serious problem here. We have our first ever Purple Friday on a game day. Do we go with blue or purple?"

You'd have to censor out the full quote, but he said, "Forget that – we're going purple."

I'm sure London doesn't remember that, but London's the coolest guy in the world, and it's a level of coolness I've never seen replicated.

London Perrantes: Getting right back into it, getting ready for that next year, and having the young guys coming in: Ty, [Jay,] Dre, and Kyle. It was a big summer for me in terms of being that teacher for those guys, being that leader, and stepping into that leader role.

And then also adding Austin Nichols to the team, which was another very frustrating thing because he would have really helped us a lot – just having that big man and be a post-presence. He was so skilled, and so naturally gifted, and something that I wish that we would have been able to play with.

Jack Salt: He was a phenomenal player, but unfortunately, that didn't work out. He would have been the starting center, but I was able to step into that role.

That's when I started to play quite a bit. I kind of found my role within the team.

During my time at UVA, I really did anything to help the team. I tried to lead in any way I could. I wasn't a huge scorer, so I just tried to help in any way.

Obviously, you've got guys on the team that are amazing shooters, and I wasn't an amazing shooter. I'm pretty open with who I am.

I would like to get my game to expand to that at some point, but I'm not oblivious to who I am and what I can do. I did what I could to help the team, and we've got guys that can do that, so I helped them do that and get open.

Bigs at UVA set a lot of screens for little, quick guards – well, not little, quick guards. Kyle's probably the only little one – and Kihei. I try to help my teammates out, and that's the way I could do it. I try not to hurt my own teammates at practice because we need them for the games.

I mean, if a guy was getting pressured full-court, I'll get him open. Like I said, anything for the team. If that helps them get down the floor and get an easy look, I will do that.

London: That year was big for me in trying to figure out ways to lead the younger guys and win at the same time. I think that we kind of needed some more inside presence, but it was a learning experience for the young guys [and a] learning experience for me, just being that sole leader.

It really just comes down to: people know. When you come into the year, you know who the leader is. So, you already have that expectation.

But then [Malcolm] grew to then finally being personable: reaching out to guys and things like that. Everybody grew as leaders, and mine was, *I have love for my teammates; all my teammates love me,* but I had to figure out a way to be able to push myself and also push them at the same time. It's a big learning experience.

I think Ty stepped into that role his sophomore year, which was big for him and gave him that confidence. Being able to learn from that year that they lost in the First Round, and bringing it back the next year, and still being that leader – [with] Dre's leadership probably stepping up [and] Kyle's leadership stepping up.

So, I think everybody's was different. It's crazy: first that it's being passed down, but I mean, being able to be in the conversation with those guys and those names is huge. Obviously, I was doing something right.

Jason Williford: I think it's just natural that you're like, *Well, what did he do? I want to get there. I watched him commit himself in a weight room. I watched him commit himself [to] getting extra shots before and after practice. I watched how he committed to his diet.* So, I just think when you have players that ultimately make it to the highest level, the guys that are following them in your program tend to mimic and do exactly what those guys did because they know it's proven – it works.

But then they're just natural leaders. I think London had a leadership quality, especially on the floor with his high feel and X-and-O knowledge. I still to this day think he's one of the most gifted feel/IQ guys that we've had.

London didn't always talk. He wasn't a great verbal guy. But [with] his actions and the way he thought the game, dudes knew, *We're in good hands with this guy.*

That's the culture. That's what you want to build. And when you have that, that's when programs are special.

London: Just being able to have Ty, and being around him as a young guy, and then trying to teach him – well, not necessarily teach him. I like to lead by example. And in games, if I see something that he's doing, or in practice, if I see something that he's doing, just talking like that.

For me as a point guard, it was a lot tougher to take on that scoring role because of the type of player that I am, and the type of offense that we were running, and then the type of guys that I had around me – having younger scorers, like a Kyle.

If I had the junior Kyle my senior year, you play in a different way. I mean, if you've got an older, more experienced shooter scoring, then I'm able to play passive and play with more assists. [I] still was able to do that [and] still had a solid year, but that was another learning experience for me. It was obviously cut short – not as successful as we wanted it to be.

But again, we had a lot of young guys, and like they say, "Take your lumps." And Coach Bennett learned from it, and the young guys learned from that year and propelled the next year – they ended up winning that ACC Championship [in 2017-2018].

Marial: Before the first game, we're on the road. Coach Bennett called me up to his room the night before, and he was like, "I'm going to go with this starting lineup. I know you wanted to come out and have a big year, which you still can."

I'm just like, *Man, whatever.*

Obviously, I never, ever disrespected him. I'm always tucking things inside and was just like, *Fuck it. Let's just play.*

That first game, I came out, had like 15, leading scorer. I started off hot that year. I came up with a few 15-point games, all double-digit games, just playing well, and we're winning, but I'm still coming off the bench.

I was like, *Won't you just let me loose?*

I thought I could really break out at this point. One of the guys in our starting lineup was struggling, and Coach Bennett didn't want to mess with their confidence.

I wasn't really hearing it at the time. I mean, I didn't want to be selfish because at the end of the day, we were all cool as far as the players, but again, we all have our own goals. I wanted to really take the next step. I thought I could really break out that year, and I felt like I was being held back a little bit.

That whole year, I was frustrated because I'm coming off the bench. And the bench – I don't care what anybody says – you come off the bench, it's just different. For one, coming off the bench when you feel like you could start, it's different. And two, the momentum is different: the feel of the game – you have to catch up.

Especially at Virginia, if you come in and you're not doing well – that could be from just someone else scoring on someone else, or if you don't even shoot and you have a few missed opportunities – boom, you're coming right back out, and the whole group will come out.

A lot of people will say coming off the bench is the same thing because it all depends on who finishes the game, but who finishes the game is who has been playing well. If you don't have a good start, and your whole lineup got taken out because you're not playing well together, then it changes everything.

I was frustrated. You have to play well, or you're not going play. You have to play well, or he's just going to go with the starters.

And that's what it all came down to at UVA: freedom – playing relaxed. You never felt relaxed because there were so many guys that were going to sub you out, and everyone was talented at the end of the day. If that lineup wasn't playing well for whatever reason, next man's up.

That whole year, I was probably the most not like myself because the first year and the second year, I was younger, and I was happy to be there, we were winning, [and] I was a younger guy on a team. [Third year,] it's like, *Alright, I showed I can play well, and I'm still not starting.*

Eventually, I start, and we win a few games in a row. I'm having my career highs, and I'm playing well, and we beat Wake Forest, and then we played at Clemson. Me and London had a really good game – we won that.

Ben Buell: [Coach Bennett is] somebody that is content learning from people just being a fly on the wall. My second year, we played at Notre Dame, and that day – or maybe it was the night before – he invited Russell Wilson's mental coach [Trevor Moawad] [to speak].

He's a pretty famous guy, and he was in town in South Bend for whatever reason, and he invited him to come [and] speak to the team – kind of on a whim. [Coach Bennett] was sitting there just listening to him, and I think it's a testament to him wanting to learn from other people and recognizing that we're all works in progress.

Marial: And then we played Duke – lose that close game – UNC, [Virginia Tech,] and Miami – we lose [four] times in a row for the first time since I've been there. So, something's got to change, right?

This is not typical of us. We've never lost three in a row since I've been there – so in years.

Coach Bennett texts while I'm in class and tells me, "We're changing the starting lineup."

It was almost like I was the reason why we're losing, even though I was still playing solid, and it definitely wasn't like I was like shooting 0-10 because no one's taking 10 shots on UVA. I was one of our better defenders, so I was like, *Man, this is not it.*

That was the rock bottom right there. I remember coming to practice like, *Fuck this.* Mind you, obviously, I'm a lot more mature and older now, but back then, I felt like all that work I'd put in… it was like, *I'm never going to get anywhere at this school* – that was my realization.

The rest of that year, I remember I told my brother, "Yo, I'm just gonna play as hard as I can [and] obviously be there for my teammates, but I'm gone."

Right then and there is when I made my decision. I even told the guys I was closest to, who I lived with, Jack and Isaiah: "Yo, I got you guys, and you're there, but I'm done. This is my last year at UVA."

It took a toll on my playing because you could tell something was different with me. I wasn't giving anybody attitude or anything. I was still practicing hard, still showing up on time, and shooting before and after practice.

I was like, *I just want to get out of here healthy, and I have to make a decision for me at this point.*

At the end of the day, no matter what anyone says, UVA is still going to be UVA; it's just on to the next class – *I gotta make sure I'm good.* And the guys that were playing ahead of me were in better positions than me.

Especially because basketball is like my everything, so I wanted to play at the next level. I wanted to play in the league, and I knew I could, and at this point, my work ethic is really high.

That second year I spent most of my time working out with Malcolm, so I really got to learn how to work. I changed my body. I was turning my mind to be a pro.

At that point, on the bench, my minutes were going lower and lower. What's crazy about this whole thing is I was like the second-leading scorer on the team – still – and I'm not even starting most of the season.

My average goes from like 10-11 points to: in a few minutes; out rest of the game. I'm playing like 4 minutes a game at this point, so I keep dropping zeros on the stat sheet.

My stats are looking worse, and I'm like, *Whatever. I'm just trying to get out of here healthy.* I was still trying to get better.

Isaiah: So, we're playing at NC State, and like four players on the team got strep throat. DT [Darius Thompson] had strep – I think he started it. I'm like, *Alright, we're playing NC State, I feel terrible, I'm pretty sure I have strep throat, but I'm gonna play because I think I can.*

I drank some milk in the morning, and it coated my throat, I guess. I'm like, *Alright, let's go.*

We played NC State. Everybody's kind of exhausted because nobody's really at full health. We pull it out – great.

Everybody gets better from the strep throat except me. I don't remember the next game [UNC], but I'm getting on the scale before every practice, and I'm slowly losing weight. I'm like, *What could be going on?*

I went to every doctor that they had at UVA, and they ran every test. Every test that came back said, "There's no real thing showing."

I have sickle-cell trait, and obviously, that will limit some blood cells, and it'll do some things to my liver (or spleen, one of those things), but I'm like, *Okay, I'm fine, I can do it.* And every game, I'm feeling like I am losing everything that I have – it's insane.

So, there's a day in class, and my throat hurts so bad, I have no energy, I'm pale, and I'm crying. I start crying in class because I don't know what's going on. I call Ethan, and he picks me up, and we shut it down for a while, like a couple practices.

We played Pitt, and I'm like, *Dude, all the muscle that I gained from Coach Curtis is all gone. I have nothing. I'm down twenty pounds. I'm slowly disintegrating.*

Marial: The ACC Tournament comes, and this is our worst year we've had since I've been there. We're not terrible. We're still a Tournament team, but it's a different flow.

We came into Tournaments [in previous years] trying to win it all; now, we're just trying to win each game, so the whole mindset of the whole team is different. We had a younger team [with] all those freshmen like Ty and Kyle, all those guys.

It was almost like that [rebuild] feel – that's what really it was like. Once we realized we weren't winning as many games, that's when you're really like, *Alright, how do you make the most of it?* No matter what anybody said, everyone knew we were not going to win it all that year.

And now the freshmen are starting: Kyle is starting, Ty is starting. I was like, *There's no way I'm coming back because if I'm not starting as a junior right now [and] if I don't know what my role is going to be going into my senior year, I shouldn't be at that school.*

Isaiah: And then we go to the Tournament, and I'm practicing, and I'm like, *I think I can do it.* The practice went fine.

I get out there the first game with UNCW, I play 5 minutes, and I feel like I played 45 minutes: *Man, this is the only thing that I have that keeps my brain okay.*

It was awful. It was the worst thing of all time. It was like mono and pneumonia. We ran every test. I don't know – that's what I attribute it to. And now, I'm done.

Marial: I was like, *Alright, it's my last run.* Again, Tournament time comes, lights are on, I'm just gonna have fun, [and] play as hard as I can.

We play UNCW. Kyle starts at the three. At this point, Darius is probably in a lot worse shape than I am because he's completely quiet. I felt like he was about to transfer – he's not playing that much.

So, the freshmen are starting now at the three. I was like, *Alright, well, I'll just go in and support these guys.* I didn't even think I was going to play at that point – even though I played in a blowout game against Notre Dame and had like 11 points.

It was funny, this was the year before they lost [to UMBC], and we're down to [UNCW] at half by damn near double digits. Kyle has foul trouble. Ty has foul trouble. I thought, *I'm not going to play,* and Coach Bennett puts me in.

I go in there, and I bring that spark and had whatever [points] at half. I'm playing really well [and] bring the lead back. I had my career high right there. I had like 20-something points, and we win.

At this point, I'm like, *Well, cool. Let's just keep it going. I'm still leaving. Have fun with these guys because at the end of the day, we're still all cool, so let me just have my last run.*

Isaiah and Jack were like, "Well damn, he's playing well now. Maybe he stays." In the back of my mind, I was like, *Ain't no way. I'm still leaving* – there's too much uncertainty.

If I would have stayed, the same shit would have happened, and I'd probably be overseas right now.

Isaiah: Next game, we played Florida, who we should absolutely demolish. That one sucked! That one sucked to watch.

They were dunkin' on us: the dude made Mamadi fall and then tried to go dunk on Jack, and Jack fouled him hard.

I'm like, "Jack, if you didn't foul him, I would've had to leave because that would have been awful for you and Mamadi."

Yeah, that one sucked.

I'm frustrated, and I'm frustrated for London most of all, because that was his time, and I think we were actually playing okay leading up to that.

My mental [game] is in the trash because I'm not eating, I'm not sleeping, and I'm not playing basketball. I'm just sitting there feeling like I'm wasting away, and we lose, and I'm still not gaining weight back.

It took me like six months after the season ended to start doing anything. We had summer practice the next year, and I was still monitored and limited. I couldn't do some of the workouts because I couldn't keep up. It took a while.

The same thing actually happened to Jack. He had mono, and he couldn't play. He couldn't get his numbers back together.

Marial: We got blown out against Florida. I was like, *Well, cool. That was a great three years.*

At this point, only Jack and Isaiah know I'm leaving. One of the coaches was asking Isaiah, "Is he out?"

I feel like they know. They've definitely known for weeks now, but I'm not showing it at all. I'm not being disrespectful. I'm still coming and playing hard and doing all that stuff. I have a blank face most of the time: just coming in, doing my work, and do my job, and getting out.

At this point, I know Jarred is transferring and Darius is transferring. They already told me, so I'm like, *Dang, they're losing three guys.*

Jarred, one morning, was like, "Yo, I'm telling them right now."

I was like, "Damnnnn!" because at the end of the day, I had and have so much respect for Coach Bennett. It was still hard to even have that conversation because we actually had a pretty good relationship off the court. I've had dinner at his house a bunch of times – always cool.

It was still like, *How am I going to tell him I'm gone?*

Jarred put the pressure on, so I texted him right then and there. There were three of us, and I didn't want to be the last person because it was going to be a rough day, regardless.

I texted Coach Bennett, "Hey Coach, can I talk to you?"

I was like, "Coach, it's tough, but I gotta make a decision for me."

And he knew. He already knew. He wished me well.

I said, "I appreciate you, Coach, for everything. Stay in touch." Boom.

Darius goes in after me, and I don't think they knew about Darius – they didn't expect it. So, all three of us: boom, boom, boom.

I think it was the best thing for both parties. I was too good not to play all year the next year as a senior, and De'Andre and the young guys, it was their time to really grow through experience and playing.

So, they wouldn't have had the opportunity to really be themselves. It would have been a whole lot of, "Alright, these guys aren't playing well, let's put him in. He's not playing well..." – all of us would have been circling. And that year, they probably wouldn't have had a successful year because there [would have been] too much in-and-out.

And you see, once I left, De'Andre was a true sixth man. Devon was there, Kyle got to grow into that role, and they all got to learn and grow, and they ended up doing what they did that year – being #1 in the country.

Summer 2017

articulated by:
Marial Shayok
Jack Salt

Marial Shayok: Once I signed at Iowa State, once I went on my visit and got to work out, I knew for a fact that, *I'm coming here*.

I'd already let them know: "I'm not going through the same stuff I went through at Virginia. I want to earn my spot, and I want to play free." That was the main thing. I felt like I was not free at all.

The most free I was at Virginia was my freshman year because I was at peace with, *Alright, this is going to be my role. There are better guys in front of me, like Malcolm and Justin. Let me just learn this year, play as hard as I can, and let's win*. After that, I wanted to really show what I could do, and I felt like I wasn't able to do that.

If you don't know how much you're going to play, and then it's dictated on if you make your first shot – that's so stressful. If you miss your first two shots, and someone behind you made their first shot, you're done for the day.

You might get like two more minutes in the second half, and it's a wrap. There's no way to play like that. You can't play like that. I don't care what anyone says – you can't play like that.

That whole season, everyone thought I would be mad. These are like my best friends. At the end of the day, I hope they do well.

I'm watching Iowa State, obviously, and then I'm watching my boys. You had all those guys: Zay [Isaiah Wilkins], Devon – and they're killin'.

I made an Instagram. I wasn't really on social media that much, but I had a year off, so I was like, *Whatever, let me just get into it*.

Every time we [UVA] did something good, one of those weirdo fans: "Bet you wish you didn't leave!"

I was like, "I don't give a shit if they win a National Championship."

I was completely at peace and completely confident with my decision because I already knew, *I'm gonna put this work in this year, and I'll eat the fruits of my labor the next year.*

My year off, I'm working out like crazy, literally three-to-four times a day. Nothing to do in Iowa, so I'm going to the gym, going home, going to the gym, going home. Before class, after class, before practice, just working out, [and] getting better.

I'll tell you this: my sit-out year [was crazy] compared to any year I was there with Malcolm (because I heard he had a crazy sit-out year, too). When you're in season, your workouts have to be a little condensed.

My sit-out year was a lot crazier than any workout I've seen or done with him because I had nothing but time. I could go as long as I wanted – getting thousands of shots a day, for real.

I took little things [from Malcolm] like how hard he goes on reps. He wouldn't count shots that hit too much rim: if it was in-and-out-and-in, it wouldn't count. It's pretty much swishes or straight in.

Malcolm was definitely a great person to have as someone to look up to – and to this day. When I was [transferring], he supported that.

A lot of people were like, "Why leave for your last year? You were playing a good amount."

He was one of the guys who was like, "Yo, go do it. You know what you got to do."

The next year, I didn't have time to watch them. I just wanted to come out and focus on Iowa State. I was finally the go-to guy on my team, the leader of my team, and I had the most experience, so I showed what I could do.

A lot of people will say, "All they want to do is score." I was like 50/40/90 [field goal/three-point/free-throw percentage] most of the season. I was efficient.

A lot of people thought I wanted to leave just to go jack shots, but I was really efficient. I was playing with another lead guy, Talen Horton-Tucker, who got drafted last year, and a lot more aggressive guys than UVA had. Mind you, we're playing a lot faster, so we're scoring in the 80's.

When I was [at UVA], it was even slower than they are now: no fast breaks, bring that ball up the court, and run Sides for 23 seconds on the court – and that wasn't me.

So, I remember I felt complete. I felt like home – it was me playing again. That was the first time I felt like I was myself since high school. I was able to do what I did that year, and play well, get to where I wanted to be, get drafted, and get to the league.

But my time at UVA was great, man. I still talk to Jack, Isaiah, Devon – Ty just hit me up to go get dinner [in the NBA bubble]. Everybody is still cool. I just saw Malcolm [and] I played against Justin a few times this year.

If I could change things, who knows what I would do. I learned how to work at UVA, I learned a lot of the fundamentals, [and] I learned how to score with limited dribbles because the spacing was different. My game got a lot sharper at UVA. I learned a lot of stuff at Virginia. Obviously, I became a way better defender.

It worked out pretty well for me because I got where I wanted to be, I got better, and I mean, I got to become damn near a family with a bunch of dudes that are good guys.

Jack Salt: I can't speak for the earlier guys, but two of my best friends transferred: Marial and Jarred. For me, I have no problem with it. They thought the system wasn't great for them and they'd work better somewhere else.

I want the best for all people I'm close with, and they thought that was best for them, and for both of them, I think it did work out better. So, if success for them is better somewhere else, that's great, but I think the guys that have stayed at UVA all did pretty well, and we managed to pull off something pretty amazing.

So, I am happy for all parties. Jarred and Marial, they went off and had successful careers, which is great. And then, I was able to be a part of a team that also had a pretty successful career. Everyone ended up happy.

NBA

articulated by:
Joe Harris
Devon Hall
Ty Jerome

Joe Harris: Everybody that comes in the NBA is super talented – the best players in the world. Everybody that is coming in is the best of wherever they came from. So, no matter if you came from Memphis, Florida, [or] UVA, you were the best player at your school, and then, when you get there, everybody is just as good, and it might be your first adversity as a basketball player.

I think what's instilled in the guys at Virginia is this level of patience. Especially early on – I mean, it's maybe a little different now because they are getting better recruits – not a lot of us were these five-star-type guys that were coming in. We had to develop and get to a level where we were respected as the same caliber of players as those highly touted guys like guys that go to Duke and Carolina.

That's sort of how I view my NBA career, though, too. I came in, [and] I knew it wasn't going to – obviously, I believed in myself – I wasn't going to solidify a niche right away, you know? You have to earn your keep and your respect in the league.

I knew it was going to take time, and there were probably going to be setbacks along the way, just like there was at Virginia early on. It was just about staying with it, trusting in it, and believing that if you keep being about the right stuff, you have those consistent habits, you're deliberate in your practice, in time, whatever you're putting in is going to come to fruition.

Devon Hall: It's a slow process, man. I've always been a proponent of, "The work will always show." So, you just gotta put your head down.

Instant gratification is something that Coach Bennett talked to me about when I was at UVA. When I came out of high school, I wasn't ready to play right away. But the instant gratification is: you're the best guy on your team in high school, and you want to play right away. You want to win, and you want to contribute [and] score points.

But when it gets to the professional level, now it's a whole different ballgame. It's like, "What's your role for this team? How can you affect the game in your role?" If you can be great at your role, you can be wealthy, you know?

It's like, *How can I do that? How can I form my game and work on my skill set to where I'm able to turn myself into a different player, adjust to the speed of the game, adjust to the game?* If I need to make tweaks here and there in my game, I will.

[In] my G-League year, I had a really good year, and it was more of me being a playmaker [and] scoring the ball. I was doing much more of that, but switch to the [Oklahoma City] Thunder – that's not what they need me to do.

They're going to need me to be able to come in, make my open shots, take care of the ball, [and] make sure I know the sets. I'm getting guys involved. They don't need me to be a playmaker.

You have pretty much got to wait your turn when it comes to UVA. You've got to grind it out [and] wait your turn.

Ty Jerome: Hundred percent he's right. I think defensively, I picked it up so much quicker than most guys [in the NBA]. I was shit out of luck because I missed the first seven weeks of the season with a bad ankle injury, but for any rookie, it's hard to recover from that – unless you're Zion [Williamson] and, you know, crazy.

But he's a hundred percent right: you look at what Dre did this year, you look at what Malcolm did as a rookie, Joe went through his ups and downs, played in the G-League for a while, but he pushed through.

Even things like that. You go through adversity. Stuff's not handed to you – you earn everything. You look at guys like Joe [or] a guy like me who missed the first six weeks, came back, had some good games, [and] got injured again.

Now, I'm still kind of pushing through and still writing my story. Or guys like Kyle – perseveres [and] scores their first NBA bucket. And I do think Kyle will get a chance and will break a full-time NBA roster.

So, that's the adversity you go through at UVA when nothing is handed to you, [unlike] at some other schools. It prepares you for the real world, whether that's basketball, business, whatever your passion is. The adversity [and] the lessons Coach Bennett teaches you, it's literally invaluable.

Joe: All the guys call for different advice. When I was coming out [of college], Mike was in the NBA, [and] you could reach out to him a little bit, but he had just gotten there.

Once you have guys that are in the NBA – especially if they have years under their belt – you start to get an idea of how things work, you know which organizations, coaches, [and] agents are reputable, things like that. You can ask them for their opinions in a trusting way about how certain guys are being viewed.

I think you can help them make easier decisions because when you're a college kid, it's kind of hard. You're sort of trapped in this bubble, and you might think you're good enough, but you're not sure, or you might think you're better than you really are – just depends. Whenever you can get outside opinions from people that you trust [and] that you know are going to be honest with you, it's always super helpful.

Again, that's the thing with the guys from Virginia: we're always looking out for one another, but you're going to give them honest input as to what they want to do. Obviously, De'Andre is a little bit different [as] a lottery pick, but the other guys want to call and get advice on certain stuff. It's the benefit of that family, that brotherhood, where you can trust the opinion of guys that are in the NBA, like Malcolm, Justin, Mike, [and] myself.

I just finished [the Yale Happiness online course]. It's been great. I kind of like filling my time with different stuff anyways. Even if I was in the offseason right now, I'd probably be doing something similar.

I'm still able to go in and work out basically every morning, and then you kind of fill your time with various stuff in the afternoon, but when all this stuff hit [Covid-19], I was like, *I might as well look into different stuff.* I had taken some classes through Harvard Business School in the past that they had offered up to the NBA Players Association. I've enjoyed it, and then they did the same thing here recently with Yale.

It's not anything super taxing. You can take it at your leisure. I didn't study psychology or anything like that at Virginia, but I find all of that stuff really fascinating and interesting.

It's all stuff that when you talk about it, you think, *Well, it's obvious,* but it is one of those things where... I think it's important to think about it on a daily basis because the whole class is predicated on what makes people happy. It talks about how when you're growing up – especially people here in America – we all have this idea of what success is in terms of making it to a certain level, having that great job, making a bunch of money, or having the corner office.

Everybody is hardwired to be competitive here, you know? You always are trying to be the best at whatever you're doing.

But the class talks about how a lot of times you get to whatever you're hoping to get to, and then you kind of assume that there's this magic switch that's going to hit, and all of a sudden, you're going to be happy. But a lot of times, you're not fulfilled at all because you've been about the wrong stuff the whole time leading up to it. It can make you happy for a little bit, but it's not sustainable, and it's not long-term happiness.

All of that stuff is sort of obvious, but I think about even in my life where my whole goal my entire life has been to make it to the NBA, and I made it, but then it wasn't like I made it, and then all of a sudden, I turned around like, *Damn, I'm the happiest guy in the world.*

It was almost the opposite. I made it, and I almost had to re-find my love for basketball because I was in disagreement with so much about what the NBA was like when I first got there.

I kind of wish I would have been able to take a class like that at Virginia or even learned about it earlier on. It's one of those things where it helps just highlight and put things into perspective. Even talking about it right now, I kind of want to revisit it because I think it's one of those things that's important to sort of refresh in your mind a lot.

Homegrown

articulated by:
Rob Vozenilek
Grant Kersey

Rob Vozenilek: The Richmond aspect is pretty cool. Even if you're a [Virginia] Tech fan, or a Carolina fan, or whatever, you still have been to plenty of UVA games with friends. You've spent tons of Saturdays on the Hill in seventh and eighth grade and running around without your parents. You've been to U-Hall. You've been to JPJ. It was pretty surreal for a little bit.

I mean, being from Richmond, there's no other place that you would want to play. I joke about it with the West Lot at Scott Stadium and sections 124, 125, and 126: if you walk on that concourse during a game, you're going to see everyone. I grew up with seats at U-Hall. I grew up going to JPJ. Coach Bennett has a huge mural in his office of the Arizona game [the first game at JPJ]. He wasn't there for it, but that's just what it is. And I can find myself in that photo.

Especially in those first couple of years, it was a ton of fun. My parents really enjoyed it. You look up into the side across from the benches, and you can spot anyone from Richmond. Sitting around The Corner, sitting up in the stands – it was a ton of fun.

As the years have gone on, there's been so many great stories. I can't imagine what Grant, or Austin [Katstra], or Jayden [Nixon] goes through being from Charlottesville – Maleek, as well. But I think certainly those guys from Albemarle [High School] and STAB [St. Anne's-Belfield School] get it a ton as well. You look at what Grant did this past year: this guy has somehow never missed a shot.

He's taking some bullshit shots, by the way. The fact that he shot one at the buzzer after a tip out or something – I was like, *We would've pulled out every single time.* I got told once not to shoot the ball towards the rim but *throw* it towards the rim because there was an extra second, and I was like, "No, I'm shooting the ball! I'm not just throwing it towards the rim."

Meanwhile, Grant's huckin' up buzzer-beaters up 20 and celebrating. I'm like, *This is ridiculous.* That was a different animal, just being from Charlottesville, being a walk-on, and literally not missing a shot ever.

Grant Kersey: It still doesn't feel real. I think I'll always be in awe of how it all happened and how grateful I am.

I was born and raised in Charlottesville, so I've been coming to all UVA sporting events – especially UVA basketball games – since as long as I can remember. That's something really cool for me to grow up coming to games and then to be involved in the program in the way I was – something I never thought would happen.

I remember being at games. During blowout games, I used to make my parents wait the whole game just because I used to love watching the walk-ons get in.

I remember waiting for Thomas Rogers their senior night when they played Syracuse and he hit that three. I was going crazy in the stands.

I can honestly say it was like a dream come true. I don't want that to sound cliché, I guess, but growing up in Charlottesville and watching games – honestly, it was a dream come true. Family's always been huge for me. So, to be able to stay at school and be close to my family was a big factor in my decision.

But it's funny: at first, I didn't want to come to UVA because I was ready to kind of get out of Charlottesville. I wanted to move away and switch it up a little bit, but then I realized, academic-wise, I'd be at such a good school, and there was a chance I could be involved in the basketball program.

I thought about going to a smaller school to play, but then I realized, *I cannot pass up the opportunity of being involved in the program I grew up watching. If I'm a manager, I'll be at practice every day. That's around the game; I don't need to play*. I was cool with that.

It's just surreal because people will see me out now, and they'll talk to me about a game or a specific shot – I never thought I would be in that situation. Kids at basketball camp will talk to me, and I remember being in their shoes – the kid talking to the guys. I never thought that would happen, but to have someone say, "You're an inspiration. My son/daughter watched your story," that's more than the game of basketball. That means so much to me, and it just makes it even better to be in the community I grew up in and want to give back to.

Year 9

(2017-2018)

articulated by:
Kevin Oberlies
Isaiah Wilkins
Devon Hall
Grant Kersey
Will Gent
Barry Parkhill
Ronnie Wideman
Ben Buell
Johnny Carpenter
Ty Jerome
London Perrantes

Kevin Oberlies: The year after we lost to Florida [in the 2017 Tournament], I went down to visit. I remember seeing Coach Bennett, and I was thankful that he was happy to see me. We talked for about five minutes.

I said, "How are we looking this year, Coach?"

And he said, "Man, I don't know."

And then they ended up winning the ACC [with] something like 30 wins? I mean, we lost to UMBC, which was tough, but I was like, *You didn't know?!*

I guess – looking back on it – you really didn't know with that team. That was a young team – that was Ty and Kyle's second year.

I just thought it was funny all year. I was like, *Man, he definitely knew.*

They were good that year.

Isaiah Wilkins: We looked up to DA because he was that [leader] for us our first year. Then you just have different guys: Malcolm, obviously, in our second year; third-year, London's leading the show; and fourth-year comes, and a lot of guys transfer, so it's a bit confusing. We were just trying to figure things out.

We knew we had Kyle [and] Ty. I knew about Dre when he redshirted because of practice, but it was good to see those guys come in. That defensive leadership role and Defensive Player of the Year in the ACC, that really meant a lot to me.

So, going into that with Devon and Jack as co-captains, it was awesome. It was the perfect build-up for me. It was exactly what I wanted to be because I like the glue guy role. It wasn't like I was adjusting. I kind of built that mold of energy, and that turned into glue, and it was perfect for me.

Devon Hall: Isaiah Wilkins, he is probably the most selfless player I've ever played with. He did not care about scoring a single point. Jack Salt, too: did not care about it; he wanted to win basketball games.

So, playing alongside of [Isaiah]… if I could play with him and I could have some autonomy in my pro career to play with him, he'd be on my team because he wants to do whatever to win. He doesn't care about shooting. He doesn't care about scoring.

He was so good on defense. He would quarterback our defense. He's in the back line pointing stuff out, telling where the coverage is – everything. He was elite defensively. He could blow a screen up, get back, three-quarter a post, post trap – this is all one possession – close out, guard, block shots – the dude is *elite.*

Jack is a bit quieter in terms of his leadership. He just leads by example. But Isaiah and I, we took on the roles of, *If there's something that needs to be said, we don't have a problem saying it and letting guys know,* and even if that's to each other.

I remember we were sitting on the bench one game, and we were arguing about a coverage – I forget when it was – and I was like, "You're wrong."

We're going back and forth, and we're using choice words. I was like, "Man, we don't have to do all this now. I'll see you in the locker room. We can fight in the locker room."

Then, next timeout, Isaiah comes to me, and he's like, "Look, I'm sorry. I was wrong about that."

I said, "Look, I'm not trippin'."

He is so competitive, and so am I. We just want to win. We want to get that right and win because we knew we were important for that team.

Isaiah: My fourth year when we had the crazy run – unranked to #1, then the #1/#16 loss – I think the thing that we really had going for us was: we were really close. Like, "Come over to my apartment after practice," and we'd play video games for eight hours.

Nine people in a small apartment, everybody brought their own TV from home, so the apartment is packed. We played Call of Duty for like twelve hours, thirteen hours.

Before practice, if you go into JPJ, there's two people playing a game against each other, whatever game it might be. There's always somebody on the sticks all the way until after practice [at] 11:00 p.m. Guys just hang out in the locker room and play the game against each other.

It made no sense, but we were just so close. We didn't really have any egos. Everybody was close, and we all wanted the next person to do great.

Marco [Anthony] had his game where he went crazy – I think it was Louisville – but it was amazing. When Devon had his games, it was great. When I had my game, it was incredible. Everybody rooted for each other, and it made it really special because we were really close.

Grant Kersey: All the guys lived in the same apartment complex. Some nights, we would go out to eat, and it'd be pretty much everybody on the team. It probably looked like a required team dinner, [but] it would just be most of us together. Everybody just got along so well, and it was just so easy, and that's kind of how it flowed for us.

Man, it was great. In our living room, we had like four TVs

because you could play Fortnite with squads of four people. We used to rotate people through – had to [get good]! If you lose, you're off the sticks, so you need to get good so you can keep playing.

We would just watch movies, play games. Me and [Kyle] are really similar: super chill, go with the flow. It's kind of whatever happens, we'll make the best of it. We just wanted to be around other people and hang out.

Will Gent: As a Virginia fan, [we had] a lot of tough losses in our history that were all fundamental pieces to reaching the pinnacle. [Coach Bennett] always talked about being thankful for the losses as well as the wins: "Hold everything with open hands and use it as a learning experience," which I thought was great.

My fourth year [was] when we lost to UMBC. At least from my perspective, it kind of felt like, *What can get worse than that Syracuse Elite Eight loss?* We were there; we had it.

Grant: I mean, talk about a change of emotions. The week before [UMBC], we'd just won the ACC Tournament. So, we're on the highest of highs right then because conference tournaments just ended, and we're one of the few teams that won their conference tournament. So, we're confident.

We're not like arrogant or anything – we obviously know in a Tournament, you lose, you go home – but we were confident in ourselves. We believed in ourselves and were just riding the high, and then all of a sudden, we're at the lowest of lows where nobody has ever been. A week later – the next weekend.

Isaiah: The UMBC game starts, and everything feels like it's going in slow motion. We're tied at halftime at 21, I think it was, but I'm not really worried yet because that's the way we play. We slow grind it – we're fine.

Some guys may have been worried, [but] I was like, *Okay, we're fine.*

I come out [after halftime], and I get my third or fourth foul. I'm on the bench, and I look up, and they're up 20.

I'm like, *Oh.*

I foul out, and then I'm like, *Okay, this is happening.*

I'm devastated – not embarrassed. I don't care about the #1/#16 necessarily, but [I'm] sad because I know that now, that bond is over.

In years past, we lost, and I'm sad, but I'm like, *I'm still coming back. I'll still see Jack next week.* I was heartbroken. I didn't even know if I wanted to play professionally after I finished because my body was hurting, and I was having mental problems, and all that stuff. I was like, *I don't even know if I'm interested.*

My whole focus is: *My time with these guys is over. I have four weeks left of school. I'm almost done with all my classes. It's over.*

That whole next three or four days, I'm just devastated that that part is over.

I ended up playing professionally and took those experiences with me, but that was the biggest part for me: *Damn. The guys who I'm closest with are international, so they can't even stay in the States. They have to go home now.* Their thing is over, so I'm like, *When am I ever going to see these guys again?*

Barry Parkhill: How many coaches would have gone out [for the UMBC postgame interview]? Maybe some, maybe not, but that's the right thing to do.

Ronnie Wideman: You know, a little bit of my job is to try to protect Tony. It's like, "No, we're not doing that."

But for Tony to sit there for a second and think, *Wait a second, I should do this* – there's been so many examples of that in the time I've been with him. It's been incredible.

Grant: After, to see the way that Coach Bennett and the rest of the staff handled that game was so amazing to me. People ask about one of my favorite memories at UVA – that's honestly one of them. Just looking back at the whole journey... the two years, that's a crazy comeback story, but it doesn't happen if we don't lose to UMBC.

The way Coach Bennett and the staff taught us how to deal with adversity and how to use it in the right way... we could've just let that get to our heads and folded. I mean, who knows what could've happened after that. It was an unprecedented moment.

But just to see the way that they handled that and how they turned it into something positive: Coach always told us, "If you learn to use it right" – talking about adversity – "it will buy you a ticket to a place you couldn't have gone any other way."

It was so true, just looking back at the full two years and our experience.

The only #16 to ever beat a #1, and we're the #1? I remember growing up always wanting the #16 to beat the #1, but I didn't want it to happen in this way.

Ben Buell: When we lost to UMBC, [Coach Bennett] said something to the effect of, "If we never make it to a Final Four, if we never win a National Championship, I'll be okay with it."

That really spoke to me because I consider myself somebody who's ambitious and has these big goals. I've always kind of been thinking about what's next and how I can get there.

Sometimes, in a way, that's not healthy. It's tunnel vision – you're not sitting there and smelling the roses. For somebody who's as competitive and ambitious as he is to recognize that right after what's the low point of somebody's career – it's really telling. That always stuck with me.

Devon: Yeah. I mean, you look at [the UMBC loss] as, *What lesson is God teaching me here in this moment?*

I know how to deal with things quicker than others – I feel like that way – and for me, it was about turning the next page because now, it was me focusing on a pro career.

It was like, *How can I deal with this not as fast as possible, but in a quicker manner,* and then worrying about, *Now, I have to prepare to become a pro [and] try to put myself in the best position to get drafted,* whatever the case may be.

And that's what I felt like God was saying: "Alright, well, I've stopped this now for you, but I'm giving you another chance to reboot and push forward. Now, here you go. You lose this. What's the lesson in this?"

And then you grow from it.

Johnny Carpenter: Devon and Isaiah – typically, they have the seniors do [the postgame press conference]. [Coach Bennett] was like, "I'm protecting you two in this."

Then he took Kyle and Ty, and before they went out for the interview, he was like, "I'm picking you two because I know you can handle this, and you guys are going to lead us through this. I am here for you; I'm here with you. If there's anything you don't want to answer, I'll answer it for you. I don't know why this happened, I don't know what's going to happen, but I know it starts right now, and with you guys, we can do this."

It's empowering, forward thinking.

Ty Jerome: Sitting on that podium was the start of the offseason. It felt like you were like below rock bottom. I remember sitting there with Kyle, and it felt like if the world ended.

Basketball is your passion. We were just running a high, lost to UMBC, and you're just at the complete bottom. You're realizing you're nowhere near where you want to be, everyone's laughing at you, you're being called a joke, you can't do anything about it for a-whole-nother year, you gotta watch March Madness – all these things.

Everything's just playing in your mind; the game is replaying in your mind. At one point, I couldn't even hear people's questions – my mind was just racing, racing, racing.

Sitting on that podium was crazy, but I'm so happy I got that experience – painful gift. Coach Bennett decided to take me and

Kyle with him on that podium – that's gotta be one of the best things that happened for us. We couldn't hide. It was: *This happened. You gotta embrace it.*

Another one of his messages was, "When you get back to campus, don't put your hoodie on and duck. Stand tall, walk around, and know you'll bounce back from it."

Stuff like that, his lessons were beyond basketball – life lessons.

London Perrantes: Obviously, that Tournament loss was not ideal. Not having De'Andre – I knew [it] was going to be a big factor. Think about losing your best player, and then you're going into the #1 vs. #16 matchup. You already have so much pressure on you in general, and then you lose one of your best players. It's tough.

I mean, it happened. It was all the part of the story, though – the storybook ending of coming back the next year and winning that Championship.

Grant: [The team] got back, and you still gotta go to class – it was the last thing we wanted to do, but we can't not go to class. The NCAA requires you to take two weeks off from basketball, and then you can start practice again.

So, two weeks later, we're starting practice, and the NCAA Tournament is still going on – that feeling of, *We're practicing when we feel like we should still be playing games. Our next season has started, and the current season still has not ended.*

I mean, I think that helped a lot, too, just because that feeling was terrible. You finish practice, and there are games on the TV still, but you don't feel like watching them.

That just added to the motivation.

We went to class, we'd go home, play Fortnite, [and] we watched all the Marvel movies. We'd just try to find something to fill the time and kind of take a break.

We didn't want to overthink it. We wanted to use it in the right way. At the same time, we each had to take our own time to come to grips with the situation and, in a way, grieve the loss.

That's the only way you get over it and use it to your advantage: to go to the next thing. You kind of have to accept it, learn from it, and keep going.

That was really interesting: the past three years were all super unique in their own way. And that's something I'm really grateful for.

Will: After UMBC, when we got back to JPJ, Ty was the last player in the locker room. I didn't realize he was still in there.

I was in the practice gym, and I was just staring at the court. I thought I was going to be emotional – going into my fourth year – whenever the season was over. I had no expectations for rising to a #1 overall seed and then even less expectations for being the first #1 seed to lose.

There's no time for emotions about it – it was just stunning. I was sort of sitting [and] reflecting. It was a more emotional time.

Once we finally got back from the trip the next day, Ty came out and was just going to get some shots up.

I was like, "Is it alright if I rebound for you? Look, I know this is over, but still, if you ever need me, I'm still going to be here."

One thing that was cool: there's a little natural sunlight, but the lights were off – something about shooting in the dark that I just like. It makes the rebounding a little trickier – I'll be honest. But yeah, there's no obligations [for me to be there or rebound].

The long-dreaded conversation that I had seen happen three years before me is: Ronnie thanks the senior managers. There's still going to be a relationship, but [the senior managers are] released of all their obligations.

For me, I was having an internal sort of struggle, [in terms of] taking this as a career option. It was like calming to me and reaffirming that I need to stay in this game. Every time I'd rebound for a guy, I knew that it was to help Virginia, but I also knew it was to help the individual.

That was the first time I ever rebounded for somebody, and there's zero benefit for me almost, and I really like that. It was definitely a very powerful way to end my managerial and collegiate career.

Ty: I think that speaks to a few things. One is the type of people we have our program: for Will to still be in the gym when he has no more obligations to the program – and he's in a jam, thinking about probably everything that UVA meant to him – and for him to say, "You know what? I got you. I'm gonna come rebound for you," and he doesn't have to.

I took time off after that, but the way I wanted to start my offseason, and the mindset I had to have going into that offseason – I felt that day, I needed to be in the gym.

As soon as we got back, it was just: *set the tone for the whole offseason*. I mean, it wasn't like I didn't take time off – I had to heal my body – but I felt that day, I just had to do something to help me clear my mind a little bit.

I remember it like it was yesterday: I was just retaking some of the shots I missed in the UMBC game, and I just kept replaying the misses and kept replaying the game in my head the whole time. Times like that are super painful times, and that's what makes the end that much more worth it.

I think the harder you work, the more confident you get [and] the more excited you get for games. But I've been both places, especially when I was younger or coming off injury. Now, my rookie year in the NBA, you feel like, *Oh, shit. I'm not as prepared as I should be.*

It's a different mindset going into the game: *Okay, I've outworked everybody.*

I think that's the best way to deal with pain because the pain comes and goes. Pain's gonna leave. But the harder you work, the next time you're able to step back on that court, you'll feel so much more confident.

Will: Yeah, he went on a tear. I got to be around for the early parts. I actually didn't leave Charlottesville until about the time when I was getting ready to go out to Vegas to give that a quick test of the water [in basketball careers] before I started my CapTech job.

Coach always talks about urgency when you play. That's always been there, but there's definitely a heightened intensity, and Ty's a very alpha male, vocal leader, very intense. Devon and Isaiah were also leaders, so [2018-2019] was the first season where [Ty] was the unquestioned leader.

Guys follow his step, and Kyle or De'Andre are right there with him, but [they have] different styles of leadership. Ty is the guy they follow into battle.

It gives me chills just talking about it.

Will Gent

articulated by:
Will Gent

Will Gent: The basketball world is really crazy. For me, I always knew that I loved [basketball] and had a passion for it, but it wasn't until I realized that there were other people like me that wanted to pursue this as a career that I really realized it was a viable option.

I had a lot of conversations with my parents and some mentors going through school and didn't really think about it too, *too* much until my last year, but there were a lot of external pressures to do the safe thing.

I was fortunate enough to get a good degree from the Engineering School, so I had some options to get your standard nine-to-five job. I don't want to say I caved to the pressure, but just from my parents helping to put me through school, I wanted to get the best job I could and make sure I could continue to give it back.

At first, I was trying to convince [my parents] that this could be a viable field. They wouldn't say it directly, but they would imply, "We're not sure it's the best idea."

When they saw the way it ended, [how] distraught I was – that career was just suddenly taken away from me [after UMBC]. I accepted the offer from CapTech in October [and] didn't start 'til like July, but it was around January where I really knew that I was really going to miss this basketball component in my life.

Actually, to clarify: going into CapTech, I knew I wanted to leave, but I wanted to honor the commitment. I mean, it was a big leap in my life. I was going to leave Virginia for the first time, probably, and start this crazy lifestyle.

It was me saying, "I'm not so sure," and my parents said, "No, this is what you love."

I got connected with the right people and got lucky – and it helps when Tony and Malcolm make a call, too – and I got hooked up here in Indiana.

It's incredible. The one knock of being a manager [at UVA] is you're still a student first, I would say. I don't think my life has ever felt as wholly more fulfilling [working in the NBA]. This is the first time in my life I'm really pouring everything into my passion.

I don't think anything will ever compare to the experience I had at Virginia as a student manager. I mean, that is, for me, what's going to start it all, and hopefully, my ultimate goal is to be a head coach at the NBA level. For me, that's sort of the rock and foundation.

Half of that, I would say, is Coach Bennett, and his Pillars, and what he did, and half of that was just the humbling experience of being a manager. I mean, I'll wake up before 7:00 a.m., walk a block to the office now at 7:00 a.m., then won't leave the gym 'til 11:00 p.m.

We have an open door policy [at Virginia], and I didn't really utilize it as much as I [could have]. I think I'm closer with Ronnie now than I was even as a manager. We always had a good relationship, but I lean on him now.

When you see the light at the end of the tunnel, you're talking to Ronnie [saying], "Hey, this is what I'm thinking," and mostly, the question is, "Can you help me here?"

Very consistently, Ronnie's perspective was, "We owe you for your service to the program."

I always felt awkward and embarrassed about that: "No, you guys are doing more for me than you know."

So, it worked out – they're willing to help, and I'm willing to help. Ronnie's sort of the communication line between us and Coach Bennett. We would see Coach all the time in the office, and we'd have conversations, and it wasn't uncommon at all.

Through that, especially in my fourth year, Coach got to know what my aspirations were, and he obviously really knows now. I got a chance to see him briefly at the [NBA] All-Star Break when I was stopping in and saying hi to Ronnie – he poked in his head and checked in.

If there's one thing I just would really want to get across: Coach Bennett – as authentic and genuine as they come.

I want to say this, coming from where we were, [the] bottom of the totem pole: you hear a lot of nice things about celebrities, and a lot of it is just publicity, but Coach Bennett is as humble and authentic as they come. I'd stand up for that guy any day – not that he would need that.

My friends make fun of me. My family makes fun of me. They know I'll do anything for that man. So, yeah. To me, he's the gold standard.

Summer 2018

articulated by:
Ty Jerome
Jack Salt
Isaiah Wilkins

Ty Jerome: I don't think there was much enjoying life going on, but I'd somehow get to class and go back to my room or Kyle's little apartment, where we'd all sit together sometimes, but we were struggling. We were all really struggling. It's embarrassing! It's really embarrassing.

Not to mention, you can't play anymore. It's super embarrassing, and you're walking around, and after a while, it starts stinging less and less. You have to realize what's important, and you have to realize what matters, but for those first four days, the first week – especially because you can't work out; no outlet – you're walking around, people are looking at you – it's bad. It's bad!

But, like Coach Bennett said, "You can't hang your head. You gotta just embrace it and know you'll bounce back from it."

Basically, our message was, "These are the same people that are going to love us next year, so, who cares?" And that's exactly what happened.

Another big piece that I'm not mentioning is how mad I was when I would hear shit like, "Coach Bennett's system can't work in March." That shit made me so mad.

I'm not a big guy who's paying attention to the media, but I remember I was sitting in a doctor's office after we lost to UMBC. I had to get an MRI on my toe because I was thinking about having surgery on my big toe (I played the whole season with turf toe and all that).

I'm sitting there in the office, and I'm reading this article that this guy wrote. It's like, "Virginia is the biggest joke of all time," or some shit like that. I was sitting there just reading it: the system doesn't work, we don't have good players, we have maybe one NBA player in De'Andre Hunter, and that's it.

Stuff like that – you're reading it, and it has to fuel you. You can not pay attention to it, but you can't sit there, read it, be a competitor, and that not fuel you.

Fast forward a year later, and we win a National Championship. I was on the podium the day after we beat Auburn. At the Final Four – I guess it was like five of us – you get your own room, and reporters kind of fill in, fill in, fill in.

It was probably about twenty-five-to-thirty reporters sitting in my room at the time, and someone asked me a question, "What do you say to the people that said Virginia's system can't work in March?"

I said, "You know, actually that guy over there wrote a whole article last year that I remember reading," and I went into it like that. He walked out of the room.

Then he found me after the National Championship and was like, "I'm so sorry."

I was like, "Just write a new article."

At that point, once we won, I couldn't care less about that dude. I didn't go looking for him or anything. When you win, there's so many more things you're thinking about than that article that happened last year, but when you lose and you're reading it, you feel it.

Jack Salt: I mean, you've got failure after failure, losing big games – that's how you become successful. You fail with a group, and you are humble enough to accept you failed and learn how you can move forward.

Obviously, you've got a lot of failures in the past, but if you look at the UMBC failure, that was a huge failure. The fact that this team bounced back and was able to be humble enough to accept: *We weren't good enough; how do we improve?*

The work ethic that was put in by everyone over that

postseason [and] that pre-season, that was just amazing. I was very thankful to be a part of that group, to experience it, and just help any way I could. It was an experience for me that I will never forget.

[Those] two weeks after [UMBC], it's a really weird thing that we don't have any basketball – we just go to class. We're regular students. You know, it was weird because it was really tough, but at the end of the day, it was a basketball game.

Coach drilled this in, and I feel like my values were pretty similar on it: "We lost a basketball game." It was bad, it was shit, unfortunate, but we have another opportunity next year.

A lot of the guys were coming back. Unfortunately, we lost two amazing leaders in Devon and Isaiah, but we had another opportunity, so it wasn't like it was over for us.

I sulked for a little while. I had my time when I was like, *Fuck. This is terrible,* but we could get back to work after the two weeks since losing, so I was like, *It's not the end of the world; we get another shot*. The mentality that was in myself and a lot of the other guys was just to work very hard, and a lot of guys did that.

The level of skill in the players on that team was phenomenal, and then Kihei coming in – I think just a combination of everything just made a beautiful run. Like I said, I'm very thankful to be a part of that team. Even though I didn't have a huge role on the team in terms of on-the-floor production, I was very happy to be a part of that group.

Isaiah Wilkins: In this past year, we lose #1/#16; the guys are extra motivated. Everybody's in the gym working. I didn't hear any nonsense or anything like that.

It makes the goal that much more clear. You don't have to do anything heroic. Some guys do, but if you win a couple of Championships, your talent obviously gets better and better every year. [Coach Bennett] cracked the code, and now it becomes a little bit more natural, which is pretty exciting for them.

Ty: Once we lost to UMBC, I sat down with Johnny and Damin Altizer – basically, he's like my skills trainer who works with a lot of guys on the UVA team now. When I first got there, we started working together. I still work with him now, and he's based out of Charlottesville.

So, I sat down with him and Johnny after we lost to UMBC, and [we] talked about what I needed to improve on, my goals for the offseason, and my goals for next season. I'm sitting there, we're talking, we're talking, and I'm just like, *You know what? This is bigger than trying to be ACC Player of the Year. This is bigger than trying to be an All-American.*

There are so many good players: start with Mike Scott, go to Joe Harris, go to Malcolm Brogdon. A million good players that have come in here and nobody has won a National Championship, and to be the first to do that would just mean... forget yourself, you're building off of an already-huge legacy.

Mindful

articulated by:
Alex Peavey

Alex Peavey: The consistency of approach is absolutely rooted in the Five Pillars and the fact that they truly measure themselves by those Pillars. There's obviously going be quantifiable goals that they set: there's certain things they want to do from the three-point line, and there's certain things they want to do defensively [or for] field goal percentage.

There's always analytics that are so huge in all of sports now, and as the analytic trend continues, to me, the lubricant of it all, the fuel, the oil in the system, is the values – and if you take that out, the engine shuts down.

It's where, I believe, when you come to a fork in the road, and you're trying to decide, *Do I do this or do I do that?* some people would say, *I'll make a decision based on what the outcome will be. Do I do this based upon the outcome, or do I do that because that will be the outcome?*

We don't know what the outcomes will ever be, but what we do know is intentions. If I hit a fork in the road, the decision I need to make as to which way to go comes from what aligns with my values now.

It was certainly there during Coach [Terry] Holland's years [as Virginia's head coach]. Values really mattered [to] that program – it was a feel-good program. It was people you wanted to pull for, and it's because their values aligned with the University's and with your own. There is diversity of people but singular focus in that set of values.

There's a comfort level in a highly competitive, chaotic world, where you know if you fall, you're gonna fall on the set of values, and the values lift you back up – it allows you to take risks, and push, and have a growth mindset.

Then maybe when you're down to Gardner-Webb [in 2019], you're like, *Here we go again,* but this is where faith in the value system allows discomfort to turn into confidence and not arrogance. That's where teams without values rely on arrogance, and then they collapse because when you get down 19 and you're arrogant: all of a sudden, you get a cramp; all of a sudden, stuff starts hurting, and your best player goes down for a phantom injury that no one else in the building sees. Not Virginia.

The value system is what makes a guy look at a score down 14 after experiencing this the year before and say, *I got faith this is the right thing to do, and I have faith that if it isn't, I'm gonna fall on a really strong foundation of values that I will have no regret living by.*

Every team wears the "Family" shirt at the Tournament, and I love it, but I also don't because not every team functions that way. It's like, "No, no, no. You can't put that on unless you are." And Virginia is.

From a mindfulness perspective, it's all about turning toward the discomfort. Like when I'm dealing with [cancer] pain on a daily basis, the way I relieve the pain is to focus on it without causing it to be worse. I turn toward the pain to then alleviate the pain. It's when we turn away from the pain that the pain gets worse.

It's the idea of, "What we resist persists." If they resisted that [UMBC] game, it would haunt them forever; instead, it fueled them. They connected two seasons, and no team has ever done that before. Every team wants to make it clear that seasons are different, and that's what I really heard different from this team.

Obviously, a lot of guys came back, but some really good players were not back. That UMBC game was as much a part of this [2019] season as the National Championship was. It's amazing stuff, but only values allow that to happen.

One of my favorite verses is Matthew 23:12: "He who humbles himself will be exalted, and he who exalts himself will be humbled." Essentially, they humbled themselves and were exalted in turn.

Or – my favorite line of the [2019] Tournament – Kyle Guy's, "I was terrified," free throws: to have humble faith is greater than the terror. To me – and I don't know what he was thinking beyond that – that's the exact right approach.

You succeed through the acknowledgment of, *This is terrifying, but I'm here for a reason. This is terrifying, but I know I can make these shots. This is terrifying, but this is what I prepared for. This is terrifying; I'm not resisting the fact that terror is present, so by not resisting it, it doesn't persist. I've checked and acknowledged that I'm terrified, and now I play basketball.*

And that goes back to that press conference [after UMBC]: the ability to turn towards the discomfort allows you to then step back into the fray because you're just acknowledging what is, whether it's fucking cancer or a free throw late in a game.

I think there's so much machismo in sports. We get so bullheaded and tough-guyed about stuff that we deny reality, and then we don't function in the context of reality. So, if Kyle Guy was trying to act like he wasn't terrified, he would've caused more internal physiological distress, which ultimately causes us to miss shots.

So, [it's] the ability to get up there and say, *Yup, this is scary, and yup, I'm gonna make these shots.* It's not about not having confidence; it's about being a realist. And they dealt with reality from the beginning all the way through.

And so, the Tony Bennett idea of [having Ty and Kyle on the podium for the UMBC postgame] press conference showed up with [Kyle's] acknowledgment of discomfort on the free-throw line [against Auburn in the 2019 Final Four] – if you put those two things together.

You tip the scale 51/49 [of "trembling courage over measured cowardice"], and then sometimes Virginia wins 51-49. The stronger-minded teams are going to hang with you, and it's gonna be 51-49; the weaker-minded teams are the ones who, with 14 minutes to go in the second half, the 1-point game with Virginia becomes a 20-point game.

It's not low-balling; it's reality. The meatheaded approach

disregards reality to a point that it undermines the ability to perform in a context of reality, and then you're not functioning in a way that maximizes the capabilities of everyone on the floor because you're acting like something's not happening when it is.

We're terrified, or, *We're getting beat, but we don't have to lose our shit about it. We can just be it and then transition back.*

The Golden State Warriors do the same thing: they have their value system that was established by Steve Kerr through the Bulls and the Phil Jackson stuff. It's non-quantifiable, and anytime they deviate in success, they tend to deviate from their values.

Year 10

(2018-2019)

articulated by:
Grant Kersey
Johnny Carpenter
Ben Buell
Devon Hall
Thomas Rogers
Rob Vozenilek
Will Sherrill
Ronnie Wideman
Barry Parkhill
Isaiah Wilkins
Ty Jerome
Jack Salt
Evan Nolte
Kevin Oberlies
Jason Williford
Joe Harris
Ritchie McKay

Grant Kersey: I tried out my second year – didn't make it. Halfway through the year, I got moved to be a practice player and a manager, then [my] third year, I try out again, [and] still didn't make it.

Coach Bennett pulls me aside after practice the night before the first game, so it's like 6:00-6:30 p.m. I was rebounding for De'Andre – he was just shooting after practice.

Coach is like, "Can I talk to you?"

In my head, I'm thinking, *Yeah, sure, but we got our season opener tomorrow, like we can talk in two days when it's an off day. We need to watch film, we need to rebound... but yeah, for sure.*

I didn't know what was going on. I had no idea.

That's when he told me that he wanted to reward my hard work and dress me for the home games, and then that progressed into away games as well. So, I was able to travel, too.

I think it was the start of the year during the National Championship season. He got a sheet of paper, and he listed the Five Pillars, and then in the background, he put everybody's name who has been involved in the program during his time here.

He rolled it up, and he got the maintenance people at JPJ to drill a hole dead center court in the cement, and he put the paper in the court, then he covered it up in cement.

It's literally directly under us, tip ball, middle of the court, every game. He did that to serve as a reminder to us of what the program is built on, and what we always fall back on, and what the team is built on.

I remember everybody came in the huddle, and he was like, "This is what I have, this is what we're doing, and this is what it stands for."

Every name: players, coaches, trainers, managers, anyone involved in the program, he had their name on a sheet of paper behind the Five Pillars – so sweet.

I mean, it's the little things like that that make it so special. That seems like a little thing, but that's huge – that's our program on a sheet of paper.

That is our program: the Pillars and the names.

Johnny Carpenter: As a program, we really wanted to foster more than just basketball. We were trying to pour into the guys individually and for their future – just connecting with the guys more. So, we did this Chair Exercise. We started in the '17-18 season, and the past two years have been the two best years we've had.

It creates an atmosphere of authentic vulnerability with guys, which isn't something men are comfortable doing because of social norms and that kind of thing. It's more off-the-court, comradery interactions that we want to build into the guys, and we want to make it less about basketball and more about getting to know you.

So, that exercise is one player [and] one staff member at a time. We maybe do it a couple times a month, or once one month and three times over the course of the next month – there wasn't really rhyme or reason to it.

A staff member and a player would go sit in this chair – it's actually Dick Bennett's Final Four chair – and Coach wants them to go as deep as they want or as shallow as they want. There is no pressure at all – you can literally say nothing if you wanted or just nod your head if you want to.

You go through your hero or heroes, a hardship, and a highlight of your life, [and] then it's open questions. The connection off the court: it's hard to describe, but you just see it. We pour into their emotional side, and the staff did a better job of showing the guys that we're not just robots – we actually care about them and not just their college careers or pro careers. We're in it with them.

That's something that really helped us push through the '17-18, '18-19 seasons: showing the guys we care. We did a ton of team-building exercises, this season in particular. We lost to Duke – shout-out to the ACC for a Saturday/Monday turnaround with home against Duke [on Saturday]; away at UNC [on Monday]. We lose at Duke, and Duke's ranked 309th in three-point shooting, and they score 12/15 threes.

Before I forget, what kind of coach has the insight to look at the schedule that far ahead of time and say, "This is the NCAA Tournament: quick turnarounds – it's about responding"?

So, we practice, go through the Duke game, watch UNC film, [and] a little bit of up and down, but we had to rest our guys. So, we bus down to North Carolina on Monday, and we're at the hotel, and we're like, "Do we have a Monday practice?"

How many teams would've probably said, "Yes"? Most of them.

We're thinking, "Should we structure our shootaround differently?" Instead of going all the way to the more basketball-end, we went the opposite: no shootaround; no nothing – ballroom walk-through. [We] walk through UNC's actions, then we're gonna play a team-building exercise, and there's a fun component of it: Name that Tune.

Frankie Badocchi is awesome on the piano, and we divide up the teams: young players, old players, and staff. The losing team, which ended up being the staff, had to serve dinner to the guys, [and] the second-place team had to serve drinks to the winners, so that was a fun thing before the team meal. Our coaches are dressed up in aprons and stuff, serving dinners and keeping it light, and we end up beating UNC.

This year, on the road, we started doing those more fun team-building exercises, and Coach would also give a really deep talk, too. He talked to them about life, beyond-basketball stuff, and I think that was something that honestly freed our guys up.

Ben Buell: At Carolina – this is maybe the first or second time we'd done this – [Coach Bennett] stopped and got everybody in a circle. He's like the most competitive person I've ever met – don't get me wrong – but he said (and I'm paraphrasing), "I'm so competitive that sometimes I get caught up in the season, and it's to the detriment of figuring out how everybody's doing."

He spent like twenty minutes just talking about life. Here we were about to play this huge game. We played Duke on Saturday, and then we were playing Carolina on a Monday. It's a massive game for the ACC Regular Season.

He was not really talking about the game at all, and we didn't even really do that much film. I was like, *Shouldn't we talk about, you know, the scouting report?*

It's just another one of these examples of him caring so much about developing people and building relationships with players and other people that will last far longer than this kind of euphoria these last couple of years.

Johnny: Our guys are so compliant because of the kind of guys we bring in, and they're so driven to be good, [and] we may have been – I don't want to say focusing too much on basketball; we were caring about them – but we really pushed to improve in the off-the-court area to take it to another level. When it's all said and done, we didn't ever want a kid to think it was all about basketball. Not to say that a kid ever thought that, but we wanted to make sure they know it's about more than just basketball.

The comradery, over time, between players, managers, [and] staff, it becomes this huge, huge family, and that was something you could see, over time, occur.

After UMBC, Coach Bennett mentioned Ty Jerome texted him saying, "I know you're always asking us, 'How're we doing?' But how're *you* doing?"

How many players think like that? And it shows, over time, it became more of a two-way street.

Ben: Our success in the last – what do we want to call it – two-to-four years is really built on this foundation of everybody who came before. The National Championship was just as much London's, Devon's, Isaiah's, Malcolm's, Anthony Gill's, all these people's, as it is Dre's, Kyle's, and Ty's. It's such this progression.

Devon Hall: It actually is a culture – a culture that's been handed down every single year. And people climb with it. It's going to be a little bit different in terms of the people you have, but Coach Bennett has established that culture. And you've got guys that come in that know it, and they try to abide by it as much as they can.

And you see what happened before you; now, it's time to try to replicate that at the highest level. And if you've got Coach Bennett there, he's going to demand the best out of you. I mean, really, it's going to be hard not to be successful at the school.

Thomas Rogers: That build-up is so real, and I hope – and I think they do – I just hope the team now realizes how special what they've done is for the program and for all of us who went through all that hurt.

The year after I left was when they were #1b to Kentucky's #1a all year, then Justin got hurt. We lost like two games in the regular season, and then we lost to Michigan State in the Second Round after we lost to them the year before, my senior year.

And then the following year, Michigan State lost to Middle Tennessee State in the First Round when they were the #2 in our Region, and we were celebrating. Then we play a Syracuse team that we'd never lost to since they joined the ACC, are up 15 with 5 minutes left, [and throw it away]. So, all that pain, it hurts.

So, my senior year, in the Sweet Sixteen, we're playing Michigan State, who was better than a #4 seed. Look at who the guys played this year [2019] in the Sweet Sixteen: Oregon, a #12 seed. I was like, *Man! If we'd had a #12 seed, we would've worked them.*

It's so circumstantial, you have to get lucky, but you have to be in a position where you *can* get lucky. Yeah, so, I hope those guys realize how special it is for everyone.

In a way, it was like, we always thought we could do it, and then they did it, and we were like, *Yeah, I knew we could do it.*

Rob Vozenilek: Every sportswriter out there can hammer the twelve months from UMBC to Minneapolis, but through no fault of their own, no one outside of the NBA cares about the previous eight years.

Will Sherrill: All the pieces that people talk about in terms of getting to the National Championship – winning and coming back from that big defeat – all those pieces were put in place over a long period of time.

So, it's great to see those guys having success because they've certainly put in the work for that coaching staff to have that success. They had that vision, and they stuck to it and had the persistence to stick to it. So, it was great to see that get rewarded.

Ronnie Wideman: Jeff White did a little article, like an alumni spotlight, about Joe Harris. Joe alludes to how people in the NBA are now recognizing that the things that Coach Bennett and this staff are teaching and emphasizing in our program translate to the NBA.

They know that what is being taught here at Virginia can and does translate to the next level. It takes time to build a program. And it's really hard.

It's really hard to build a program. It takes time, effort, consistency, discipline – all those things. Once you feel you've "built a program," to then sustain the success... I don't know if it's harder, as hard... I don't know... but it's hard.

Especially as competitors, as you build it, you can continue to hope. You know where you're trying to get to, have that focus of big picture stuff, and try to keep things in perspective.

Then, when you kind of "get there" (again, it's a relative term), to sustain that level of success with expectation? Man, that's hard – expectation can do a lot to somebody.

Tony does such a tremendous job of channeling the pressure of expectation – because that's pressure. I mean, the #1/#16 game? That's pressure. The expectation is for you to easily win the game and move on.

There's pressure. I mean, I can't explain it – literally can't find words for the tense pressure in moments leading up to the Gardner-Webb game. And then, at halftime, you just simply can't describe it. But there's pressure there.

Barry Parkhill: That is the only game I didn't go to because I just was very confident we'd move on. And I get really, really wound up when I watch our guys on TV. I feel like I'm rooting for my own family. And I'm a little bit superstitious, but that game – I never had any doubt at halftime. And we sort of crept back in at the end of the first half – never had any doubt.

Isaiah Wilkins: It's actually super stressful watching [us now]. I understand why people were stressed watching us, but I cut the games off sometimes. I'm like, *I'm bad luck. I'm bad luck, and I'm ruining the game.*

When they were playing Gardner-Webb, and they were down at halftime, I cut the game off. I was in Greensboro, and I'm like, *I won't watch it. I'm bad luck.* Then they won.

Thomas: I was in the office that day. It was like a Thursday at noon or something. I was so nervous. Obviously, the guys were, too. I was like sweating. I felt like I was gonna be sick again.

UMBC was more like, "What the fuck is happening?" whereas Syracuse [two years] before was more painful because we thought we had it, and we lost it. UMBC was like: we never had it. It wasn't a sadness; it was a shock.

So, this year, I was like, *Please don't let it happen to these guys again. That would destroy someone.* I'd be curious to know what Tony said to them at halftime.

Barry: I'm sure they looked back on their experience the year before and [said], "This is not going to happen again. You guys got to just go out and take care of business." And they did.

Ty Jerome: The biggest thing was we'd been there. Having UMBC, we knew we couldn't panic – that was the biggest thing. We panicked at UMBC, and we were like, "Relax. We've been down before this year against better opponents. We're fine."

Basically, I said, *If we're losing again, I'm going down aggressive as hell.*

So, [we] came out of a timeout, I think I came off a screen, hit a little step back, threw it to Kyle, [and] Kyle hit a three. We started getting stops. Kihei hit a three, and when we cut [the lead] to 6 at halftime, it was like, *Alright, we're going to win this game by 20.*

How calm we were in the locker room at halftime was crazy compared to UMBC. We were tied against UMBC at halftime: coaches came in screaming, we're looking at each other, nobody looks confident – it was bad.

And Gardner-Webb, we're down 6, and we're just like making jokes, like, "Yo, we're about to win this game by 30," and they scored [20] points in the second half. We just knew it.

They were actually a solid team, [but] we just knew it. We weren't going to lose that game. And [the] same went for Oklahoma: we just knew we weren't going to lose. If Carson Edwards doesn't go for that crazy-ass performance, I don't think anyone would've come close to beating us. People remember the ends of those games, but I think everyone forgets the big-ass leads we had with like 4-5 minutes left.

Carson has to go crazy for them to come back – that happens once in a lifetime. He's a special player – don't get me wrong – but you don't have those performances often.

So, for us to respond and win that game, it's special. For Kihei to make that pass and Mamadi to hit that shot is crazy. I remember thinking, *He's hitting those big ass shots,* and the players we had were just like, *Let's respond.*

Jack Salt: Actually, that was the one game of the Tournament that I played a lot. I was in the game at that point – that was amazing. I was so happy. The joy... I can honestly say I have so much joy when anyone I'm close to does well.

For me, seeing Mamadi hit that shot, I was happy. And then I was also happy when Kyle hit those free throws and also happy at Braxton's block and Dre's three. I mean, there's so many moments with guys' individual, huge, clutch plays, and to have all those three games back-to-back-to-back was insane.

Ty: Funny story – it's on topic, but it's out of rhythm. Dre and I would sit there after we lost to UMBC, and finally, like four-to-five days later, we watched the UMBC highlights.

Then we went back, and we watched the Elite Eight game when Virginia blew that lead to Syracuse and Malachi Richardson was going crazy. When he's going crazy, similar to what Carson Edwards did in the second half, they flashed to Coach Bennett, and they look at his face, and they flash to Coach Bennett's dad in the stands, and they showed his face.

When you go back and watch the Purdue highlights when

Carson Edwards is hitting those threes, they flash to Coach Bennett's dad, and he has the exact same face. It is the exact same face when Malachi Richardson was going crazy. He's just like, *Oh my goodness. No way.*

You could take a picture of both, and it'll be the same face.

So, in the moment [against Purdue], it's like, *We're meant to lose now,* and then to come back, and for it to go our way. You need a little bit of luck to win a Championship – for the ball to bounce our way – and you gotta make big plays, and Kihei and Mamadi made a huge play. So, that was pretty cool.

Johnny: Ten years to the date [Coach Bennett] got hired at Virginia, we go to the Final Four. To go to the Final Four, we had to beat Purdue – his dad had to beat Purdue to go to the Final Four. We had three Saturday/Monday turnarounds, and from the very start, Coach said, "This is the NCAA Tournament, this is the NCAA Tournament, this is the NCAA Tournament."

Before the Florida State game, he said, "This is our chance at a title fight," then he comes back and was like, "No, that was a conflicting message – it's not about that."

After that game, we all said, "Coach, we're gonna get our title fight. It's just not this fight. It's not the ACC Championship Game."

And then the Final Four comes, and inside the arena, instead of walking onto the court, you have to walk up the stairs – like walking into a boxing ring. So, Coach was like, "This is our title fight. Right here."

Ty: Auburn, I think we're up 10 or 12, and I picked up my fourth foul – like an idiot. I had to sit, and I'm sitting on the bench, and they just come back, come back, come back.

I go back in the game, [and] I think we're tied up or down 2. Everyone kept their composure. The side out-of-bounds play: we run that play every day in practice [and] go over that play every day in practice. Kyle got fouled, and he made three big free throws.

People forget. They talk about, "Oh, the luck, the luck," but the play I picked up my fourth foul, before I fouled him, I'm in the post, and I'm getting fouled, and if the ref gives us that foul call, I'm still in the game, I knock down two free throws, we're up 12, and we probably win by 15.

That's the thing about going on a Championship run: you need a little bit of luck. One whistle could change the game. We didn't get the whistle that play, but then we end up getting the whistle on the missed double-dribble call, whatever you want to call it. We got the whistle down the stretch. I was [fouled], but nobody realized that first whistle that we don't get.

My third foul was a questionable call, too. So, those two whistles we don't get, which lets them come back, and then we get the next one. Like I said, it speaks to the composure we had. Kyle making those three free throws is crazy.

Once he hit the first one, I knew – because there's no way he's missing two in a row, so worst case: we go to overtime. He's one of the best shooters – if not the best – that I've ever been around. Not many guys shoot it like him, even at the NBA level.

Evan Nolte: I went to the Final Four game the other week [in 2019], and there were like seventy-year-olds crying after we won the Championship. It was the coolest thing ever. I could definitely notice a difference in the support in general. Some of those games in JPJ, I mean, people were so loud when we get on the defensive end and the shot clock is going down.

You could tell people really embraced and understood the style of play that Coach Bennett brought, and after a little bit of success, I felt like people were fully bought in, and every time they could not wait until we had another team under 10 seconds on the shot clock so they could all stand up. That was definitely really cool.

Kevin Oberlies: I flew out to that Championship Game from San Diego. I was not going to miss it. We watched the Auburn game out here, and then I booked a flight the next day. You know, one of those like twenty-hour trips.

Barry: At the Championship Game – I think this says a lot – there were a lot of former players there. Not just guys who played for Tony. And there was a reception at a local restaurant before the Auburn game, and there are a boatload of former players from a lot of different eras. There was also a lot of Tony's guys here. And I think that says a lot right there: whether it's guys who played for Tony or former players, he's just created a welcome environment.

Thomas: We obviously went to Minneapolis, which was awesome. [We] wouldn't have gone to a game before then because after the Syracuse game a couple years ago and UMBC – it's just a high risk and medium reward. Outside of the National Championship Game, I'm always level-headed going into the game, but afterwards, I'm just… crazy.

Ty: Fast forward to Texas Tech, and same thing: we're up 10 with 5 minutes left, Dre gets the and-1 around the 5-minute mark. We're going crazy, and all of a sudden, they start coming back.

Basketball is a game of runs, so it's going to happen. But Texas Tech was – I think – the least dramatic of it all because they helped when I drove, and that was just a stupid play of them, and Dre makes a big shot. No referee involved – that's just them making a bad play; us making a good play.

[I] missed the floater down 1, [and] Coach Bennett was like, "Same play." That just speaks to the confidence he had in all of us – not just me. [We] ran the same play again – I think we ran it for the next five plays in overtime.

Jason Williford: When we won it all, ultimately, we're on that stage, and I'm at the back of the podium. In fact, I don't think I'm in any of the pictures that they took with the team. Like, I must have been off goin' *nuts*. But I'm on the back of the podium, and they give me the Championship trophy.

Somehow, I get the trophy, and I just turn around, and there's nothing but a wall of fans behind us. And as the team and everyone is talking out front, I've got this trophy, and I'm sharing it with – I just wanted to be with the crowd. I wanted to be with all the fans. And that meant the world to me to be able to look at all of that orange and blue in that arena and to share in that moment with the fanbase, the alumni, and all of the basketball alumni that were at that game.

That was the most special moment for me. It's still surreal, but when you grow up at Virginia, bleeding orange and blue, loving everything about your experience at UVA, that was the pinnacle of success. And being able to lift that trophy and do it with all of those Wahoos all over the place – that was fun. And I want to do that again.

Jack: It was amazing. I remember trying to be really present in the moment. It was easy to get caught up in a bunch of stuff at that point, but I was just there, looking around, seeing all the guys that I played with in the past, some guys that were before me, and just looking around.

For me, just to think where I was in New Zealand to somehow be on this National-Championship-winning team, just to be a part of this group, this Virginia family, I was just happy. I was happy, I was looking around, I was soaking it in, and it was a very good experience for me.

Devon: Ultimate comeback story – it's the worst of the worst and then the high of the high. I was actually at the game in Minnesota. I mean, it felt like a win for me. I felt like I won.

I was so happy for the guys. I wanted them to celebrate, and I wanted them to know they just created the wildest and the best memory you can when it comes to college basketball. I was just happy. I was super happy. I was smiling from ear to ear in the stands.

There was a lot of alumni there. I was just talking to them about that journey, and losing to UMBC, and then doing this. We were kind of setting a platform for other guys that come in.

I've gone back and played pickup. I like seeing guys that are younger come into their own as a player, like Jay Huff [and] Mamadi. I like to see Kihei because Kihei's just a little *dog*. It's good to see those guys come into their own, and I did that so I was able to flourish, and I want to see those guys flourish as well.

Grant: On and off the court, [Mamadi] just loves life, and he's so easy to be around and just makes everybody feel better [and] everybody happier. But it's cool to see just because while he has that side of him, he hates to lose, he's super motivated, [and] he'll work hard, so he has the perfect balance.

He'll be hard on you when he needs to be hard on you, but he'll also encourage you and motivate you, and he always does it in the right way. [He figured] out the balance of what he needed to do in the game and how to also make his teammates better, too.

Ben: When we won the National Championship, I remember so vividly standing there on the stage and thinking, *This is incredible.* I don't want to say it was anti-climactic – because it wasn't – but I recognized that the joy came in the journey to get there.

No matter how amazing this ultimate victory was, I took far more joy in beating Purdue to go to the Final Four, and that moment at Carolina, or the rafting trip we took in the summer before.

People are like, "How can that be what really sticks to you?" But it is. It was the memories and the relationships that you built with people over time [more] than it was reaching this pedestal.

After winning the National Championship... it's almost the moment that stands out to me more than the buzzer going off and all that stuff. In the locker room after, [Coach Bennett] got us all in a big circle, and it was all of us and then some alumni like Justin Anderson, Joe, Malcolm, and Ron Sanchez.

He put the trophy down the middle, and he said, "Look around and just soak this moment in because only the people in this circle can really, truly comprehend the progression of that season from losing to UMBC, all that entailed, that offseason, the natural highs and lows of the regular season itself, getting to the

Final Four, getting to the National Championship, and recognizing that those relationships are what're going to carry you the rest of your life."

Like, "This moment, it's kind of fleeting." It was amazing – don't get me wrong; it always will be – but I think everybody would agree: I took far much more joy from the relationships and those small moments I built with those people.

Ty: I'm getting goosebumps just thinking about that because that's another moment when you realize it's bigger than you. You're in a circle with Justin, Joe, I don't know if Malcolm was in there, and then, you know, we just won the National Championship after everything that happened to us. I have a video on my phone of that moment. I still go back and watch it.

Coach Bennett has worked for ten years – he finally won the National Championship. We celebrated – don't get me wrong – but instead of going crazy, he huddles us up and is like, "Don't let this change you. Be super humble."

Like, who else does that? That's what makes you realize what type of people you're around and how special the people around you are. That makes everything that much sweeter.

That's when I think people reveal their true colors, right? When they're at the highest of highs or the lowest of lows, and you've seen him in both, and his reaction was the same. He was going back to his faith.

When we lost to UMBC, he sat on the podium, and he answered every question. He said, "We got outplayed. We gotta be better as a team. I gotta be a better coach."

Humble, thankful (still), [he] told us to remain thankful, super passionate, told us to stay unified, and told us to serve each other. [He] literally told us all those five things when we lost.

After we won, he told us, "Remain super humble, be so thankful, you won because you served each other, continue to do that." And obviously, you had to be super passionate and unified.

With the lowest of lows and the highest of highs, his message is the same. It was the same every day. That just shows the type of person he is. It shows that it's not fake; it's real. It's really him, and it's really what that program is built upon.

Joe Harris: I mean, it was amazing. Even though we didn't play, we still felt a part of it, and I think that's a testament to Coach Bennett, and his program, and what he's built.

People talk about certain schools having a brotherhood within the basketball program, or a family sort of atmosphere, but with Coach Bennett and Virginia, it is genuine.

Everybody is a family. No matter in what capacity, you were a part of the basketball program. You're automatically bonded and part of a family.

You even see it now. If I'm in Charlotte, I'm going to go out to eat with Marcus Conrad and Ron Sanchez, people like that: guys that were part of the program but no longer are. But, you know, Marcus was a manager there. Coach Sanchez, he was the assistant coach while I was there, and it's the same thing wherever we go. Everybody is sort of connected, you know? And it's a true, genuine, authentic family atmosphere.

Johnny: I go on a jog through Charlottesville after we won the National Championship, and it's hot, I'm tired, and I need to shave, so I go over to this parking lot by McCormick Road by the first-year dorms. I was like, "Oh, I'm just gonna cut through the cemetery and see if I can get to old dorms," which ended up being under construction.

So, I'm coming back, and there was one headstone with this huge piece of paper on it, so I go over to see what it says, and you can't really read it because it's been weather-beaten and there's leaves and flowers and grass and dirt on top of this thing. I look at it closely, and you can read across the top, "National Champs."

So, somebody put it on their loved one's grave, but they had that Virginia Basketball connection with that loved one, and I see this on the grave, and I'm like, *Man, talk about unifying. Someone came back because those memories meant so much to them that they had to put that down.*

Ritchie McKay: I'll give you one. My dad passed away in 2000. What was really interesting to me was to see the relationship between Tony and Dick and how incredibly wise his dad was. Tone was a great blend of his mom and his dad together.

I always marveled at the respect and the appreciation that he had for his father. It reminded me of just how much I valued my dad. How wise Dick was. He would write letters to Tone – handwritten letters – that reminded me so much of my dad and what he provided for me. And when Tony would share some of those letters with me, man, it moved me to... yeah.

It's a beautiful relationship, yet Tone wanted so much to be Tony and not be compared to his dad. So, that picture at the Final Four after that Purdue game, [their] exchange, that was one of my neatest moments in being in this profession because of what I just described. Eating popcorn solo in a movie theater, I watched that relationship – how beautiful it was.

And then lastly, Laurel Bennett – you know how they say, "Behind every great man, there's a greater woman"? It's true. She's the one person in his life that's not afraid to tell him the truth – well, his dad is another person, and *maybe* I was another person. But Laurel has a wisdom and discerning spirit that has really influenced his life for the better!

I'll close with this: trust God with your life, and trust others. Whenever you can find a man in your life that will tell you the truth, hold on to him and don't let him go.

Ty: Another big thing was: the first day we were able to come back to school in August [2018], we already have practice. We get there, and Coach Bennett is like, "We're just in the film room today. We're not getting dressed."

We sit there, we're all in the film room, [and] we're not

practicing. I'm like, *What are we doing? Why can't we just practice? I want to play. I want to at least play a little bit.*

Coach Bennett has a TED Talk [from Donald Davis], and he puts it on. Basically, the message is: "If you use adversity the right way," – the guy was talking about his story – "If you use it the right way, it can give you a ticket to a place that you couldn't have gone without it."

It's like, *That's what this UMBC thing is.* If you use it the right way, it can buy you a ticket to a place you could not have gone without it: how it fuels you, the experience it gives you, sitting on a podium, all those things. We talked about that TED Talk all year.

Coach Bennett was giving a speech at our banquet, September 13th, [2019]. He has the ticket of the UMBC game and the ticket of the Championship Game. He was telling a story: "I told the guys, if you use adversity right way, it can buy you a ticket to a place you couldn't have gone without it," and he holds the UMBC ticket up next to the Championship ticket.

So, that stuff is pretty cool. It's literally like a movie – or a book.

references

"2009-10 Virginia Cavaliers Schedule and Results." Sports Reference. Accessed June 29, 2021. https://www.sports-reference.com/cbb/schools/virginia/2010-schedule.html.

"2011-12 Virginia Cavaliers Schedule and Results." Sports Reference. Accessed June 29, 2021. https://www.sports-reference.com/cbb/schools/virginia/2012-schedule.html.

"2012-13 Virginia Cavaliers Schedule and Results." Sports Reference . Accessed June 29, 2021. https://www.sports-reference.com/cbb/schools/virginia/2013-schedule.html.

"2013-14 Virginia Cavaliers Schedule and Results." Sports Reference. Accessed June 29, 2021. https://www.sports-reference.com/cbb/schools/virginia/2014-schedule.html.

"2014-15 Virginia Cavaliers Schedule and Results." Sports Reference. Accessed June 29, 2021. https://www.sports-reference.com/cbb/schools/virginia/2015-schedule.html.

"2015-16 Louisville Cardinals Roster and Stats." Sports Reference. Accessed July 2, 2021. https://www.sports-reference.com/cbb/schools/louisville/2016.html.

"2015-16 Virginia Cavaliers Schedule and Results." Sports Reference. Accessed June 29, 2021. https://www.sports-reference.com/cbb/schools/virginia/2016-schedule.html.

"2016-17 Virginia Cavaliers Schedule and Results." Sports Reference. Accessed June 29, 2021. https://www.sports-reference.com/cbb/schools/virginia/2017-schedule.html.

"2018-19 Liberty Flames Roster and Stats." Sports Reference. Accessed June 29, 2021. https://www.sports-reference.com/cbb/schools/liberty/2019.html.

"About Us." KFC Yum! Center. Accessed July 12, 2021. https://www.kfcyumcenter.com/arena-information/about-us.

"Allen Fieldhouse." Kansas Jayhawks. https://kuathletics.com/, June 3, 2021. https://kuathletics.com/facilities/allen-fieldhouse/.

"Arizona vs. Virginia - Game Summary - November 12, 2006." ESPN. ESPN Internet Ventures. Accessed July 2, 2021. https://www.espn.com/mens-college-basketball/game/_/gameId/263160258.

"Cal State Long Beach vs. Virginia Box Score, November 20, 2015." Sports Reference. Accessed June 29, 2021. https://www.sports-reference.com/cbb/boxscores/2015-11-20-virginia.html.

"Cameron Indoor Stadium." Duke University. Accessed July 13, 2021. https://goduke.com/news/2005/11/29/209837009.aspx.

Clemmons, Anna Katherine. "'A Chance to Breathe'." SBNation. SBNation, January 3, 2019. https://www.sbnation.com/2019/1/3/18165248/kyle-guy-virginia-umbc-ncaa-tournament-anxiety.

Cooperman, Jackie. "The Man Responsible for Russell Wilson's Mental Conditioning." Worth, November 19, 2019. https://www.worth.com/the-man-responsible-for-russell-wilsons-mental-conditioning/.

Coyle, Daniel. "The Talent Code." Daniel Coyle. Accessed June 29, 2021. http://danielcoyle.com/the-talent-code/.

"Foreigner - Juke Box Hero (Official Music Video)." YouTube. YouTube, March 11, 2016. https://www.youtube.com/watch?v=Ic02W1bWeFU.

"Gardner-Webb vs. Virginia Box Score, March 22, 2019." Sports Reference. Accessed July 2, 2021. https://www.sports-reference.com/cbb/boxscores/2019-03-22-15-virginia.html.

Harrell, Eben. "How 1% Performance Improvements Led to Olympic Gold." Harvard Business Review, October 30, 2015. https://hbr.org/2015/10/how-1-performance-improvements-led-to-olympic-gold.

"Harvard vs. Virginia Box Score, December 21, 2014." Sports Reference. Accessed June 29, 2021. https://www.sports-reference.com/cbb/boxscores/2014-12-21-virginia.html.

"Isaiah Wilkins." 247Sports. Accessed July 2, 2021. https://247sports.com/Player/Isaiah-Wilkins-25911//high-school-42000/.

Khurshudyan, Isabelle. "Virginia's Justin Anderson Breaks Finger, Expected to Miss Four to Six Weeks." The Washington Post. WP Company, February 8, 2015. https://www.washingtonpost.com/sports/colleges/justin-anderson-breaks-finger-out-4-6-weeks/2015/02/08/1383d492-af4e-11e4-ad71-7b9eba0f87d6_story.html.

Leung, Brian J. "NCAA Tournament: Following Virginia Loss, Tony Bennett Says to His Team, 'Joy Is Coming.'" Streaking The Lawn. Streaking The Lawn, March 28, 2016. https://www.streakingthelawn.com/2016/3/27/11314840/ncaa-tournament-following-virginia-loss-tony-bennett-says-to-his-team.

"Mamadi Diakite." Basketball Reference. Accessed June 29, 2021. https://www.basketball-reference.com/players/d/diakima01.html.

"North Carolina vs. Harvard Box Score, March 19, 2015." Sports Reference. Accessed June 29, 2021. https://www.sports-reference.com/cbb/boxscores/2015-03-19-harvard.html.

"Oregon vs. Virginia Box Score, December 17, 2010." Sports Reference. Accessed June 29, 2021. https://www.sports-reference.com/cbb/boxscores/2010-12-17-virginia.html.

"Psalm 30:4-6 - English Standard Version." Bible Gateway. Accessed June 29, 2021. https://www.biblegateway.com/passage/?search=Psalm+30%3A4-6&version=ESV.

"Radford vs. Virginia Box Score, December 7, 2010." Sports Reference. Accessed June 29, 2021. https://www.sports-reference.com/cbb/boxscores/2010-12-07-virginia.html.

"Ritchie McKay Coaching Record." Sports Reference. Accessed June 29, 2021. https://www.sports-reference.com/cbb/coaches/ritchie-mckay-1.html.

TEDxTalks. "How the Story Transforms the Teller | Donald Davis | TEDxCharlottesville." YouTube. YouTube, December 23, 2014. https://www.youtube.com/watch?v=wgeh4xhSA2Q&t=1s.

Thayer, Ernest Lawrence. "Casey at the Bat." Poets.org. Academy of American Poets. Accessed June 30, 2021. https://poets.org/poem/casey-bat.

"Tony Bennett." Basketball Reference. Accessed July 2, 2021. https://www.basketball-reference.com/players/b/benneto01.html.

"Virginia vs. Georgia Tech Box Score, February 8, 2014." Sports Reference. Accessed June 29, 2021. https://www.sports-reference.com/cbb/boxscores/2014-02-08-georgia-tech.html.

"Virginia vs. Maryland - Game Summary - March 4, 2012." ESPN. ESPN Internet Ventures. Accessed June 30, 2021. https://www.espn.com/mens-college-basketball/game/_/gameId/320640120.

"Virginia vs. Minnesota Box Score, November 29, 2010." Sports Reference. Accessed June 29, 2021. https://www.sports-reference.com/cbb/boxscores/2010-11-29-minnesota.html.

"Virginia vs. North Carolina Box Score, March 12, 2016." Sports Reference. Accessed June 29, 2021. https://www.sports-reference.com/cbb/boxscores/2016-03-12-north-carolina.html.

"Virginia vs. Tennessee - Play-By-Play - December 30, 2013." ESPN. ESPN Internet Ventures. Accessed July 1, 2021. https://www.espn.com/mens-college-basketball/playbyplay/_/gameId/400502759.

"Virginia vs. Washington Box Score, November 22, 2010." Sports Reference. Accessed June 29, 2021. https://www.sports-reference.com/cbb/boxscores/2010-11-22-washington.html.

Thanks a lot to Coach Bennett, who respectfully declined an interview request but who inspires a host of people, myself included.

And thanks a lot to these folks for background interviews:

Luke, William, Gray, The Wiltshires, The Brothers Cha,
Anders, Riley, Austin, Matt, Sam, Julia, Bill,
Townshend, Buck, Hart, Dick, Jack, Tommy, Trey, and Collin.

Made in the USA
Las Vegas, NV
16 November 2021